Evangelical Hermeneutics

Edited by
Michael Bauman
and
David Hall

Evangelical Hermeneutics

Edited by
Michael Bauman
and
David Hall

CHRISTIAN PUBLICATIONS, INC.
CAMP HILL, PENNSYLVANIA

Christian Publications
3825 Hartzdale Drive, Camp Hill, PA 17011

Faithful, biblical publishing since 1883

ISBN: 0–87509–603–4

Printed in the United States of America

95 96 97 98 99 5 4 3 2 1

Table of Contents

Preface

The editors are pleased to thank the Publisher, Dr. K. Neill Foster, for making these essays available. We also wish to publicly thank the individual contributors and *The Evangelical Theological Society*, at whose annual meeting (1994) these were originally presented. The essays contained in this volume are the fruit of some of the finest and most promising evangelical minds. The subject considered by this work is one of perennial importance. Of course, not every conceivable question has been addressed. Yet, we do believe that significant contributions have been made by this volume, and that these chapters will guide many by proper hermeneutical considerations.

When such scholars come together from such a variety of backgrounds and specialties the result is normally salutary. However, in this case we believe the essays to be of extraordinary value. We have tried to adhere to our domain, but one will quickly note that broad societal issues have also been considered. One of the strengths of this volume is its attention to cultural and historical developments not only within theology, but outside of theology as well. These essays strive to benefit from other helpful studies, while rejecting the methodologies—ancient or modern—that are lacking in potency. We seek to stand with earlier Christians who were commanded to "Test everything. Hold on to the good" (1 Thessalonians 5:21). We only ask our readers to apply the same judgments to our work.

We thank *The St. Croix Review* for permission to reprint "The Case for a Conservative Hermeneutic." We dedicate this work to our wives, our colleagues, our students and our fellow church members.

Michael Bauman
David W. Hall

May 8, 1995

The Ethics of Meaning: The Case for a Conservative Hermeneutic

Michael Bauman

"I should be glad if I sent my reader away with a new sense of responsibility to the language."

C.S. Lewis, *Studies in Words*

If you are a student, please read carefully.

I will explain how you can prevent any teacher who believes that a text means what the reader says it means rather than what the author says it means from marking any of your work wrong ever again, regardless of whether your work is in the form of short answers, essays, or research papers.

The payment I seek for doing so is not primarily financial. Rather than money, my reward is to stifle those literary critics and those literary theories that undermine Western tradition, at least those parts of Western tradition preserved for us in language and in texts. In other words, the wealth I seek is not monetary. I want to preserve the wisdom, the truth, and the freedom that our forefathers bequeathed to us in our culture's foundational documents.

Put differently, I want to hear the voices of the founding fathers in the Declaration of Independence and in the Constitution, not the voices of activist liberal judges who think that heeding the intentions of the framers is simply to fall slave to the dead hand of the past. I also want to hear the voices of the poets and the sages, who speak to us across the centuries in the greatest works of verbal art ever produced, not the deconstructive ramblings of the self-appointed destroyers of language and literature who seem to occupy so many seats of power and influence in the humanities departments on so many college campuses. Finally, and most importantly, I want to hear the voice of God and the voices of His apostles and prophets in the Bible, not the voices of modernist exegetes who think that the Bible's meaning has nothing to do with the intention of either the God who inspired it or the people who wrote it.

I want to do so, on the one hand, because I value the theological, political, and cultural legacy left me by those men and women who made the civilized world what it is. I am firmly persuaded that the best of the past deserves—indeed requires—our protection, especially now, when the mindless mantra chanted on so many American campuses seems to be "Hey-Hey, Ho-Ho, Western Civ. has got to go!" I do so because I value the patrimony of freedom, of truth, and of salvation left for us in the texts that make both civilization and hope possible. I do so because I agree with Confucius that when words lose their meaning, people lose their freedom.

I want to do so, on the other hand, because I value the teaching profession, which, without a suitable hermeneutic, becomes impossible, as the following considerations make evident.

The Hermeneutics of Pedagogy

Before I keep the promise I made at the outset of this

essay and explain how to insulate yourself from all your professor's criticisms, and before I tell you how to preserve the meaning of the most important and enduring texts in the world, I want to tell you a story.

Some years ago, a good friend of mine was caught in a London downpour. Fighting his way slowly, but resolutely, along some unfamiliar English side street, and bitterly longing for the umbrella he somehow had misplaced, my friend turned a fog-shrouded corner and on an overhead shop sign spied the words "umbrellas recovered." "Ah," my friend thought to himself, "perhaps this man can help me recover mine!"

A moment's reflection, however, revealed the folly. No matter how intensely my friend wished otherwise, "recovered" meant "repaired" or "refurbished," not "retrieved." The meaning of that word was the one intended for it by the shopkeeper who made the sign, not the meaning imagined or desired by the drenched pedestrian who was reading it. That is how shop signs, telephone books, love letters, travel brochures, and—Dare we say it?—even novels and epic poems are written and should be read. A text means what its author intends it to mean, not what a reader wants it to mean. In Alexander Pope's words, one ought "to read every work of wit in the same spirit as its author writ." That is the meaning of meaning. If something on an umbrella shop sign is unclear, perhaps a quick perusal of the information displayed on the shop window will help, or else a glance inside. That is the beauty and function of context.

I stand over against those literary critics, activist judges, and modernist biblical exegetes who mistakenly insist that a text, whether poetry or prose, has a life of its own, or that what a text means is what it means to the reader and not what its author intended it to mean. That is, I deny the hermeneutical assumption that a text can be rightly understood apart from solid grammatical/historical exegesis. I do so because, methodologically, any interpreter who maintains otherwise must necessarily compromise himself every time he turns away from the text at hand and opens a dictionary in order to trace down a term with which he is unfamiliar. And who among us has not done so? My desire, of course, is not to steer readers away from the *Oxford English Dictionary*; it is to steer them away from the unfortunate hermeneutical inconsistency that has racked modern literary criticism—the sort of criticism that tells us a great deal more about the presuppositions and world view of the reader than it does about the great works of writers like Dante, Erasmus, or Milton.

As a student and devotee of literature myself, I want to know more about great authors and great books, not about the predilections and prejudices of people who read them many centuries after the fact. The interpreter's work is to point out and to elucidate the literature at hand, not to foist upon it the interpreter's own peculiar world view or that of the one small segment of contemporary society that interpreter represents.

In short, I oppose non-intentionalist and non-historical exegesis.

Who cannot see the hermeneutical fortress that non-intentionalist and non-historical readers try to build for themselves? By positing, on the one hand, an autonomously existing text, subject neither to time nor place, and by positing, on the other hand, a subjective meaning for that text, a meaning unrestrained by either authorial intention or historical milieu, critics who deny authorial intention insist, in effect, that any text's meaning reduces to whatever *they* say, though, what they say seldom, if ever, accords with what other readers of the same school say. By adopting this autonomous, indeed libertine, hermeneutical subjectivity, modern critics assert both that the text itself is independent (nothing controls *it*) and that so are they (nothing controls *them*). They no longer need hearken, they think, to Spenser when they read *The Faerie Queene*, to Shakespeare when they read *Romeo and Juliet*, to James Madison when they read the

Constitution, or even to the apostle Paul himself when they read the epistle to the Romans. The meaning of all texts, new or old, great or small, sacred or secular, is now to be concocted free hand, by anyone so inclined.

But I, for one, ardently oppose this arrogant intrusion into the texts of others. I oppose the shameless hijacking of someone else's words for our own self-seeking ends. The time has come to put both the text and the modern interpreter back under authority. I believe it is of more than etymological significance that the word "authority" derives from "author." In short, I am saying that to call authorial intention a fallacy is itself a fallacy.

Yet, nearly all the literary critics with whom I have ever spoken say precisely that: authorial intention is a fallacy.

But, if authorial intention is a fallacy, if meaning is the reader's prerogative, then graded instruction of any kind is an injustice because it credits the student with the instructor's insight, on the one hand, and it holds the student responsible for the instructor's mistaken meanings, on the other. If authorial intention is not the measure of meaning, then teachers can no longer count students wrong when *the teachers themselves* are responsible for what the students' test answers or research papers actually mean. After all, no student ought to get a lower grade simply because the instructor gave that student's answer or essay an incorrect or inappropriate meaning. One could quite as easily give the student's writing the correct meaning so that the student in question, indeed all students, might make the Dean's list every semester.

If the professor gives the student's words what the professor deems an incorrect meaning, then the error ought to be charged to the *professor*, not the student. In that case, teachers who give their students F's are failing their own courses. Under such a method of interpretation, the incorrect meaning of all mistaken answers on all tests is the responsibility of the grader.

Furthermore, because in this system of interpretation meaning is the prerogative of the reader and not the author, no professor can properly prevent any student from giving the professor's course syllabus, the professor's lectures, the professor's assignments, or the professor's test questions whatever meanings the *student* sees fit. On the basis of the professor's own hermeneutical principles, no objection could be effectively raised against such a student practice. Nor could any teacher ever again chide any student for failing to follow instructions, because the teacher's instructions mean not what the teacher intended them to mean but what the student determined they ought to mean.

The professor cannot escape this difficulty by saying that authorial intention applies to syllabi but not to epic poems or to elegies because syllabi are prose and epics and elegies are not. Both this dichotomous view and the double hermeneutic to which it gives rise assume that words mean not only a *different thing* in a prose passage than in a poetic one, but that words mean in a *different way* in a prose passage than in a poetic one, neither of which is demonstrable. Such professors argue as if subordinate clauses and indirect objects somehow functioned differently in a line from Keats than they do in a line from Faulkner, which is nonsense.

Put differently, if my professor told me I could be graded down on a test or a paper and that mistaken answers could be attributed to me rather than to him because my answers were in prose, I would simply write all my answers in iambic pentameter (or, more troublesome for the instructor, in free verse)—then, on the instructor's own basis, all errors revert to the instructor because the instructor's own theory of interpretation states that in poetry meaning is the prerogative of the reader.

And if a professor who holds that prose meaning differs from poetic meaning were unable to say definitively and precisely what exactly poetry is, and if that professor could not objectively or conclusively distinguish what was truly poetry from what was merely poetic—that is, if that professor affirmed that whether or not a text was poetry was a matter of private judgment and not a matter of absolute fact—then that professor still could not extricate himself from his pedagogical dilemma because identifying a student's answer as prose and not as poetry would be a subjective literary judgment on the part of the professor and would reflect more on that professor than on the student. In such a case, the professor would be able to count the student's answer wrong only because that professor had subjectively categorized that student's answer as prose. If the student insists that his answer is poetry, the professor's attribution of error to the student remains self-condemning.

Thus, if you are a student, pay close attention to what I am about to say. It will ensure that you never again miss another question on any test or receive a poor grade on any essay or any paper from any teacher who denies authorial intention or who says that poetry means subjectively but that prose does not.

According to your professor's own rules of interpretation, when you are assigned to write an answer or a paper about a poem, that poem means what *you* say it means, not what anyone else says it means—not even the poet or your professor. By the professor's own rules, meaning is your prerogative. The text means what you say it means.

If your professor says that prose texts mean objectively and that poetic texts do not, then write all your answers in poetic form. In that way, all wrong answers are the result of your professor's interpretation, not your intended meaning. If your professor wants to continue to mark himself or herself wrong, that is up to your professor. But your professor cannot continue to mark *you* down because of your professor's own mistaken meanings. If your professor wants to grade you, he must deny his own interpretive method, and he must relinquish his hegemony over the meaning of your texts and begin to read everything in a new way.

In short, if authorial intention is wrong, then you are not; only your professor is. If authorial intention is not wrong, then all those who have opposed it up until now are wrong, which includes most modern professors of literature.

Some professors try to extricate themselves from this hermeneutical and pedagogical mare's nest by insisting that the meaning of a text lies neither with the author nor with the reader, but with the text itself. But this unabashed textual positivism will not do. It conveniently overlooks the obvious fact that a text has a meaning (indeed a text has existence) only because an author put it there. A text does not somehow create its own meaning. Nor does a text create itself; an author has a meaning and creates a text in order to preserve that meaning and to communicate it. Neither texts nor meanings are autonomous. To think otherwise is to apply to textual meaning Satan's error in *Paradise Lost*, which is to ascribe to something not God that it is "self-begot, self-raised/By [its] own quick'ning power" (*Paradise Lost* V, 860-1).

Put differently, to assert that a text is autonomous is bad theology because a text is the product of a writer. Because that writer is necessarily subject to the limitations of time, space and causation, one simply cannot ascribe to any creation of a creature (i.e., one cannot ascribe to the text) the self-sufficiency and independence that reality and theology deny to the creature himself (i.e., the author).

The Hermeneutics of Conservatism

You see (to move from theology to economics), Adam Smith was right.

Prosperity follows in the wake of the division of labor. As long as every worker is constrained to satisfy all his needs and desires for himself, his lot in life will be significantly poorer. He cannot raise his own sheep and cotton in order to provide all his own clothes. He cannot extract his own iron ore from the earth and then smelt it and shape it in a steel mill of his own construction and operation in order to make his own automobiles and passenger trains. He cannot grow his own bananas and coconuts so that he will have tasty little morsels to sprinkle on his cereal or his ice cream. He cannot produce, direct, and act in his own television programs and movies, or build and operate his own television sets and movie theaters in order to keep himself entertained. He cannot design, develop, test, and deploy his own system of nuclear weapons in order to protect himself from foreign aggression. In order to have a more pleasant, more prosperous, and more secure existence, he needs the things that others can provide for him better than he can provide them for himself. Because the division of labor affords a degree of specialization, expertise, and efficiency not available in alternate economic systems, some people are able to do for others what others are not able to do for themselves nearly so well, if at all. As a result, those who engage in the division of labor are far better off than those who do not.

By the same token, I propose that we all are better off, not only pedagogically but *in virtually every way,* if we employ a division of labor with regard to our fundamental texts, whether literary, political, or sacred. If each one of us had to write our own *Paradise Lost,* our own *Canterbury Tales,* our own *Divine Comedy,* our own *Reflections on the Revolution in France,* or our own Psalms, rather than permitting Milton, Chaucer, Dante, Burke and David to do so for us, we would each be immeasurably impoverished. We could never do for ourselves what that collection of great minds and valiant spirits has done for us in their world-shaping texts. As it is in economics, so it is in hermeneutics—prosperity follows close upon the division of labor.

In hermeneutics, the division of labor runs like this: The author has in mind something he thinks is true or beneficial and which he desires to communicate. He selects language and a genre that he deems appropriate for his message, which he then writes down. A reader, interested in what he imagines this text will say, picks it up and begins to read. If the author has formed his mental concepts clearly and cohesively; if he has selected his terms and his genre with careful precision; and if the reader has expended the effort needed to understand the text from the author's point of view (that is, if the reader has properly discerned the author's intended meaning); genuine communication occurs. In such a case, the notions received by the reader from the text will closely approximate the intentions built into it by the writer.

But if the author's ideas were not clearly defined in his own mind; or if the author has chosen terms and a genre ill-suited to his purpose; or if the reader has been careless in his work as an interpreter; or if he feels it his prerogative to ignore the intentions of the writer altogether; a failure of communication predictably results. In such cases, what the reader claims to get from the text is not gotten from the text at all. It is simply manufactured *ad hoc* in the reader's own mind. That failure to communicate results from a breakdown in the division of labor within the literary enterprise. It results, on the one hand, from writers not taking seriously their proper task of clear conception and precise articulation. It results, on the other hand, from readers abandoning their proper task of consuming meaning in favor of usurping a role not truly their own—that of producing meaning. That wrongheaded method of procedure does not work well in the marketplace, where buyers and sellers freely exchange goods and services; it does not work well in the classroom, where students study Wordsworth and Shakespeare; it does not work well in the judge's chambers, where judges interpret the Constitution and its attendant amendments; and it does not work well in the pulpit, where preachers interpret and expound the word of God.

As long as we require the reader to do the job of the writer, and as long as we continue to confuse the role of the interpreter with that of the author, we will remain culturally, politically, and spiritually poorer because this backwards-working hermeneutic lays upon every one of us the tremendous burden of reinventing our entire cultural heritage anew. It lays upon us the necessity of reinventing the meaning not only of our foundational texts, but of all texts whatsoever, because (according to this theory of reading) no text has a meaning until the reader gives it one. The Bible means nothing; the Constitution means nothing; *Hamlet* means nothing; traffic signs mean nothing; marriage vows mean nothing; even the perverse scrawls on rest room walls mean nothing until the reader gives them a meaning—a meaning quite cut off from, perhaps even antithetical to, the author's intention.

To consign the manufacture of meaning to the reader requires the reader to create the meaning of all texts *de novo*, to reinvent the literary wheel, the legal wheel, and the theological wheel each time the reader picks up a text. To insist that texts mean what their readers say they mean and not what their authors intended them to mean effectively strips the reader of his entire cultural patrimony by forcing him to create for himself what the apostles, the prophets, the sages and the framers have made for him already but (according to this view) foolishly preserved for him in the form of a text, not realizing that simply by preserving it for him in verbal form they have actually sequestered that patrimony from him forever and sentenced him to remake the great works of the Western world all over again, freehand.

If this hermeneutic is correct, no messages are possible. No sentence you ever heard, no statement you ever read, had any meaning until you gave it one. Though perhaps you thought otherwise, if this method of interpretation is correct, Plato has never spoken to you in the *Republic*, nor Thomas in the *Summa*, nor God in Christ. Your wife, your husband, your Lord, have never really whispered "I love you." It was only your own voice all along. You simply did not recognize it. You have never really talked to anyone; you talked only to yourself using someone else's words. If this hermeneutic is correct, all conversations, despite their appearance, are monologues.

If this hermeneutic is correct, you are surrounded by a

world of empty texts, waiting for you not simply to discover their meaning, but to invent it.

If this hermeneutic is correct, no text has been, or ever could be, misconstrued. If this hermeneutic is correct, no author and no speaker can raise any complaint about being misunderstood or misrepresented. The meaning of their words, according to this theory, is simply not their prerogative. Over the meaning of their own words, they exercise no claim.

According to this theory of interpretation, the position I advocate—the idea that authorial intention, not the reader's interpretation, is the true measure of meaning—is fundamentally and expansively wrong.

According to this misguided theory of interpretation, you can tell me, now that I am finished with this essay, just what I meant by it, but did not realize or intend. I invite you to do so.

Tell me what this essay really means.

Then I'll tell you what your interpretation really means—and it will surprise you.

I guarantee it.

I know you won't mind.

Legal Hermeneutics and the Interpretation of Scripture

John W. Montgomery

The Hermeneutical Impasse

What divides Christian theology and turns the theological landscape into a battlefield today is not so much confessional differences as hermeneutical perspectives. On the one side, regardless of denominational commitment, are those who insist on interpreting the biblical text in its natural (not necessarily literal) sense; on the other, those who flatly deny that any such objective interpretation is possible and who therefore see the text as a reflection of its original environment and in dialectic interaction with the contemporary interpreter. It may almost be reduced to: Billy Graham ("The Bible says . . .") vs. Robert Funk's Jesus Seminar.

One might even go so far as to claim that biblical hermeneutics constitutes the great gulf dividing the church at the end of the twentieth century. As illustrated by Robert Campbell, O.P.'s companion volumes, *Spectrum of Protestant Beliefs* and *Spectrum of Catholic Attitudes*,[1] far more basic than Protestant-Catholic doctrinal differences today is the cleavage between those who take revelational sources as objectively true and those who relativize and subjectivize them. The conservative-liberal split on how to read the Bible cuts across all denominational lines, and directly or indirectly colors the theology and church life of every church person. Clearly, if the Bible does not mean what it appears to mean and does not teach what it seems to teach, the door opens wide for an infinite number of new interpretations, teachings, and styles of church life.

The essential difference between historical-grammatical interpretation and the new hermeneutic is not difficult to describe. The former, set out in such classic treatises as Milton S. Terry's *Biblical Hermeneutics*, maintains that the scriptural text can be objectively known, that it has a clear, perspicuous meaning, and that that meaning can be discovered if the text is allowed to interpret itself, without the adulteration of the interpreter's personal prejudices. Professor Eugene F.A. Klug summarizes this approach, which dominated the field of scriptural interpretation at least from the Reformation to the rise of modern biblical criticism, as follows:

> It is a fundamental principle to assume that there is one intended, literal, proper sense to any given passage in Scripture ("sensus literalis unus est"); also that the Scripture is its own best interpreter ("Scriptura Scripturam interpretat' or 'Scriptura sui ipsius interpres"). . . . The literal sense thus always stands first and each interpreter must guard against cluttering that which is being communicated with his own ideas, lest the meaning be lost.[2]

In diametric contrast to this classic hermeneutic is the so-called "hermeneutical circle" of Rudolf Bultmann and the contemporary followers of *formgeschichtliche Methode* and related higher-critical philosophies. Here, the text and the interpreter are locked together in such a way that a purely objective, "presuppositionless" understanding of the text is out of the question. The interpreter always brings his own understanding to the text, and interpretation is the product *both* of the text working on the interpreter *and* the interpreter working on the text.[3] And this will be true not only of the current interpreter vis-à-vis the text but also of the original writer or editor of it: neither the events described in the text nor the resulting description of them can ever represent objective truth in any absolute sense. A text is ultimately inseparable from its *Sitz im Leben* in the widest sense of that term.

Philosopher Roy J. Howard thus sets forth "three important aspects of contemporary hermeneutics": (1) "There is no such thing as presuppositionless knowing." (2) "Just as there is no uniform stance from which to begin thinking, so there is no uniform term in which to end it. Hermeneutics is willing to rethink the dialectical logic of Hegel but not to accept his conclusion of an absolute mind." (3) "Hermeneutics' recognition that intentionality is present and operative and effective on both sides . . . and in a dialectical way. This effectiveness might be resident in the social condition of the researcher (cf. Habermas and Winch) or in the very logic of his research activity (cf. Von Wright), or in the choice and manner of the questions he addresses to experience (cf. Gadamer)."[4]

The impasse between classical and contemporary hermeneutic approaches is well illustrated by the current controversy engendered by Adrian Desmond's and James Moore's biography, *Darwin* (1991). The authors set Darwin in his 19th century context, relating the development of his theory of organic evolution to the social influences that played upon him. Evangelical reaction has been mixed: On the one hand, there is joy that evolutionary theory is now less able to be regarded as scientific fact than as "the contingent product of complex inferences between the Victorian natural and social orders"; on the other, there is much disquiet that such sociological reductionism is the very thing that has characterized the treatment of the Bible by the modern critics! Moore, in responding to the evangelicals on the latter point, puts it bluntly: "Can texts interpret themselves? If the Bible's don't, why *a fortiori* should Darwin's?"[5]

To determine whether or not texts such as Scripture can or cannot interpret themselves, we may perhaps benefit from a perspective other than that afforded by theology or even the liberal arts. Theological discussions of the hermeneutical impasse tend to become mired in dogmatic considerations; and philosophical, historical; and literary treatments of the question are often highly abstruse and far removed from the practicalities.

In the present essay we shall offer assistance by way of legal hermeneutics—and that for two reasons. First: Lawyers—perceived through the centuries as motivated by filthy lucre and woefully deficient in moral character and spirituality—can hardly be thought to be offering surreptitious theological solutions to the hermeneutic dilemma! Secondly, and far more important: As I have pointed out elsewhere,[6] law is necessitarian, coloring all aspects of societal life; so its solutions to fundamental problems carry powerful weight. On the interpretation of contracts, wills, statutes, and constitutions hang the lives and property of all of us. A legal hermeneutic will not represent mere academic theory: It will have developed a necessary response to resolving peaceably the otherwise intractable conflicts within society. A legal hermeneutic, in short, constitutes the interpretive cement by which society is kept from fragmenting.[7] The plain consequence is that the theologian has every reason to observe law's hermeneutic methodology with care.

How Lawyers Construe Documents

It is a truism that written instruments have played and continue to play a central role in legal activity. Legal historian Frederic William Maitland argued that the "forms of action"—the documentary writs—were the most important single factor in the development of the Anglo-American common law tradition.[8] As early as the 17th century, written evidence of contractual relations, as compared with purely oral contracts, was deemed so important that in certain key areas only contracts in writing or evidenced by written memoranda could any longer be enforced.[9] Written instruments such as contracts, deeds, wills and trusts, legislative statutes, and constitutions represent the very essence of the law, and their proper interpretation is a *sine qua non* for the effective operation of the machinery of justice.

Not surprisingly, therefore, canons for the proper construction of legal documents were developed early in the history of the law and remain with us to this day. The Oxford *Concise Dictionary of Law* lists the six "principal rules of statutory interpretation" as follows.

> (1) An Act must be construed as a whole, so that internal inconsistencies are avoided.
> (2) Words that are reasonably capable of only one meaning must be given that meaning whatever the result. This is called the *literal rule.*
> (3) Ordinary words must be given their ordinary meanings and technical words their technical meanings, unless absurdity would result. This is the *golden rule.*
> (4) When an Act aims at curing a defect in the law any ambiguity is to be resolved in such a way as to favor that aim (the *mischief rule*).
> (5) The *ujusdem generis rule* (of the same kind): when a list of specific items belonging to the same class is followed by general words (as in "cats, dogs, and other animals"), the general words are to be treated as confined to other items of the same class (in this example, to other *domestic* animals).
> (6) The rule *expressio unius est exclusio alterius* (the inclusion of the one is the exclusion of the other): when a list of specific items is not followed by general words it is to be taken as exhaustive. For example, "weekends and public holidays" excludes ordinary weekdays.[10]

In the law of contracts, the *parol evidence rule* sets forth the same hermeneutic philosophy: Integrated writings cannot be added to, subtracted from, or varied by the admission of extrinsic evidence of prior or contemporaneous oral or written agreements; extrinsic evidence is admissible to *clarify* or *explain* the integrated writing, but never when it would *contradict* the writing.[11] The construction of deeds follows the same approach: the parties "are presumed to have intended to say that which they have in fact said, so their words as they stand must be construed."[12] And at the loftiest point of American constitutional interpretation the identical philosophy prevails; thus Chief Justice John Marshall in *Gibbons* v. *Ogden*:

> As men whose intentions require no concealment, generally employ the words which most directly and aptly express the ideas they intend to convey, the enlightened patriots who framed our Constitution, and the people who adopted it, must be understood to have employed words in their natural sense, and to have intended what they have said. If, from the imperfection of human language, there should be serious doubts respecting the extent of any given power, it is a well-settled rule that the objects for which it was given, especially when those objects are expressed in the instrument itself, should have great influence in the construction. . . . We know of no rule for construing the extent of such powers, other than is given by the language of the instrument which confers them, taken in connection with the purposes for which they were conferred.[13]

Concerning the interpretation of legal documents in general, Lord Bacon summed up aphoristically.[14]

> Non est interpretatio, sed divinatio, quae recedit a litera. (Interpretation that departs from the letter

> of the text is not interpretation but divination.) Cum reciditur a litera, judex transit in legislatorum. (When the judge departs from the letter, he turns into a legislator.)

More recently, Sir Roland Burrows drives the same point home with admirable clarity:

> The Court has to take care that evidence is not used to complete a document which the party has left incomplete or to contradict what he has said, or to substitute some other wording for that actually used, or to raise doubts, which otherwise would not exist, as to the intention. When evidence is admitted in connection with interpretation, it is always restricted to such as will assist the Court to arrive at the meaning of the words used, and thus to give effect to the intention so expressed.[15]

Now it is certainly true that among contemporary thinkers in the fields of political theory and jurisprudence (philosophy of law) the classical hermeneutic approach just described has not received uniform approbation. The most radical of today's legal philosophies, the Critical Legal Studies (CLS) movement, which reached its high water mark in the 1970s in the work of Roberto Unger and Duncan Kennedy, argues in deconstructionist fashion against the face-value of virtually all legal instruments. Carrying American Legal Realism's doubts about the objectivity of legal operations virtually to the point of existential solipsism, CLS regards the legal interpreter as all-important, the text as infinitely malleable grist for the mill of political activism.[16] But CLS has been decisively shown to be incapable of practical application in the legal field, since its position undercuts the very Rule of Law.[17] The impact of CLS on day-to-day judicial activity has been virtually nil.

Professor Ronald Dworkin, H.L.A. Hart's successor in the chair of jurisprudence at Oxford, maintains that interpretation, in law and other fields, is essentially concerned with *purpose*: "but the purposes in play are not fundamentally those of some author but of the interpreter. Roughly, constructive interpretation is a matter of imposing purpose on an object or practice."[18] On the surface, this suggests that Dworkin is prepared to sacrifice the text to the interpreter, but he insists that "constructive interpretation" does not mean that "an interpreter can make of a practice or work of art anything he would have wanted it to be."[19] The text or object of interpretation is a residual given which limits what the interpreter can do to it.

Moreover, Dworkin is so unhappy with American Legal Realism and so horrified by Critical Legal Studies—and quite rightly, in our view—that he has set forth his "one right answer" thesis: the view that, in deciding cases, judges can indeed arrive at a single correct answer, based objectively on the existing legal tradition.[20] Such a view, inconsistent though it may be with Dworkin's concept of "constructive interpretation," nonetheless shows that he is at heart an objectivist who refuses to sacrifice the integrity of the legal documentary tradition to the subjective whims of the interpreter.

The most powerful contemporary theoreticians of legal hermeneutics are certainly those in the "original intent"camp—thinkers who argue (as did Chief Justice John Marshall) that texts must be understood in their original sense, not twisted to fit the interpreter's agenda. Robert Bork, for example, admits to the difficulty of psychoanalyzing the Founding Fathers to discover what they really "intended" in framing the American Constitution (the dilemma thrown up by liberal constitutionalists such as Laurence Tribe), and so prefers the expression "original understanding": "What we're really talking about [is] not what the authors of the Bill of Rights had in the backs of their minds, but what people who voted for this thing understood themselves to be voting for."[21]

If, however, trying to determine the "original intent" of the author over and above his text poses extreme problems (Sibelius, for example, was hopeless at explaining the true intent and significance of his *Finlandia*!), the same dilemma attaches to the original audience of the text: they, too, may have misunderstood it—for any number of personal, societal or cultural reasons.

Thus the most sophisticated academic analysis of legal interpretation would appear to focus on the Wittgenstein-Popper approach: the analogy of the shoe and the foot. Interpretation is like a shoe and the text like the foot. One endeavours to find the interpretation that best fits the text (allowing the text itself to determine this). Here, "intent" or "understanding" is decided by the text itself.[22]

Such an approach fully supports the principle that the text must be allowed to interpret itself—in the sense that when different or contradictory interpretations of it are offered, each will be brought to the bar of the text to see which fits best. Interpretations therefore function like scientific theories which are arbitrated by the facts they endeavour to explain: the facts ultimately decide the value of our attempts to understand them.[23]

In the Wittgenstein-Popper model, the interpreter of course brings his prejudices (*aprioris*, presuppositions, biases) to the text, but it is the text that judges them also. And the meaning of the text is not to be established by extrinsic considerations, for that would yield an infinite regress. (If the given fact or text has no inherent meaning and one must appeal beyond it for its true signification, then that must *also* be true of the extrinsic facts to which one appeals. "Bigger bugs have littler bugs upon their backs to bite them/And littler bugs have littler bugs/And so—*ad infinitum*.") Of course, extrinsic considerations can be used to clarify ambiguity, but never to contradict the clear meaning of a text.[24]

Free Legal Advice for Theologians

What has our discussion of legal hermeneutics to do

with the interpretation of Scripture? Could it not be argued that Christian faith is a matter of grace and not law and that therefore the preceding analysis, interesting as it may be for the history of ideas, is irrelevant to the Bible interpreter?

Hardly, for (1) the Bible—as a matter of fact—presents *both* gospel *and* law, and, as Luther stressed, the theologian's task is not to eliminate either one for the sake of the other, but properly to distinguish them;[25] and (2) a confusion of categories occurs when we do not recognize that Scripture, which indeed centers on grace and salvation, is first of all a collection of *writings*. If we do not employ a proper hermeneutic to discover what the Bible says, we cannot be sure of its message at all, whether it deals with grace or law.

Legal hermeneutics offers the most powerful reinforcement for traditional, grammatical-historical interpretation of Holy Writ. And why is such reinforcement important? Because of the tragic departure from such standards of literal, textual interpretation of the Bible in the church today. Modern theology has done perhaps its greatest harm to classical Christian faith through the new hermeneutic. In general, modern interpreters refuse to be held to the fundamental rule of classical biblical hermeneutics that "Scripture must interpret itself." Because the contemporary theologian does not regard the Bible as a qualitatively unique divine revelation, he constantly employs extra-biblical materials (ancient non-biblical Near Eastern documents, modern scientific and social theories, etc.) to structure and recast the scriptural data.

Thus the Creation account in Genesis is construed—on the basis of extrinsic evolutionary considerations—not to intend to teach *how* the world came about (but only *that* God created it), in spite of its clear and repeated stress on the creation of each species "after its kind"; alleged scientific "impossibilities" transmute the account of Noah and the Flood—which could hardly teach more plainly a universal deluge—into a minor Near Eastern drizzle; ancient extra-biblical literary parallels are allowed (by fallacious *post hoc, propter hoc* reasoning) to contradict the veracity of Jesus' own affirmations of the Mosaic and Davidic authorship of Old Testament books; and modern rationalistic antipathies to the supernatural provide hermeneutic justification for construing our Lord's miraculous ministry as little more than a morality play. These are but illustrations of the fact that practitioners of the new hermeneutic operate on the general assumption that no biblical text is capable of objective interpretation but must be construed in a "dynamic life-relation" with extra-biblical materials of the past and present and with the presuppositions of the contemporary interpreter.[26]

Here indeed we have the "divination"—as opposed to interpretation—Lord Bacon warned against. Such an approach is the death of all meaningful understanding of Scripture—as it would be in reference to legal documents too, were jurists to enter on the same suicidal hermeneutic course. They do not, of course, since if they did they would be disbarred or removed from the bench; our courts would crumble. And the society which depends on the Rule of Law would collapse with them—or be transformed into something closer to barbarism and anarchy than to civilization.

In theology, however, defrocking is virtually impossible today (witness the late Bishop James Pike and the just-retired Bishop of Durham); and the effects of textual destruction are far less visible. Apathy and invisibility, however, have never prevented fatal diseases from spreading or reduced the numbers of their victims. We conclude, therefore, with two words of advice for the theologian interpreting Scripture today: *Gardez bien*![27] (Guard the good.)

Endnotes

[1]Published by Bruce in Milwaukee in 1968 and 1969 respectively. The present writer was one of the five contributors to *Spectrum of Protestant Beliefs*.

[2]Eugene F.A. Klug, " 'Sensus Literalis'—das Wort in den Wörtern, eine hermeneutische Meditation vom Verstehen der Bibel," 12/5 *Evangelium* (December, 1985), 165-75.

[3]Cf. Bultmann's seminal essay, "Is Exegesis Without Presuppositions Possible?," conveniently available in English translation in Kurt Mueller-Vollmer, ed., *The Hermeneutics Reader: Texts of the German Tradition from the Enlightenment to the Present* (Oxford: Basil Blackwell, 1986), 241-48.

[4]Roy J. Howard, *Three Faces of Hermeneutics: An Introduction to Current Theories of Understanding* (Berkeley: University of California Press, 1982), 165-66. On the varieties of contemporary higher criticism, see Steven L. McKenzie and Stephen R. Haynes, eds., *To Each Its Own Meaning: An Introduction to Biblical Criticisms and Their Application* (London: Geoffrey Chapman, 1993).

[5]James Moore, "Cutting Both Ways—*Darwin* Among the Devout: A Response to David Livingstone, Sara Miles, and Mark Noll," 46/3 *Perspectives on Science and Christian Faith: Journal of the American Scientific Affiliation* (September, 1994), 169-72.

[6]John Warwick Montgomery, *Human Rights and Human Dignity* (Richardson, Texas: Probe, 1986), 134-36.

[7]In legal literature there are occasional references to possible connections between legal hermeneutics and theological interpretation—for example, Per Olof Ekelöf, "Teleological Construction of Statutes," 2 *Scandinavian Studies in Law* (1958), 88-89—but the subject remains undeveloped. Moisés Silva, in his brief work, *Has the Church Misread the Bible? The History of Interpretation in the Light of Current Issues* (Grand Rapids: Zondervan Academic Books, 1987), includes as fields creating "Today's Hermeneutical Challenge" (chap. 1): Philosophy, Literary Criticism, Linguistics, History, Science and Theology. Law is conspicuous by its absence!

[8]Frederic William Maitland, *The Forms of Action at Common Law* (Cambridge: Cambridge University Press, 1936).

[9]The so-called Statute of Frauds, 29 Car. II, c.3, s.17 (1676). Though modified in various particulars, sections of this historic Statute remain in force today in all common law jurisdictions.

[10]Elizabeth A. Martin, ed., *A Concise Dictionary of Law* (Oxford: Oxford University Press, 1987), 189. For a fuller discussion of these canons, see, *inter alia*: Herbert Broom, *Legal Maxims*, ed. W.J. Byrne, 9th ed. (London: Sweet & Maxwell, 1924), chap. 8

("The Interpretation of Deeds and Written Instruments"), 342-444; P.B. Maxwell, *The Interpretation of Statutes*, ed. G. Granville Sharp and Brian Galpin, 10th ed. (London: Sweet & Maxwell, 1953); Rupert Cross, *Statutory Interpretation*, ed. John Bell and George Engle, 2nd ed. (London: Butterworths, 1987).

[11]Cf. *Uniform Commercial Code*, sec. 2-202.

[12]Charles E. Odgers, *The Construction of Deeds and Statutes*, 4th ed. (London: Sweet & Maxwell, 1956), 21. The cited statement offers a direct challenge to and refutation of the so-called "intentional fallacy" as commonly practiced in contemporary biblical interpretation; see John Warwick Montgomery, ed., *God's Inerrant Word* (Minneapolis: Bethany, 1974), 30-31, 41.

[13]*Gibbons* v. *Ogden*, 9 Wheaton, 187-89 (1824).

[14]Francis Bacon, *The Advancement of Learning*, II. 20. viii.

[15]Roland Burrows, *Interpretation of Documents*, 2nd ed. (London: Butterworth, 1946), 13.

[16]Roberto Unger, *The Critical Legal Studies Movement* (Cambridge: Harvard University Press, 1986); Mark Kelman, *A Guide to Critical Legal Studies* (Cambridge: Harvard University Press, 1987); Peter Fitzpatrick and Alan Hunt, eds., *Critical Legal Studies* (Oxford: Basil Blackwell, 1987).

[17]See especially J.W. Harris, "Legal Doctrine and Interests in Land," in *Oxford Essays in Jurisprudence, Third Series*, ed. John Eekelaar and John Bell (Oxford: Clarendon Press, 1987), 167-97.

[18]Ronald Dworkin, *Law's Empire* (Cambridge: Harvard University Press, 1986), 52.

[19]Ibid.

[20]Ronald Dworkin, in *Law, Morality and Society: Essays in Honour of H.L.A. Hart*, ed. Hacker and Raz (Oxford: Oxford University Press, 1977), 58-83.

[21]Robert Bork, interview in "Bork v. Tribe on Natural Law, the Ninth Amendment, the Role of the Court," *Life*, (Fall Special, 1991): 96-99. For his position in detail, see Bork, "Neutral Principles and Some First Amendment Problems," 47/1 *Indiana Law Journal* (Fall, 1971); Bork, *The Tempting of America* (New York: The Free Press, 1990); and cf. Ethan Bronner, *Battle for Justice : How the Bork Nomination Shook America* (New York: W.W. Norton, 1989).

[22]For examples of the contribution of Wittgensteinian analysis to legal hermeneutics, though centering more on the *Philosophi-*

cal Investigations than on the *Tractatus Logico—Philosophicus,* see Jim Evans, *Statutory Interpretation: Problems of Communication,* corrected ed. (Auckland, New Zealand: Oxford University Press, 1989), 16-19, 25-26, 29-30, 188.

[23]See John Warwick Montgomery, "The Theologian's Craft," in his *The Suicide of Christian Theology* (Minneapolis: Bethany, 1970), 267-313.

[24]The corresponding principle of classical biblical hermeneutics is that extra-biblical materials may be used *ministerially,* but never *magisterially,* in the interpretation of the sacred text. On the English legal scene, the opinion prevails in some quarters that the recent House of Lords decision in *Pepper (Inspector of Taxes)* v. *Hart and Others* (*Times* Law Report, 30 November 1992) erodes the fundamental hermeneutic principle that statutes must interpret themselves, since it allows the record of Parliamentary debate ("Hansard") to assist in interpreting them. However, *Pepper* emphatically does not displace the classic rule, for the decision expressly makes "a limited modification to the existing rule, subject to strict safeguards." These are: (1) use of Hansard is allowed only "as an aid to construing legislation which [is] ambiguous or obscure or the literal meaning of which led to absurdity" and only "where such material clearly discloses the mischief aimed at" by the legislation; and (2) even in such instances, it is highly unlikely that any use can legitimately be made of a Parliamentary statement "other than that of the minister or other promoter of a Bill." Thus *Pepper* is little more than a gloss on the *golden rule* and the *mischief rule* of the classic canons of legal hermeneutics (see rules 3. and 4. in the list corresponding to note 10, *supra*).

[25]See C.F.W. Walther, *The Proper Distinction Between Law and Gospel,* ed. W.H.T. Dau (St. Louis, Mo.: Concordia, 1928); John Warwick Montgomery, "Luther's Hermeneutic vs. the New Hermeneutic," in his *Crisis in Lutheran Theology,* I, 2nd ed. (Grand Rapids: Baker Book House, 1973), 45-77—also in his *In Defense of Martin Luther* (Milwaukee: Northwestern Publishing House, 1970), pp. 40-85; and John Warwick Montgomery, *Law & Gospel: A Study for Integrating Faith and Practice* (Merrifield, VA: Christian Legal Society, 1986), especially 5-10, 23-26.

[26]On the scholarly problems with form- and redaction-criticism, see the references in John Warwick Montgomery, Letter to the Editor, 3/12 *Ecclesiastical Law Journal* 45-46 (January,

1993); and John Warwick Montgomery, "Why Has God Incarnate Suddenly Become Mythical?," in *Perspectives on Evangelical Theology: Papers from the 30th Annual Meeting of the Evangelical Theological Society*, ed. K. S. Kantzer and S. N. Gundry (Grand Rapids: Baker Book House, 1979), 57-65.

[27]The Montgomery clan motto.

The Globalization of Biblical Hermeneutics

Craig L. Blomberg

In my first year of doctoral studies I found myself sharing a small office with a Singaporean. We got into a discussion of cultural differences and he was describing the old Chinese tradition of newlyweds living with in-laws. I remarked that it was hard for me to imagine living that way and, after all, did not the Bible teach that "a man shall leave his father and mother. . . ?" Courteously but pointedly, he reminded me that extended families more often than not lived together in biblical times, so that *his* culture was closer to the biblical practice in this respect than mine was.[1] I had not learned the term yet, but I had experienced a classic example of a lesson in the "globalization" of biblical hermeneutics.

Globalization as a topic in North American theological education has become a prominent issue at least since Don Browning's ATS address in 1986.[2] More than 70 seminaries or graduate schools of theology on this continent have participated in various programs relating to the topic. Perhaps the most ambitious of these has been the Hartford-based Plowshares program of international travel, cross-cultural immersions and theological reflection, which has produced an extensive collection of essays edited by Evans, Evans and Roozen and published by Orbis a year ago.[3]

But the concern for globalization far outstrips the world of theological education. For example, a relatively new academic journal, *Biblical Interpretation,* was designed in part to address concerns of globalization, and its inaugural fascicle included several articles about globalizing *hermeneutics.*[4] Similar concerns have regularly surfaced at the annual Society of Biblical Literature/American Academy of Religion consultations entitled "The Bible in Asia, Africa and Latin America."

So what is globalization? To a large degree, it depends on whom you ask, but it seems to me that five topics consistently recur with greater frequency than any others: issues of liberation theology, feminism, economics, religious pluralism and the contextualization of the gospel. I have addressed each of these briefly in an article in the Evans, Evans and Roozen volume, in light of the relevant biblical data, so I shall not repeat myself here.[5] Instead, I wish to suggest a definition for globalized hermeneutics that is both narrower and broader than this pentad of concerns. It is broader because it is not limited to the five topics just mentioned; it is narrower because it presupposes a long-standing evangelical hermeneutic. After setting my definition into the larger context of contemporary hermeneutical discussion, I shall give six illustrations, all gleaned from the New Testament, though I have no doubt that many profitable Old Testament examples could easily be adduced.

Definition and Contexts

For my purposes, I shall begin defining the globalization of hermeneutics as "asking a given portion of Scripture new questions, or suggesting new answers to old questions, which a particular interpreter has not previously considered because of the inevitably parochial nature of his or her interpretive communities and the historical and social conditioning those communities have created."

Defined in this way, globalization has probably occurred any time there has been a paradigm shift in the thinking of a given exegete, as, for example, when a classic Wesleyan-Arminian asks, "What would happen if First John 2:19 were treated as the explanation for all apparently apostate Christians?"[6] or when a classic dispensationalist (or other cessationist) reflects afresh on the significance of people other than apostles working miracles in New Testament times or of orthodox Christians uttering prophecies well into the third century.[7]

But these potential paradigm shifts, enacted repeatedly within relatively homogeneous subcultures, are not usually in view in contemporary discussions of globalization, so we must add to our definition: "When those questions and answers are suggested to the interpreter by representative voices of a different nationality, ethnic group, gender, socio-economic stratum, or even religion than those which have normally dominated the guild of biblical interpretation." Here, of course, we immediately confront major pitfalls. In some "politically correct" circles today, such voices have so overwhelmed traditional ones that a globalized reading of Scripture should actually work in reverse—challenging radical liberationists, liberal feminists or even members of other world religions, to consider more seriously historic, orthodox Christian readings. But given the obvious cultural and even subcultural homogeneity of evangelicalism, that is not likely to be *our* problem.

A more serious danger, at least from an evangelical perspective, is that the venture of globalizing hermeneutics turns into one in which novelty and creativity are prized more than legitimacy; or, worse still, that "validity in interpretation" (to use Hirsch's famous title[8]) is seen as an impossible goal because of an overriding relativism endemic to the interpretive task.[9] This is a topic worthy of far more serious attention by evangelicals than it has received, particularly because it is pervasive in contemporary worldviews. Most recent conservative hermeneutics textbooks unfortunately seem to presuppose that a modernist or even pre-modernist paradigm remains dominant, so that the challenges of reader-response criticism, deconstruction, social-scientific theories of interpretation, and the like, receive little or no sophisticated attention.[10]

My goal in this short paper, however, is not so ambitious. Rather, it is to suggest that we have a lot to learn from interpreters of a wide variety of cultures if we are willing to read expositions we might otherwise ignore, and raise questions we might otherwise never explore. Specifically, my thesis is that many contemporary students of Scripture, outside of the guild that has tended to dominate our circles, may in various ways actually live in cultures closer to the biblical ones than evangelical, white, male, affluent Westerners, and therefore may at times understand features of the biblical environments that we more naturally miss. If, as I take it, we are fairly agreed that the foundational task of interpreting Scripture is to recover some combination of authorial intent and textual meaning,[11] first of all through whatever textual clues the author has left behind, but secondly also through other germane historical-cultural background, then we should welcome the potential insights of those who may stand in a position closer to the original biblical settings than we do. Perhaps by asking some of the questions they ask and interacting with their answers, we may at times stand a better chance of recovering the true meaning of the text. And, to the extent that contemporary application is made easier when ancient and modern cultures are more directly analogous, the *significance* of passages for today's world may also be more readily clarified.[12] I proceed with my illustrations. The first is relatively detailed; the remaining five, more abbreviated.

New Testament Examples

1. The Epistle of James

Protestant discussion of James' letter has been overwhelmed by the legacy of Martin Luther's concern for the issue of faith vs. works. Surveys of the secondary literature consistently disclose that about a third of all the studies of specific passages in this epistle focus on 2:18-26.[13] Yet in the immediate literary context, these verses flow out of James' discussion of rich and poor in 2:1-17, and in the rest of the letter this latter topic is clearly more dominant (cf. esp. 1:9-11, 4:13-17 and 5:1-6). These and other passages actually give fairly explicit information about the Christian community to which James was writing: largely comprised of marginalized day laborers, working for wealthy landowners who were at times withholding their subsistence wage and committing either literal or judicial murder (i.e., by sending some of the fieldhands to debtors' prison—5:6). This led to quarrels within the community (4:1-3) and the temptation to show favoritism to the rich in an attempt to alleviate the suffering of the marginalized (2:1-4). Yet among recent evangelical commentators, only Peter Davids has explored this *Sitz im Leben* in any detail.[14] And even he shrinks back from some of the possible implications of James' advice to this oppressed community, as he strongly dissociates 5:7-11 from any "Zealot option," largely equates the poor with the pious, and sees James' thrust as primarily one of encouraging his readers to pray and wait patiently for divine intervention.[15]

I confess that is not what comes to my mind when I read the words: "as an example of patience in the face of suffering, take the prophets *who spoke in the name of the Lord"* (5:10) and "you have heard of Job's perseverance" (5:11, italics added). In the Old Testament, when the prophets spoke out about the suffering of their day, it was with forthright calls for social justice and with potentially inflammatory rhetoric to denounce the corrupt religious and political leaders who had neglected the poor and needy in the land (as classically in Amos and Micah).[16] And who could legitimately equate the perseverance of Job with passivity—he who complained bitterly to his friends and to God about his fate and yet refused to renounce his faith? I agree that James is not promoting violence, but I suspect he is as far removed from the Essene option as from the Zealot one, creating instead a "centrist position" that might be called the "prophetic option"—encouraging God's people to trust in the Lord's coming as the ultimate solution to social injustice but calling them to work for it by eschewing favoritism and forthrightly proclaiming and modeling God's righteous standards in the present age.

Yet the only major works I can turn to for sustained exposition and application of these themes are not written by mainstream evangelicals. In my opinion, the two best are *The Scandalous Message of James* by Elsa Tamez, a Mexican professor of biblical studies at the Seminario Bíblico Latinoamericano in San José, Costa Rica, and *Poverty and Wealth in James* by Pedrito U. Maynard-Reid, a Jamaican scholar and Seventh-day Adventist pastor.[17] I cannot accept all of the exegetical positions promoted in either work. For example, I dispute that the rich persons in 1:10-11 are necessarily unbelievers or that the merchants of 4:13-17 are to be linked closely with the rich oppressors of 5:1-6.[18]

But I certainly find much I can approve: Tamez's description of James as enjoining "militant patience," which includes non-violent resistance to oppression, reflected also in the choice of the term hupomone;[19] her balanced interpretation of the poor in 2:5, which ignores neither their dependence on God nor their lack of material possessions;[20] and Maynard-Reid's insistence that 5:1-6 "opposes the structures that enable the rich to increase their wealth at the expense of the poor—structures that fatten some and allow them to live in luxury while others are exploited and live in misery and filth, eking out a mere existence."[21]

Surely there are striking parallels between the plight of the landless, migrant workers of several contemporary North and South American countries, including places in which Christianity has grown rapidly, and the situation of James' church. Yet we hear few applications of our much-vaunted plain-meaning hermeneutic to 2:14, which employs the negative adverb *moy* with a rhetorical question to make clear that a person who has the awareness of the plight of hungry or inadequately clothed fellow believers, along with the ability to help, and yet does not do so, *cannot be saved.*

Worse still, when a brave voice in our circles occasionally dares to speak, as in a recent article in this society's journal, in the context of the larger issue of lordship salvation, at least one respondent tries to bypass the problem by limiting *sozo* in James to "practical sanctification" rather than also embracing "positional justification."[22] Yet in five short verses, workless faith will be likened to demonic belief, not a standard model for the "not-yet fully sanctified but still-genuine Christian"! There are very adequate ways to exegete James without pitting him against Paul and the biblical doctrine of justification by faith, but this is not one of them.[23]

I submit we have much to learn from our Latin American sisters and brothers whose more direct parallels to the biblical milieu make them less likely to get so far off track, at least on this issue. To return to Tamez:

> If the letter of James were sent to the Christian communities of Latin America today, it would very possibly be intercepted by the National Security governments in certain countries. The document would be branded as subversive because of the paragraphs that vehemently denounce the exploitation by landowners (5:1-6) and the carefree life of the merchants (4:13-17). The passage that affirms that "pure, unspoilt religion, in the eyes of God our Father is this: coming to the help of orphans and widows when they need it, and keeping oneself uncontaminated by the world" (1:27) would be criticized as "reductionism" of the gospel or as Marxist-Leninist infiltration in the churches. The communities to

> which the letter was addressed would become very suspicious to the authorities.[24]

Have North American evangelicals also "intercepted" the letter of James by refusing to stress the socially and spiritually subversive message of his epistle?

2. Matthew 2

Is James an aberration? Maybe it is too easy an example of the need for globalized hermeneutics. Consider then one of our favorite Christmas stories, the account in Matthew 1-2. Are our students and our churches in touch with the original meaning of the text here? We have all encountered the problems of non-biblical legends turning magi into kings, insisting that there were three, putting them at the manger, and so on. But have we heard the dissonant overtones that do resonate from the passage—a comparison of two kings, one a usurper and one legitimately born to be king (2:1-2)? Have we grappled with the fact that the conservative religious authorities were outraged at the birth of their Messiah, while pagan Persian astrologers found Him and paid Him lavish homage (2:3-12)? Is there any tie-in with the genealogy of Matthew, which begins with Jesus as son of Abraham (1:1)—the father of the Jewish nation to be sure, but also the one through whom all peoples on earth would be blessed (Genesis 12:3)? Of the various explanations for the unusual inclusion of the five women in that genealogy (Tamar, Rahab, Ruth, Bathsheba and Mary), the one that works the most consistently for all five is that each was shrouded in the suspicion (not always justified) of having engaged in illegitimate sexual relations. Yet God was sending a deliverer for "those kinds of people" as well.[25] Does that recast the not-too-distant debate between Dan Quayle and Murphy Brown in a somewhat different light?

Yet, again, to find a detailed exposition of the infancy stories, in both Matthew and Luke, that does justice to both the spiritual *and* social dimensions of the "liberation of Christmas," we have to go outside evangelical circles, for example, to the incisive book by that title from Richard Horsley.[26] Then we may suspect that when all Jerusalem was troubled along with Herod (Matthew 2:3), it was because that city was dominated by wealthy and corrupt Jewish leaders (and their families) personally installed by Herod, whose jobs could be on the line if a legitimate king appeared.[27]

Powerful rulers today who wield great authority by wedding religion and politics and denying justice to the oppressed should similarly recognize the birth of the Christ child as a threat to their position and be called to repent, change their ways, and worship him. Not surprisingly, Horsley's pacifist commitments[28] lead him to explore some of the same contemporary Latin American analogies as Tamez and Maynard-Reid did but also to contrast the message of the infancy narratives with the domestication of these texts in both secular and ecclesiastical culture in North America.[29] He concludes:

> The infancy narratives of Jesus, on the other hand, once freed both from the domesticating cultural context of "the holidays" and from rationalist dismissal as "myth," can be read again as stories of people's liberation from exploitation and domination. *The people who may respond most immediately are probably those whose situation is similar to that portrayed in the stories.* But for the modern-day citizens of "Rome," uncomfortable about their intricate involvement in the web of the new forms of domination, they also offer a challenge and inspiration to regain control of their own lives in response to God's liberating initiative in the birth of Jesus [italics mine].[30]

Asking different questions of the text again enables the retrieval of a dimension of its probable original meaning *and* contemporary significance which we have often missed.

3. John 3-4

Suppose we turn to a portion of the New Testament often assumed to be almost entirely "spiritual" in nature. Even liberation theologians have not found much to do with the Gospel of John.[31] If there is a promising chapter for them, it must be John 4, with the Samaritan woman as the heroine, despite the three strikes against her due to her gender, ethnicity and six men. Yet one may read extensively in both the standard commentaries and more recent liberationist literature without finding anyone asking or attempting to answer the question, "Why did this woman have five husbands in the first place, and why was she now living together outside of marriage with a sixth partner?"[32]

The vast majority simply assume that *she* was at fault, but that Jesus was willing to give her a chance at a fresh start nevertheless. But women in her world rarely had the right to initiate one divorce, much less five. It is at least plausible and perhaps even probable, that four men had legally "dumped" her, and that the fifth, as so often happened, had abandoned her without granting a divorce, so that she was forced to come under the protection of a man more informally in this sixth relationship. I am indebted for this suggestion to my former colleague, now academic dean of the Conservative Baptist Seminary of the East, Alice Mathews, in a popular level study of women in the Bible.[33] I have found partial parallels in Kenneth Grayston's recent commentary on John[34] and in Gilbert Bilezikian's study of gender roles in Scripture,[35] but little else.

Someone who does seem to have captured the correct balance, not surprisingly again from a woman's perspective, is Denise Lardner Carmody, who speaks of Jesus paying little heed to the woman's past, with its five marriages, "whether because of forces beyond her control or because of her own inclinations," but rather helping her realize that "she need not think of herself as a being condemned to haul water and pleasure men." Rather, "she could be a witness to salvation, a sharer and proclaimer of great good news."[36]

Is it coincidence that Jesus' dialogue with Nicodemus (John 3:1-15) comes shortly before his conversation with the Samaritan woman? I doubt it, and here many commentators point out the contrasts between a Jewish man who was "learned, powerful, respected, orthodox, theologically trained" and a Samaritan woman who was "unschooled, without influence, despised, capable only of folk religion."[37] How striking that the first went away baffled, while the second became a witness to bring many of her people to Jesus. Perhaps we should not be so quick to judge her pre-Christian character either; she may have been more of a tragic victim than an immoral slut. But this fresh perspective demands that we be willing to listen to and consider the voices of contemporary persons, in this case certain women, who may be better able to read the text from the perspective of the Samaritan. Then we might encounter interpretations that may strike us as highly probable, but which traditional ways of reading the text have obscured.[38]

4. Revelation 13 and Romans 13

A fourth example pairs another of John's writings with one of Paul's. It has been remarkable for me to watch the abrupt swing of the pendulum in various grass roots conservative Christian circles from the overuse to the underuse of Romans 13 before and after the Clinton election. Evangelical scholarship is somewhat more nuanced. Cranfield stresses that the submission enjoined of believers to the government is not to be equated with "uncritical, blind obedience to the authority's every command."[39] Harrison suspects Paul deliberately avoided the verb "obey" precisely because "a circumstance may arise in which [the believer] must choose between obeying God and obeying men (Act 5:29)."[40] Porter even suggests that the word translated "governing" in the NIV (from the Greek *huperecho*) should be interpreted to refer to authorities who are qualitatively superior, in this case with respect to their "justness",[41] though it is not clear if its standard usage allows it to be narrowed quite this much.

But it is rare for North American evangelicals to reflect on the juxtaposition of Romans 13 with Revelation 13—in the former the state seems to be divine; in the latter, demonic![42] For this task we have to turn, for example, to Allan Boesak, writing at the height of apartheid in South Africa, who alleged that the "authority" that has been established by God in Rom. 13:1b refers to a power and not to the government itself. As he puts it, "the . . . words, 'For there is no authority except from God,' do not mean that government comes from God, but rather that the *power,* the authority which the government represents is established by God." From this follows the corollary that "a government has power and authority *because, and only as long as,* it reflects the power and authority given by God" (italics his). In Revelation 13 this is clearly not the prevailing state of affairs.[43] Boesak's observations are grammatically possible, though not demonstrable; they are at least worth pondering.

More persuasive is the perspective of long-time U.S. evangelical (even premillennial) missionary-teacher to Central America, Ricardo Foulkes, who writes in his Spanish commentary on Revelation:

> we affirm that, to the extent that a government inspires terror in evildoers (whether they be drug-dealers, greedy bankers, traffickers in arms or brutal militarists), it surely deserves the obedience of the Christian; but to the extent that a government inspires terror more so in those who do good (and in the Bible, those who practice good works are defined essentially as people who give food to the hungry and drink to the thirsty, a welcome to

> strangers and clothing to those who do not have it, and who visit the sick and imprisoned) and use the "sword" to silence and intimidate them, it deserves the disobedience of the Christian (translation mine).[44]

Here is an exposition which takes adequate account of Romans 13:4.

I wish I could reproduce in its entirety the powerful poem "Thanksgiving Day in the United States" by the Guatemalan woman, Julia Esquivel, reflecting on the parallels between the sins of Babylon in Revelation 17-18 and godless Western materialism and environmental abuse. All I can do is give you a sample from the beginning and the end:

> In the third year of the massacres by Lucas and the other coyotes against the poor of Guatemala, I was led by the Spirit into the desert. And on the eve of Thanksgiving Day I had a vision of Babylon: The city sprang forth arrogantly from an enormous platform of dirty smoke produced by motor vehicles, machinery and contamination from smokestacks. It was as if all the petroleum from a violated earth was being consumed by the lords of capital and was slowly rising, obscuring the face of the Sun of Justice and the Ancient of Days. In between the curtains of dollars going up in smoke, the spectre of skyscrapers stretched upward insolently pretending to reach the clouds. In the darkness, millions of lights confused the ignorant as in the times of Babel. Each day false prophets invited the inhabitants of the Unchaste City to kneel before the idols of gluttony, money, and death: Idolaters from all nations were being converted to the American Way of Life. . . .
>
> Then, in tears, I prostrated myself and cried out: "Lord, what can we do? If they have no time to

> hear the truth and even less to seek it for themselves? They are a people too ignorant and too comfortable. Come to me, Lord, I wish to die among my people!" Without strength, I waited for the answer. After a long silence and a heavy darkness, He who sits on the throne to judge the nations spoke in a soft whisper in the secret recesses of my heart: "You have to denounce their idolatry in good times and in bad. Force them to hear the truth, for what is impossible to men is possible for God!"[45]

Are we denouncing the materialist idolatries of our age—through our writing, teaching, pastoring? Or are our personal and institutional financial priorities too indistinguishable from the secular world around us so that we are part of the problem rather than part of the solution?

5. Philemon and Galatians

Anyone concerned about racial reconciliation in this country had better take seriously the painful truths underlying Bill Pannell's at times overstated and even outrageous rhetoric in *The Coming Race Wars?*[46] The frustration for a professor wanting to expose students to African-American *New Testament* scholarship (one of Pannell's more modest requests) is simply how little there is (this is not true in many other areas of the theological curriculum). One important exception is the work of Cain Hope Felder.[47] One example of the globalization of hermeneutics from a volume of essays Felder recently edited encourages us to consider interpreting Philemon more in light of Galatians than Colossians. Had Walter Kaiser written this article, he would have dubbed it a use of "the analogy of antecedent Scripture,"[48] and it probably would have been widely acclaimed!

We may be able to agree that we see

> in Paul's almost dizzying display of family lan-

guage even Paul struggling with the fact that a gospel that subverts the fundamental distinction between Jews and Gentiles would not leave the issue of slavery alone. Here, I think, is a chance for black exegetes to claim Philemon as their own and as an indication of good news and of a new arrangement for blacks.[49]

6. The Parables

I would be remiss if I did not say something in my final example about one culture at times perhaps closest of all to biblical cultures—contemporary Middle-Eastern peasant village-life. No one has done more in recent years to illuminate possible historical backgrounds to Jesus' parables than Ken Bailey. Based on a career of Christian ministry in the Middle East, Bailey has excelled at collecting insights from traditional Palestinian and Arab practices that have been preserved down through the centuries.[50]

Thus we are indebted to him for suggesting that God's lavish love for sinners in the parable of the prodigal is highlighted by the father's *running* down the road to greet his son—an entirely undignified action for a well-to-do head of household,[51] that *anaideia* in Luke 11:8 probably means "shamelessness" rather than "importunity" (an interpretation possibly reflected in the revised NIV choice of "boldness" over its previous use of "persistence"),[52] and that *men* in Jesus' world beat their breasts (as the tax collector does in Luke 18:13) only as a dramatic gesture in times of extreme emotion.[53] Numerous similar insights abound.

Conclusions

I have hardly scratched the surface of possible examples of cultural insights that interpreters from other parts of the world or from outside of our guild have contributed to an understanding of the Bible. Undoubtedly, not all of the examples I have given are equally compelling. And I confess to have read a lot of "chaff" in order to uncover this "wheat." But then that seems to be true these days in the reading of the scholarly literature of any interpretive community! My plea is really a modest one—that we expand our horizons and read widely from sources that have not traditionally received much attention in the hegemony of German-English-American historical-critical studies. This may encourage us to consider other languages, most notably Spanish and Portuguese, as a valuable area of study. Numerous profitable contextualized essays have appeared, for example, in recent issues of the evangelical Guatemalan journal *Kairos* and its Brazilian counterpart *Vox Scripturae* or in the fledgling publications, *Jian Dao* from Hong Kong and the *Stulos Theological Journal* from Indonesia.

We need, further, to read the results of international colloquia like those produced by the five outstanding WEF volumes edited by Don Carson,[54] and then to create more such fora, and not always limit them to evangelicals.[55] We need to continue to travel and teach overseas and in our inner-cities and to come not merely imposing our own agendas and theological literature but listening to others' concerns and helping them to create their own appropriately contextualized studies.

If there was a "big idea," as Haddon Robinson would use the expression,[56] that came to me from the decade of the ICBI, it was that all the commitment in the world to inerrancy does not resolve numerous complex hermeneutical questions, though it obviously rules out certain options. Whatever you may be thinking of the authors of the globalized interpretations I have given, one thing they all share is the firm conviction that they are unpacking the actual meaning and/or significance of the text. These are not representatives of those branches of liberationism or feminism or any other ideology that so often begin with praxis or impose their own artificial interpretive grids on certain passages.[57] They have each done historical-grammatical research on the text and are convinced their interpretations are defensible at the level of the biblical world.

They merely believe that their own contemporary circumstances put them in closer touch with the setting of the texts they are investigating, so that analogies from their modern experiences stand a good chance of reflecting what the people in the biblical world were experiencing as well. They may sometimes be wrong in these judgments, but so may we when, often far less self-consciously, we anachronistically read modern Western images into the texts we expound. At the very least they deserve a hearing; at more times than we may like to admit, they may even be right![58]

Endnotes

[1] A theme now helpfully explored at length in Rodney Clapp, *Families at the Crossroads: Beyond Traditional and Modern Options* (Downers Grove: IVP, 1993).

[2]Published in "Globalization and the Task of Theological Education in North America," *Theol Educ* 23 (Autumn 1986), 43-59. Subsequent issues have provided helpful suggestions and bibliographies across the theological disciplines for would-be practitioners; see *Theol Educ* 29.2 (1993) and 30.1 (1993) *passim.*

[3]Alice F. Evans, Robert A. Evans and David A. Roozen, eds., *The Globalization of Theological Education* (Maryknoll: Orbis, 1993).

[4]*Biblical Interpretation* 1.1 (1993), esp. 67-87, 96-110.

[5]Craig L. Blomberg, "Implications of Globalization for Biblical Understanding," in *Globalization,* 213-28, 240-45. Cf. my additional reflections in idem, " 'Your Faith Has Made You Whole': The Evangelical Liberation Theology of Jesus," in *Jesus of Nazareth: Lord and Christ,* ed. Joel B. Green and Max Turner (Grand Rapids: Eerdmans, 1994), 75-93; and idem, "On Wealth and Worry: Matthew 6:19-34—Meaning and Significance," *CTR* 6 (1992): 73-89.

[6]As, e.g., in D.A. Carson, *The Farewell Discourse and Final Prayer of Jesus* (Grand Rapids: Baker, 1980), 98 (though I am not implying that Carson is a converted Arminian!)

[7]On which, see, respectively, Jack Deere, *Surprised by the Power of the Spirit* (Grand Rapids: Zondervan, 1993); and Cecil M. Robeck, Jr., *Prophecy in Carthage* (New York: Pilgrim, 1992).

[8]E.D. Hirsch, Jr., *Validity in Interpretation* (New Haven: Yale, 1967).

[9]See further the discussion of postmodernist and poststructuralist reading strategies in William W. Klein, Craig L. Blomberg and Robert L. Hubbard, Jr., *Introduction to Biblical Interpretation* (Dallas: Word, 1993), 117-51, 427-57.

[10]Though see the important, detailed appendix in Grant R. Osborne, *The Hermeneutical Spiral* (Downers Grove: IVP, 1991), 366-415.

[11]Cf., e.g., the diversity within unity on this topic throughout Walter C. Kaiser and Moisés Silva, *An Introduction to Biblical Hermeneutics* (Grand Rapids: Zondervan, 1994).

[12]Cf. further, Klein, Blomberg, Hubbard, *Interpretation*, 401-26.

[13]E.g., 23 out of the 75 entries in NTA for 1972-93—30.6%. The percentage rises to 36.8% (21 out of 57 articles) if we omit the years 1986-90 when interest temporarily waned. Otherwise the averages remain remarkably consistent over the years.

[14]Peter H. Davids, *The Epistle of James* (Grand Rapids: Eerdmans, 1982), 28-34 *et passim*.

[15]Ibid., 181-88.

[16]For outstanding balance on this issue, see M. Daniel Carroll R., *Contexts for Amos* (Sheffield: JSOT, 1992).

[17](New York: Crossroad, 1990); and (Maryknoll: Orbis, 1987), respectively.

[18]Tamez, *James*, 42-43; and Maynard-Reid, *James*, 69; for counterarguments, see, e.g., Douglas J. Moo, *The Letter of James* (Grand Rapids: Eerdmans, 1985), 67-70, 153-59.

[19]Tamez, *James*, 14, 52-56.

[20]Ibid., 44-45.

[21]Maynard-Reid, *James*, 97.

[22]Earl D. Radmacher, "First Response to 'Faith according to the Apostle James' by John F. MacArthur, Jr.," JETS 33 (1990), 40; cf. John F. MacArthur, Jr., "Faith according to the Apostle James," *JETS* 33 (1990), 13-34. No other use of this verb in James supports such a distinction: *sozo* in 1:21 comes in a context of declaring workless religion deceived and useless (v. 26); in 4:12, salvation is the opposite of destruction, in 5:15 physical healing is in view, and in 5:20, salvation is rescue from death.

[23]See any of the standard evangelical commentaries (e.g. Davids, Moo, Martin, Adamson, Kistemaker, Baker, Stulac, Burdick, Hiebert), ad loc.

[24]Tamez, *James*, 1.

[25]For a fleshing out of the points of this paragraph, see Craig L. Blomberg, "The Liberation of Illegitimacy: Women and Rulers in Matthew 1-2," *BTB* 21 (1991), 145-50.

[26]Richard A. Horsley, *The Liberation of Christmas* (New York: Crossroad, 1989).

[27]Ibid., 49-52. Cf. the discussion of the recent recognition of the corruption of Sadducees, in particular just before the time of Christ, in Markus Bockmuehl, *This Jesus: Martyr, Lord, Messiah* (Edinburgh: T & T Clark, 1994), 69-71, 109-12, and the literature there cited.

[28]Cf. his particularly candid self-disclosure in Richard A. Horsley, "Ethics and Exegesis: 'Love Your Enemies' and the Doctrine of Non-Violence," *JAAR* 54 (1986), esp. 27 and n. 15.

[29]Ibid., 127-43.

[30]Ibid., 161.

[31]But see David Rensberger, *Johannine Faith and Liberating Community* (Philadelphia: Westminster, 1988).

[32]An exception is the revival of the allegorical interpretation of the passage, as reflected, e.g., in Richard J. Cassidy, *John's Gospel in New Perspective* (Maryknoll: Orbis, 1992), 34-35.

[33]Alice Mathews, *A Woman Jesus Can Teach* (Grand Rapids: Discovery House, 1991), 24-26.

[34]Kenneth Grayston, *The Gospel of John* (Philadelphia: Trinity, 1990), 42.

[35]Gilbert Bilezikian, *Beyond Sex Roles* (Grand Rapids: Baker, 1985), 99.

[36]Denise L. Carmody, *Biblical Woman: Contemporary Reflections on Scriptural Texts* (New York: Crossroad, 1988), 105.

[37]D.A. Carson, *The Gospel of John* (Grand Rapids: Eerdmans, 1991), 216.

[38]For detailed elaboration of this line of interpreting John 3-4, see my "The Globalization of Biblical Understanding: A Test Case—John 3-4," forthcoming.

[39]C.E.B. Cranfield, *A Critical and Exegetical Commentary on the*

Epistle to the Romans , vol. 2 (Edinburgh: T & T Clark, 1979), 662.

[40]E.F. Harrison, "Romans," in *Expositor's Bible Commentary*, ed. Frank E. Gaebelein, vol. 10 (Grand Rapids: Zondervan, 1976), 136-37.

[41]Stanley E. Porter, "Romans 13:1-7 as Pauline Political Rhetoric," *FNT* 3 (1990), 123-24.

[42]An exception comes from the recent work of systematic theologian Stanley J. Grenz (*Theology for the Community of God* [Nashville: Broadman, 1994], 304): "The structures, therefore, have the potential not only to be the instruments of angels; they can also become the tool of demons. The New Testament presents human government as a case in point. Paul speaks of the civil sphere—and specifically of the Roman magistrate—as God's servant, for it provides for the punishment of the wicked and the rewarding of the good (Romans 13:1-7). The Book of Revelation, in contrast, presents the same Roman civil structure as demonic, manipulated by Satan himself in his attempt to injure the church through persecution."

[43]Allan A. Boesak, *Comfort and Protest* (Philadelphia: Westminster, 1987), 106.

[44]Ricardo Foulkes, *El Apocalipsis de San Juan* (Buenos Aires: Nueva Creación; Grand Rapids: Eerdmans, 1989), 156.

[45]Julia Esquivel, *Threatened with Resurrection* (Elgin, IL: Brethren Press, 1982), 79-91.

[46]William Pannell, *The Coming Race Wars?* (Grand Rapids: Zondervan, 1993).

[47]See esp. Cain Hope Felder, *Troubling Biblical Waters: Race, Class, Family* (Maryknoll: Orbis, 1989); idem, ed., *Stony the Road We Trod: African-American Biblical Interpretation* (Minneapolis: Fortress, 1991).

[48]See, e.g., Walter C. Kaiser, Jr., *Toward an Old Testament Theology* (Grand Rapids: Zondervan, 1978), 18-19.

[49]Lloyd A. Lewis, "An African American Appraisal of the Philemon-Paul-Onesimus Triangle," in Felder, *Stony*, 246.

[50]See esp. Kenneth E. Bailey, *Poet and Peasant* (Grand Rapids: Eerdmans, 1976); idem, *Through Peasant Eyes* (Grand Rapids: Eerdmans, 1980); and idem, *Finding the Lost* (St. Louis: Concordia, 1992).

[51]Bailey, *Poet*, 181-82.

[52]Ibid., 119-33. I say "possibly" because Bailey also attributes the shamelessness to the sleeping man not to the asker. Bailey is probably correct in his understanding of the term, but the NIV is probably correct in attributing the quality to the person asking for bread. See further J. Duncan M. Derrett, "The Friend at Midnight: Asian Ideas in the Gospel of St. Luke," in *Donum Gentilicum*, ed. Ernst Bammel, C.K. Barrett and W.D. Davies (Oxford: Clarendon, 1978), 83.

[53]Bailey, *Eyes*, 153.

[54]All initially published by Paternoster: *Biblical Interpretation and the Church* (1984); *The Church in the Bible and the World* (1987); *Teach Us To Pray* (1990); *Right with God* (1992); *Worship: Adoration and Action* (1993).

[55]Cf. the esp. challenging collection of essays in R.S. Sugirtharajah, ed., *Voices from the Margin: Interpreting the Bible in the Third World* (London: SPCK, 1991).

[56]See Haddon W. Robinson, *Biblical Preaching* (Grand Rapids: Baker, 1980), esp. 31-45.

[57]Evangelicals have not always adequately recognized the vast differences among interpreters who get lumped together under categories such as these. For a modest attempt to begin the necessary process of subdivision, see Klein, Blomberg and Hubbard, *Interpretation*, 447-57.

[58]I am grateful to my colleagues on the faculty of Denver Seminary for their reading and constructive critique of a previous draft of this paper.

The Foundation of Reformation Hermeneutics: A Fresh Look at Erasmus

David S. Dockery

Interest in the study of Erasmus and his thought continues to grow, both among Roman Catholics and Protestants, spanning the fields of literature, history, biblical studies and theology. In these same fields, the dominant questions facing representative scholars are matters that are hermeneutical in nature. We therefore study the hermeneutics of Erasmus for a twofold reason: 1) to learn who the true Erasmus was instead of the caricature of cowardice so often presented, and 2) to learn from this pioneering figure in the field of biblical criticism and hermeneutics in order to see how his approach was developed and received in his own day, and to see how it might possibly speak to the hermeneutical concerns of the present.

Erasmus was a transitional figure who was both Renaissance man and reformer and simultaneously neither Renaissance man nor reformer. As Erasmus' concern to study the original sources increased, so his hermeneutic developed. From this starting place, Erasmus drifted from his Renaissance views toward a new area where he found himself calling for the reform of the church. Yet, this movement propelled him from one sphere in which he was king into another where many of his most cherished beliefs were intensely challenged. Erasmus was, then, not only a transitional figure, but also independent, seemingly ambivalent, and without a supporting community.

The transition initiated by Erasmus formed the grounding and provided the significant intellectual equipment for the Reformation. The Reformation was a frightening experience for Erasmus, for it compelled him to choose sides in the ensuing religious struggle. Erasmus chose not to align himself with the Lutheran movement, though initially he was quite sympathetic with Luther. Instead he remained a critic of the church's wrongdoings as he sought to reform the church from within. But that choice, in the long run, was tragic for Erasmus and his followers because neither the Lutheran Reformation nor the Roman Catholic renewal could find a place for him and his ideals. Paradoxically, both movements were deeply indebted to the thought of Erasmus for impetus and direction.

Instrumental to both movements was a hermeneutical revolution that found its source in Erasmus. Erasmus desired to seek the simple, original meaning of the biblical text and to make it meaningful for the common man or woman. He thus stood in contrast to the medieval schoolmen, who created elaborate systems of biblical interpretation and theology that were beyond the comprehension and interest of the intellectually uninitiated.

The purpose of this chapter is to understand the basis of this hermeneutical revolution. In order to do so, we examine the background of Erasmus from the perspective of his Christian humanism and biblical scholarship. We then shall analyze the hermeneutics of Erasmus noting its sources and attempting to show the historical development in his hermeneutical thought. Finally, we will examine the impact of Erasmus upon Reformation and post-Reformation hermeneutics. This will include an attempt to discover the significance of Erasmus for hermeneutical studies in our own day.

Erasmus as Christian Humanist and Biblical Scholar

A. Christian Humanist. The leading Christian humanist of the Reformation era, who wished to reform the church through scholarly effort, was Desiderius Erasmus (ca. 1466/9-1536).[1] Erasmus was the most distinguished of many humanists seeking to simplify Christianity, to exalt reason and to emphasize morality over ritual. The New Testament was the authority for bringing about this much needed reform.

Erasmus, the illegitimate son of a Dutch priest, became a scholar of international reputation honored by popes, princes and university scholars as a genius, prophet, and servant of Christ.[2] In 1516, he published his critical edition of the Greek New Testament, a momentous event in the history of biblical scholarship because it was a necessary tool for anyone who wished to move beyond the Latin Vulgate. Also, he laboriously prepared painstaking translations of the early Christian fathers, which made it possible for scholars to compare the church in the 16th century with the church of the first four centuries.[3]

Brilliantly he showed his abilities to write literature of various genres ranging from the ironic and witty *Praise of Folly* (1509) to the serious and challenging manual for Christian discipleship, *The Enchiridion* (translated *The Christian Soldier's Handbook*, 1501) to the *Colloquies* and *Adages* (of which there are more than 4,000) in which he exposed human weakness, vice, superstitions and legalistic approaches to Christian piety.[4]

Erasmus, a cautious and careful reformer, attempted to provide his students and readers with a *philosophia Christi* that represented a clear account of genuine Christianity as he understood it. In this philosophy of Christ, Jesus serves as a pattern to be imitated and followed. For Erasmus, Christianity was a simple matter, not perfunctory legalistic acts of devotion or complicated scholastic systems of theology. Erasmus wanted to purge the church of these errors, which he believed obscured, even obviated, the simplicity of New Testament Christianity. He maintained that the primary means for bringing about this task included education, illumination and persuasion.

B. Biblical Scholar. Erasmus represented a break with medieval theology and thus the beginning point of the Reformation and contemporary biblical studies. With Erasmus, we find the first flowering of New Testament exegesis, based on criticism and philology,[5] through which the Renaissance—while restoring the link with the Alexandrian school of interpretation—was to prepare the way for contemporary exegesis. Erasmus represents a departure from the typical medieval hermeneutic and his hermeneutic must be defined as a fresh endeavor. This fresh approach, unlike Luther's hermeneutic, was not a deliberate reaction against medieval traditions,[6] but an attempt to return to the earlier sources, thus bypassing the medieval schoolmen.

Erasmus was a Renaissance man, a product of the movement. As the word "Renaissance" indicates, Erasmus was devoted to the rebirth of antiquity. Beyond this, he desired to Christianize the Renaissance movement so that the result would be not only an intellectual awakening but a genuine spiritual rebirth for the people of his times.[7] This new age was to be an age combining the very best of the classical and the Christian world, a classical world molded into a Christian pattern, a Christianized classical world.

Erasmus began his scholarly career as a thorough-going Renaissance scholar, totally immersed in the ideas of antiquity. But he moved definitely and deliberately toward a Christian humanism, even to the point that he could be identified with the Renaissance movement only with certain reservations; that is, that classical studies rather than being the *summum bonum* of literature must be adapted or made serviceable to Christianity. For Erasmus, the deepest meaning of cultured literature was not found in its intrinsic value but in its benefits for theology.[8]

Following his initial visit to England in the years 1499-1500, a definite change took place in Erasmus' thinking. The change did not move him away from his commitment to the original sources (*ad fontes*), but toward the Holy Scriptures as the chief among sources. This shift was occasioned primarily by the influence of John Colet, under whom Erasmus had studied during his time at Oxford. Colet had been lecturing on the Pauline letters at Oxford since 1496. He determined to discover the historical meaning of the biblical texts and this hermeneutical approach shaped the formation of Erasmus' pioneering hermeneutics.[9]

Erasmus as Biblical Interpreter

A. The Sources of Erasmus' Hermeneutics

The two primary influences upon Erasmus' approach to biblical interpretation came from his study of the Church Fathers and from his association with John Colet. Erasmus enthusiastically approached the ideas of Colet. During his days at the University of Paris, he had been introduced to the idea of original meanings of authors. His association with Colet encouraged him to direct his attention to the Scriptures. His reading of the Church fathers had greatly influenced and shaped his developing theology which was grounded in a "spirit-letter" or "spirit-flesh" dichotomy, a tradition that can be traced back to Origen and the Alexandrian fathers. It will be helpful for us at this stage to understand the approaches of these two significant figures, Origen and Colet.

1. Origen of Alexandria (ca. 185-254). Several important Christian writers of the second and third centuries engaged incidentally in New Testament studies, but the first important scholarly interpreter was Origen. He brought "the touch of a master to what had hitherto been nothing much more than the exercise of amateurs."[10] Origen understood biblical inspiration in the Platonic sense of utterance in a state of ecstatic possession. Therefore it was appropriate that the words imparted in this way should be interpreted mystically if their inner significance was to be known.[11]

Whereas Erasmus contended that there was letter and spirit in the Bible just as there is flesh and spirit in men and women,[12] Origen distinguished three senses of Scripture—literal, moral and allegorical—as corresponding to the three aspects of men and women, body, soul and spirit.[13] Although Erasmus was aware of Origen's threefold division of humanity, and on occasion enumerates these three senses, he does not clearly incorporate the tripartite approach into his hermeneutics, rather combining the allegorical and moral.

As Erasmus' hermeneutical method developed, he distanced himself from Origen and moved toward the model of Jerome (who had a twofold approach), stressing the literal over the allegorical. Yet it should be recognized that in the *Enchiridion,* Erasmus named Origen as the interpreter, next to Paul, who best disclosed the hidden meaning of Scripture. So it is apparent that Erasmus never completely abandoned certain aspects of the allegorical hermeneutics, even while developing his *sensus literalis* concept of Scripture.[14] Yet, it is the literal-grammatical-historical sense that most excited Erasmus and shaped his pioneering hermeneutics.

2. John Colet (ca. 1467-1519). Erasmus' career as biblical interpreter was influenced more by John Colet than by any other person, ancient or contemporary. Colet received the bachelor of arts and master of arts degrees at Cambridge. Following his study there, he traveled in Italy and then returned to lecture at Oxford while working on his doctoral degree.[15] Whether Colet developed his hermeneutical system at Cambridge or elsewhere is difficult to know with certainty. What is known for sure is that Colet's treatments of the biblical materials in his 1499 lectures were a departure from the medieval system of interpretation.

Prior to Colet, medieval exegetes concentrated upon organizing a body of doctrine, point by point, based on a conflation of biblical texts and supporting quotes from the Church fathers. Colet went to the text of Scripture itself and its direct interpretation. He focused upon the document and the author rather than the doctrine and the tradition.[16]

Erasmus greatly admired this approach and sought to add his characteristic emphasis of the original sources, which in this case was the Greek New Testament. Colet lectured from the Latin Vulgate, but Erasmus wanted to move beyond the Vulgate to interpret the Greek and Hebrew texts. So at this stage in his life, Erasmus devoted himself to the mastery of the Greek language. By the time that Erasmus had penned the *Enchiridion*, he had a vision for the reform of Christianity and biblical studies that would be accomplished by calling the church back to the Bible, the sourcebook of its faith. In order to understand Erasmus' hermeneutical contributions, it is necessary not only to see the insights derived from Colet concerning the historical meaning of Scripture, but also his dependence upon Origen's spiritual sense, even though this aspect of Erasmus' hermeneutics declined as his views developed and matured.

B. The Two-Sided Aspect of Erasmus' Hermeneutic

1. *Sensus Literalis*. To discover the philological-historical meaning of a biblical passage, one must first apply the method of textual criticism. The original words of the author must be recovered as far as possible by the restoration of the text. Erasmus sought to do this by emending the text of the New Testament, which had suffered considerable textual corruption since the time of Jerome. The result of this effort was the *Novum Instrumentum* (1516), the first critical edition of the New Testament.[17]

One of the oft-neglected elements in the study of Erasmus' approach to textual criticism is its Christological significance. Because Erasmus saw the sources as the means by which reform could be initiated, he realized too that *more* was needed than merely the conscientious study of the sources if the reform was to be implemented. This "more" was Christ himself. The *philosophia Christi* was the purest source for reform. But only through studying the sources could the desired reform be accomplished, for it is in the sources that Christ lives, breathes and speaks.[18]

Erasmus established hermeneutical principles beyond the initial steps of textual criticism, which as far as possible sought to determine the meaning of the actual words of the text. These hermeneutical principles included aspects of literary and historical criticism. When interpreting any biblical passage, Erasmus noted that the interpreter:

1) should weigh not only what is said but also by whom it is said.
2) should observe to whom the words were said.
3) should see what words were used at what time and on what occasion.
4) should note what precedes and what follows the words under consideration, that is, the historical and literary context must be known.
5) should have a knowledge of Hebrew, Greek and Latin as well as the disciplines of dialectic, arithmetic, music, natural science, history and especially grammar and rhetoric (both of which were preferred to dialectic).[19]
6) should handle the ambiguities and apparent contradictions by textual emendation and knowledge of grammar. If difficulties still remain, then obscure passages should be correlated with other passages to bring illumination to the problematic texts, which often led to allegorical interpretations. Also, these difficult passages should be viewed from within the circle of orthodox Christian doctrine, the teachings of Christ and common sense (= law of nature; for Erasmus, the law of Christ and the law of nature were in essential agreement).[20]

7) should at this point look to the Fathers[21] (the Greek Fathers are preferred to the Latin Fathers) and the classical writers for additional insight for the literal *and* spiritual meaning of the text.[22]

Following these principles, the interpreter should be able to discern the original sense of the biblical author. However, it is vital to realize that Erasmus was willing to acknowledge that even after applying these principles and the tools of philology and grammar, the meaning of some passages still remained obscure. Erasmus differed at this point with certain reformers, who stressed the perspicuity of Scripture. Erasmus remained willing to live with the tension of some unanswered problem texts. He did not want to remove the text from its historical setting simply for the sake of harmonization, but rather preferred to wrestle with the meaning of the text as it stood. He declared that some texts remained obscure and for this reason various interpretations existed among the fathers. Because of the difficulties that remained in the interpretations of some passages, in spite of Erasmus' genuine optimism for philological-historical hermeneutics, he maintained a cautious reverence for the mystery of the biblical text.

2. Spiritual-Allegorical-Tropological Hermeneutics. The obscurity of certain passages was increased by the fact that texts have not only a simple, historical sense, but also a deeper, spiritual sense.[23] However, Erasmus, like Origen, failed to recognize that figures of speech interpreted figuratively were, in reality, the literal sense. In fact, Hugh of St. Victor (ca. 1096-1141) had recognized and established that figures of speech belonged to the literal sense of interpretation.[24]

Whenever the words, interpreted literally, remained obscure or in conflict with the teachings of Christ, Erasmus suggested that the literal meaning must be shifted to the allegorical sense. Especially was this the case with the stories, primarily in the Old Testament, that contain morally offensive acts. Also, accounts, which while not morally offensive, were less valuable if interpreted literally rather than allegorically such as the story of Eve and the serpent (Genesis 3) and the historical accounts in the Kings and Chronicles.

Erasmus was careful not to *prove* important doctrines on the basis of allegorical interpretation, but believed they could be used to *confirm* certain theological truths. For example, the vision of the dry bones in Ezekiel 37 interpreted literally refers to the regathering and renewal of the people of God. Yet, Erasmus believed that a spiritual interpretation of this passage could usefully serve as a confirmation of the truth of the resurrection.[25]

J.B. Payne has outlined Erasmus' purposes in using a spiritual-allegorical hermeneutic:

> 1) to veil mysteries from the impious;
> 2) to exercise the minds of the pious since they are more avid for what is hidden and acquired with labor than for what comes to them easily;
> 3) to fix the divine truth in their (the pious) memory through imagery.
> 4) to lead by degrees to perfect knowledge.[26]

Erasmus, always the teacher, affirmed a pedagogical theme in the use of allegorical interpretation. The Old Testament, through types and enigmas, prepared the world for the light of the gospel. This approach paralleled the teaching method of Christ, who gradually revealed to His disciples the more sublime mysteries, not immediately, but through the progression of aphorisms, parables, signs and wonders. In so doing, Jesus led them from a recognition that He was a teacher—to the fact that He was a prophet—to the fact that He was Messiah. This pedagogical theme followed the accommodation concept in Origen's understanding of allegory.[27] Thus, God, in Holy Scripture, accommodated Himself to the weaknesses of His children, babbling and stammering with them as a parent to an infant.[28]

As we might expect from a moral theologian, Erasmus was ultimately concerned with the application of piety and therefore stressed the tropological meaning of the biblical texts. The goal of exegesis, as understood by Erasmus, was not the gathering of information, but the transformation of character that took place in the interpreter through the process of interpretation and learning.[29]

So important was the tropological/moral sense for Erasmus that he was seemingly willing to disallow the historical meaning of a text in order to receive pious truth. The moral teaching, however, must be consistent with some other portion of Scripture if it is not consistent with the present context being considered by the interpreter. Erasmus attempted not to violate the literal-historical sense, yet the dominant consistency in his interpretation was the moral sense of the passage. The tropological sense was exceedingly more important and simultaneously easier to grasp. It did not require the imagination required of the allegorical interpretation.[30]

For Erasmus, certain passages were difficult to interpret historically because of the ambiguities or obscurities in the passage or because of the seemingly immoral acts in the stories of biblical characters. Not all passages can be interpreted allegorically for numerous reasons. However, all passages can be accommodated to the tropological sense of Scripture and moral principles can be discerned. Therefore, the interpreter needs not only training to use the tools of literary and historical criticism or the imagination and insight to determine allegorical meanings, but a clean heart and pure mind to seek the ultimate goal of Scripture.

3. The "Both/And" Tension. It is important to remember that the "early" Erasmus emphasized the spiritual-allegorical sense of Scripture. In the *Enchiridion,* Erasmus placed so much emphasis upon the spiritual meaning of the text, that the literal was almost entirely de-emphasized.[31] With his increasing preoccupation with philological and historical exegesis, his appreciation for the literal sense was heightened and developed.[32] This literal-historical sense was present in the preface of the *Novum Instrumentum*, where he affirmed that the literal should not be scorned for it serves as the foundation upon which the spiritual can be built.[33] In his mature writings, Erasmus wanted to understand carefully the historical meaning of the text before proceeding to the allegorical, seeking to demonstrate the unity between the letter and spirit, the historical and allegorical.[34] Erasmus only rejected the historical sense when seeking to discern literary, historical or moral difficulties, considering such a rejection a moral necessity.

In the "later" Erasmus, the stress was placed upon the historical sense while calling for prudence and restraint, as well as simplicity in allegorical interpretation. In the *Ecclesiastica* (1535), Erasmus sought balance between the two aspects of his "both/and" hermeneutic. He observed that those on the verge of moving to a Christianity similar to legalistic Judaism excluded tropes and allegories from the Scripture, making the letter the law, calling that spiritual which Paul called carnal. Likewise he chided those who subverted the foundational meaning of Scripture, who rejected it because it was supposedly the lowest sense, when there was no necessity to do so.[35]

Erasmus did not simply return to the Alexandrian exegesis of the brilliant Origen, neither did he exceed the allegorizing of Origen nor neglect the strengths of Origen altogether. At the same time, the historical interpretation developed from John Colet was not employed to the extent that the allegorical or tropological sense was ignored. There was development from the early Erasmus in the *Enchiridion* who praised Origen without qualification to the later Erasmus who used Origen's method primarily out of necessity. The mature Erasmus attempted to retain the literal and spiritual senses, while stressing the priority of the moral sense. He combined in a tension-filled manner the philological-historical concepts of Colet and the allegorical approach of the Platonizing Origen. It was because of the richness and soundness of Erasmus' method that he became the positive influence for reformers (Luther and Calvin), puritans (Tyndale, who had been his student) and contemporary biblical scholars as well.

Erasmus as Model for Biblical Interpretation

A. The Reformers. In Erasmus, it has been said that Greece rose from the dead with the New Testament in her hand. Erasmus brought a breath of fresh air to biblical studies with his decided emancipation from untenable traditions. The English martyr, Bilney, owed his conversion to Erasmus' edition of the Greek New Testament. Tyndale, Coverdale and Luther all used it as well. Erasmus' famous words were quoted by his disciple, Tyndale, as he faced the disputation with the church theologians: "If God spare my life ere many years, I will cause the boy that driveth the plough to know more of Scripture than thou dost." One has to recognize the time period in which Erasmus first uttered that statement for its impact to be grasped. It was in an era when even Luther was 26 years old before he read a complete Bible. Erasmus was calling for a bold reformation where even common persons could read for themselves the wonderful news of God's gospel.[36]

In a certain sense, Erasmus had a right to reject the ridicule, *Erasmus lutherissat.* When his influence is properly understood, it can be affirmed that *Luther erasmissat.* Erasmus made an important break with medieval scholastic approach to theology and hermeneutics, but not in a reactionary manner. The break was through a combination of Christian commitment, Renaissance scholarship and the implementation of John Colet's hermeneutical insights. The genius and ability of Erasmus as a biblical scholar and moral theologian served as a model for Luther and other Reformers, thus paving the way for the acceptance of Luther's German translation of the Bible and the accompanying hermeneutical principles.

That Luther is the father of Protestant biblical interpretation is affirmed,[37] but Luther's way was paved by

Erasmus. Luther advanced Erasmus' hermeneutics, especially focusing upon the perspicuity of the text's message and the referencing of all Scripture to Christ.[38] Luther published hermeneutical principles in 1521 and 1528 with his German translations of the Bible. These two lists can be summarized as follows. He insisted:

1) on the necessity for grammatical knowledge;
2) on the importance of taking into consideration the times, circumstances and conditions;
3) on the observance of the context;
4) on the need of faith and spiritual illumination;
5) on keeping what he called the "proportion of faith" for maintaining the perspicuity of Scripture (often called the analogy of faith principle);
6) on the reference of all Scripture to Christ.[39]

Luther's commitment to the necessity for grammatical knowledge, the consideration of circumstances and conditions, the observance of the context, and the reference of all Scripture to Christ certainly reflects Erasmus' hermeneutics. Luther's stress on the christological aspects of interpretation, which included the themes of justification and redemption in Christ, differed from Erasmus' christological principle that focused on the teachings of Jesus. Moreover Luther's primary goal as interpreter was to overthrow the fourfold medieval exegesis.[40] As much as Luther disliked allegorical interpretation, even going so far as to refer to it as the harlot and dirt of the earth, he was not always faithful to his commitments and principles.[41] Perhaps the most consistent interpreter among the reformers was John Calvin, who best reflected the *sensus literalis* of interpretation developed by Colet and Erasmus.

In contrast to Calvin, Luther's interpretations tended to be subjective, directed toward the individual believer. Accordingly, Luther's hermeneutical principles at times led to extremes and to subjectivism. Luther stressed the religious feeling or the existential dimensions of subjective faith over against the object of faith, thus often losing sight of the historical sense.[42] Erasmus differed from Reformation hermeneutics, though he provided the framework and impetus for it. Yet the path that Luther and Calvin followed, which was previously rugged and troublesome, had been prepared and made more smooth by Erasmus.

B. Significance for Contemporary Biblical Hermeneutics. In post-reformation theology since F. Schleiermacher (1768-1834), no area of study has aroused more interest for student and scholar alike than biblical-theological hermeneutics.[43] Having developed the hermeneutic of Erasmus and shown its relation to the Reformation, we turn here to Erasmus' impact upon post-reformation thought. Such an examination will not solve the current hermeneutical debate, but it will provide insight concerning present-day discussions.[44] The present-day debate can be seen, in an oversimplified sense, as a discussion between objective hermeneutics and descriptive hermeneutics. The two outstanding representatives of these approaches are E.D. Hirsch, Jr.[45] and H.G. Gadamer.[46] Hirsch advocates an objective hermeneutic based upon the author's original intention. Gadamer is concerned to deal with the text, apart from its author, as a mediation of meaning. It is beyond the scope of this essay to develop this section fully, but it is important for our purposes to note that both the objective (literal-historical sense) and the descriptive (spiritual-allegorical) are represented in Erasmus.[47]

Erasmus' principles for a literal-historical hermeneutic stressed historical meaning, context, occasion, intent and tone of the work.[48] So, likewise, the contemporary interpreter in the objective school sees the primary task of interpretation as historical, in the sense that he or she endeavors to discover what texts and contexts meant to their authors in their relationship with their readers.[49]

Even as Erasmus moved from the allegorical principles of Origen toward a more objective interpretation, he did not neglect the descriptive hermeneutic entirely. Erasmus maintained that the text was capable of deeper meanings beyond the historical sense.[50] In the same way, the descriptive hermeneutical school maintains that the text is not a fixed, univocal depository of meaning, but an exposition of something that exceeds it. The text has a fullness of meaning that by its very nature, can never be exhausted. Thus it is sometimes the case that the meaning mediated by the text actually exceeds the conscious intention of the author.[51]

Though I reject Gadamer's hermeneutic, I appreciate the emphasis on helping modern readers find meaning—or what I would prefer to call "significance"—in the text. Thus in Erasmus there is a groundwork for an avenue toward "understanding" in the present hermeneutical debate. The author's meaning in the writings can be determined through dedicated effort to reach back and read the text in its original context and setting. But at the same time, the biblical text is a word to bring transformation to the lives of the present members of the believing community. Both dimensions of the hermeneutical task must be affirmed. In doing so, following Erasmus, two interrelated phases should be implemented: 1) the literary-historical and 2) the spiritual-theological.[52] The first is prior and deals with the external features of the text and the situation in which the text has been placed by its authors. The second is concerned with the inner life of the text, that is, how the text impinges on the members of the community, past and present.

In this view, the norms and principles essential to historical and literary methodologies are incorporated into the spiritual-theological interpretation, serving to guide and oversee the spiritual or moral sense. Erasmus has established a paradigm for contemporary biblical studies in establishing the historical sense as foundational to, but not separate from, the spiritual aspect of Scripture. The task of the contemporary interpreter, standing upon the shoulders of Erasmus, is to go to the author's meaning in the historical situation before coming back again to speak to the present.

Conclusion

Erasmus' work was the contribution of an innovative pioneer moving beyond tradition and supplying impetus for Reformation and post-reformation studies. His brilliance and courage paved the way for the direction of biblical studies for the following four hundred years. He exposed the religious abuses of the church and the excesses in the theology and biblical interpretation, while remaining an ally of popes and cardinals. He was prince of the Renaissance humanists, yet a conceptual and reforming theologian. He delivered biblical exegesis from the dictatorship of the Church tradition, yet he was a premier student, translator and editor of the patristic writers. He was a pious moralist, yet a scholarly biblical critic. His words were more powerful than deeds and his many-sided abilities are worthy of appreciation.

As the chief founder of modern biblical criticism and Reformation hermeneutics, he must always hold a cherished position among the interpreters of Scripture. With Erasmus, we find an innovator in his historical sense of scriptural interpretation and in his attachment to the human content of biblical theology. His conception of critical philology was the basis of his hermeneutics and biblical research.

Erasmus was the finest example of Renaissance scholarship emphasizing the original sources. The ultimate source to which he returned was the Greek New Testament. Coupled with the return to the sources, his was a truly historical understanding of ancient texts. But Erasmus sought not only the historical or literal meaning of texts, but he desired that the texts bring edification to the readers through the moral-spiritual sense of Scripture. Yet, while holding this "both/and" tension of the literal and spiritual senses of Scripture, Erasmus' hermeneutics developed toward a more critical-historical and philological approach as his method matured. In the "both/and" hermeneutics of Erasmus, we find the groundwork for the advances that have occurred in contemporary biblical studies, as well as a paradigm for determining historical meaning and contemporary significance in the current hermeneutical discussions.

Endnotes

[1]His Dutch name was Gerrit Gerritszoon, but he gave himself the Latin name, Desiderius Erasmus. For interesting biographical accounts of Erasmus, cf. J.P. Dolan, ed., *The Essential Erasmus* (New York: Meridian, 1964), 7-23; R.D. Jones, *Erasmus and Luther* (New York: Oxford University Press, 1968); R.H. Bainton, *Erasmus of Christendom* (New York: Crossroad, 1969); P. Smith, *Erasmus* (New York: Ungar, 1923); R. Clouse, "Erasmus" *New International Dictionary of the Christian Church,* edited by J.D. Douglas (Grand Rapids: Zondervan, 1978), 350-51.

[2]Erasmus' influence was immense. In England, John Colet (ca. 1467-1519), Dean of St. Paul's at Oxford and Thomas More (1478-1535) were in warm sympathy with his aspirations. In fact, they were involved in influencing and shaping Erasmus' thought on these matters. Cf. Frederick Seebohm, *The Oxford Reformers: John Colet, Erasmus and Thomas More* (London: Longmans, Green and Co., 1896); and W.E. Campbell, *Erasmus, Tyndale and More* (London: Eyre and Spottiswoode, 1949). In France, he was admired by Guillaume Bude (1468-1540) and Lefevre d'Etaples (1455-1529). In Spain, Cardinal Ximenez was one of his most ardent patrons. In Germany and in Holland, Erasmus' influence had a crucial contribution to make in the development of both Protestantism and reforming Roman Catholicism. Perhaps one of the great tributes to Erasmus was found engraved on the tomb of Andrew Zebrzydowski, bishop of Krakow, who died in 1560, where the words *magni illius Erasmi discipulus et auditor* were found. After studying with Erasmus in 1528, he considered himself among the disciples of Erasmus. Indeed John Colet said following the publication of the Greek New Testament in 1516, "The Name of Erasmus will never perish." Cf. J.C. Olin, ed., *Christian Humanism and the Reformation: Selected Writings of Erasmus* (New York: Harper and Row, 1965), 1.

[3]See the survey in R.T. Jones, *The Great Reformation* (Downers Grove: InterVarsity, 1985), 24-26; also cf. J. Huizinga, *Erasmus and the Age of Reformation* (New York: Harper and Row, 1957).

[4]A fine summary of these writings can be found in W.R. Estep, *Renaissance and Reformation* (Grand Rapids: Eerdmans, 1986), 78-93.

[5]Note the creative discussion in H.J. DeJonge, "Novum Testamentum A Nobis Versum: The Essence of Erasmus' Edition of the New Testament," *Journal of Theological Studies* 35 (1984): 394-413; also see the contribution by Edwin Yamauchi to this discussion.

[6]L. Bouyer, "Erasmus in Relation to the Medieval Biblical Tradition," *The Cambridge History of the Bible*, 3 vols., ed. by G.W.H. Lampe (Cambridge: Cambridge University Press, 1969), 2, 492-93; R.F. Surburg, "The Significance of Luther's Hermeneutics for the Protestant Reformation" *Concordia Theological Monthly* 24 (1954): 241-61.

[7]D. Erasmus, "The Paraclesis," *Christian Humanism and the Reformation*, 94-95.

[8]P.S. and H.M. Allen, eds., *Opus Epistolarum Erasmi*, 11 vols. (New York: Oxford University Press, 1906-47), 2136-185, *"Prouexi linguas ac politores litteras, magno rei theologicai bono."*

[9]Cf. J.H. Bentley, *Humanist and Holy Writ* (Princeton: Princeton University Press, 1983), 115-17; also cf. J.W. Aldridge, *The Hermeneutics of Erasmus* (Richmond: John Knox, 1966), 16, who observes that Erasmus maintained multiple sources including classical philosophy and the Church fathers, but the Scriptures were the chief source.

[10]R.P.C. Hanson, *Allegory and Event: A Study of the Sources and Significance of Origen's Interpretation of Scripture* (London: SCM, 1959), 360. It should be noted that the most inclusive work to date on Erasmus' hermeneutic, Aldridge, *The Hermeneutics of Erasmus*, generally ignores this allegorical/spiritualistic aspect of Erasmus' hermeneutic.

[11]F.F. Bruce, "The History of New Testament Study," *New Testament Interpretation*, ed. by I.H. Marshall (Grand Rapids: Eerdmans, 1977), 26.

[12]B. Smalley, *The Study of the Bible in the Middle Ages* (New York: Oxford, 1952), 1-25; also see the "Enchiridion" *Essential Erasmus*, 47-49.

[13]Hanson, *Allegory and Event*, 235-37; J.N.D. Kelly, *Early Christian Doctrines*, rev. ed., (San Francisco: Harper and Row, 1978), 73.

[14]Erasmus, "Enchiridion," *The Essential Erasmus*, 37, 39.

[15]Cf. the innovative work by W.R. Godfrey, "John Colet of Cambridge," in *Archiv für Reformationgeschicte* (Stuttgart: Mohr, 1974), 65, 6-18.

[16]A. Rabil, *Erasmus and the New Testament: The Mind of a Christian Humanist* (San Antonio: Trinity University Press, 1972), 43-44.

[17]Cf. K.W. Clark, "Observations on the Erasmian Notes in Codex 2," *Studia Evangelica* 53 (1959), 749-56; also cf. J.H. Greenlee, *Scribes, Scrolls and Scripture* (Grand Rapids: Eerdmans, 1985).

[18]Aldridge, *Hermeneutics of Erasmus*, 14.

[19]Erasmus was careful to examine the idiomatic expressions (particularly Hebraisms) proper to the language of the Bible which are particularly confusing when encountered in New Testament texts: hyperboles and other expressions to be taken in a wide sense. He did not forget that irony must be taken into consideration, including certain sayings of Jesus. He also insisted on the danger of taking words in a sense they may have had in Classical Greek, but which was not the way they were used in the New Testament. Cf. Bouyer, "Erasmus and Medieval Biblical Tradition," 504.

[20]This Christological center should be differentiated from Luther's Christological method by observing that Erasmus' focus was upon the teaching Christ in the Gospels and for Luther the emphasis was upon the redeeming Christ of the epistles. Cf. I.D.K. Siggins, *Martin Luther's Doctrine of Christ* (New Haven: Yale University Press, 1970) and J.B. Payne, *Erasmus: His Theology of the Sacraments* (Bratcher, 1970), 54-70.

[21]It is of interest to observe that Erasmus was not afraid to differ with and be independent of the fathers, even those he greatly admired like Ambrose, Jerome and the highly esteemed Origen. The fathers were never the final authority in the interpretation of Scripture for Erasmus. Though the fathers were given a place of high esteem and value by Erasmus in interpreting Scripture and though they remained the standard for interpretation, they were never the final authority. The Holy Scriptures were the final irrefutable authority for Erasmus. While Erasmus held to a high view of Scripture and emphasized biblical authority, he did not equate biblical inspiration with biblical infallibility and noted some minor errors or mistakes in Scripture, but he sought to deal with these difficulties through al-

legorical interpretation. Cf. Aldridge, *Hermeneutics*, 93-95.

[22]These principles are summarized and expanded in J.B. Payne, "Toward the Hermeneutics of Erasmus" in *Melanges, Scrinium Erasmianum*, vol. 2, ed. by J. Coppens, cited in Payne, *Erasmus: His Theology*, 45, 46, 252.

[23]The medieval scholastics distinguished four senses of Scripture: the historical or grammatical, the allegorical, the tropological and the anagogical without distinction. Payne notes that Erasmus, while quite methodical, was inexact in his terminology, cf. Payne, *Erasmus*, 48-49.

[24]Smalley, *The Bible in the Middle Ages*, 93-101. This was perhaps Erasmus' only digression in the development of his hermeneutical method.

[25]Payne, *Erasmus*, 49.

[26]Ibid., 49-50.

[27]Hanson, *Allegory and Event*, 224-231.

[28]Ibid.

[29]Again, here he followed Origen who maintained the moral meaning of Scripture as the most important level of interpretation. Cf. J.L. Gonzalez, *A History of Christian Thought*, 3 vols. (Nashville: Abingdon, 1970), 1, 220.

[30]Payne, *Erasmus*, 52.

[31]Erasmus, "Enchiridion," 47-49.

[32]Aldridge, *Hermeneutics*, 98ff.

[33]According to Smalley, *Bible in the Middle Ages* 95, Hugh St. Victor was perhaps the first to emphasize the historical sense as the foundation for the allegorical sense and to criticize the Gregorian tradition with its sublime disregard for the literal meaning of Scripture. Cf. also, B. Smalley, "The Bible in the Medieval Schools," *The Cambridge History of the Bible* 2, 197-220. Origen did not regularly stress the need to build the allegorical upon the literal, cf. Hanson, *Allegory and Event*, 242-58.

[34] H.R. Boer, *A Short History of the Early Church* (Grand Rapids: Eerdmans, 1976), 92-94; Bruce, "History of New Testament Study," 25.

[35]Erasmus, "Ecclesiastica," LB, V, 1028c, cited in Payne, *Erasmus*, 51.

[36]For discussions of this information, see F.W. Farrar, *History of*

Interpretation (London: Macmillan, 1986), 316-17. Erasmus' statement can be found in the "Paraclesis."

[37]A.S. Wood, "Luther as Interpreter of Scripture," *Christianity Today* 3 (November 24, 1958), 7; cf. B.L. Ramm, *Protestant Biblical Interpretation* (Grand Rapids: Baker, 1970), 53-57.

[38]Luther's "Christological Principle" was founded upon the ideas of justification and redemption (see note #20). Cf. J.S. Preuss, "Luther on Christ and the Old Testament," *Concordia Theological Monthly* 43 (1972), 490-93; and H. Bornkamm, *Luther and the Old Testament*, ed. by V.I. Gruhn (Philadelphia: Fortress, 1966).

[39]Farrar, *History of Interpretation*, 232.

[40]It is important to note that Erasmus never dealt with the eschatological or analogical aspects of interpretation. The finest work on the fourfold hermeneutic of the medieval schoolmen is B. Smalley, *The Bible in the Middle Ages*.

[41]Bornkamm, *Luther and the Old Testament* 248; cf. J.T. Mueller, "Luther and the Bible," *Inspiration and Interpretation*, ed. by J.F. Walvoord (Grand Rapids: Eerdmans, 1957); also W.J. Kooiman, *Luther and the Bible*, trans. by J. Schmidt (Philadelphia: Muhlenberg, 1961).

[42]T.D. Parker, "The Interpretation of Scripture: A Comparison of Calvin and Luther on Galatians," *Interpretation* 17 (1963), 68-69.

[43]S.N. Gundry, "Evangelical Theology: Where Should We Be Going?" *Journal of the Evangelical Theological Society* 22 (1979), 13, states, "Hermeneutics is the unfinished item on our agenda of theological prolegomena. It must be seriously addressed by all evangelical theologians and biblical scholars in the immediate future. Without a hermeneutical consensus, any hope for a consensus in theology and ethics is merely wishful thinking."

[44]Cf. the inquisitive discussion, "Was Erasmus a 'Modernist' Before the Event?" in L. Bouyer, *Erasmus and the Humanist Experiment* (London: Chapman, 1959), 137-51.

[45]E.D. Hirsch, Jr., *Validity in Interpretation* (New Haven: Yale University Press, 1967).

[46]H.G. Gadamer, *Truth and Method*, trans. by G. Borden and J. Cummings (New York: Crossroad, reprint, 1985). On page 473 of this work, Gadamer observes that nowhere is the debate over contemporary hermeneutical problems so lively as in the area of modern theology.

[47]In the present debate, there are some who seek to hold the "both/and" tension in a way similar to Erasmus without neglecting either side, e.g. A. Thiselton, *Two Horizons* (Grand Rapids: Eerdmans, 1980) who wants to affirm an objective reading of the text in its historical setting while recognizing descriptive (reader-response) reading for contemporary interpreters.

[48]Bouyer, "Erasmus and the Medieval Biblical Tradition," 502.

[49]R.M. Grant, *A Short History of the Interpretation of the Bible* (New York: Macmillan, 1963), 186.

[50]Bouyer, "Erasmus and the Medieval Biblical Tradition," 503-04.

[51]Gadamer, *Truth and Method*, 264.

[52]Cf. the discussion in W.G. Doty, *New Testament Interpretation* (Englewood Cliffs: Prentice Hall, 1972).

Hermeneutical Methods in the Westminster Standards

John A. Delivuk

Some controversies repeat themselves in church history. Today we are seeing a replay of the controversy over how to interpret the Bible. Because we can gain important insights by studying what believers have said in the past about hermeneutics, the goal of this discussion is to learn what the Westminster Standards, particularly the Westminster Confession, can teach us about biblical interpretation. Because of space limitations we shall examine only a few major aspects: "good and necessary consequence," the role of reason, the analogy of faith and the role of the Holy Spirit in biblical interpretation.

The Meaning of "Good and Necessary Consequence"

While "good and necessary consequence" is a generally accepted method by evangelicals today, it was the most controversial hermeneutic used by the authors of the Confession. Good and necessary consequence serves both as a method of interpretation and as a criterion for evaluating hermeneutical conclusions. Good and necessary consequence means that the Bible has implications that are equally authoritative and binding with Scripture's literal statements. There are two requirements for these implications: They must be morally good and consistent with the rest of the Bible, and they must be certain—not possible or even probable implications (the members of the Westminster Assembly believed that there was absolute truth and that men could know it). This position set the Westminster Divines in opposition to the positions held by the Sectarians and the Anglicans in the 17th century. Jack Rogers argues for the distinctive hermeneutical position of the Assembly from attacks by those on both sides of the Assembly theologically, the Anglican Arminians on one side and the Sectarians and Anabaptists on the other. The Anglican position was represented by Richard Hooker. Hooker asserted that the Bible gave only general principles, but few details of religious life. One pillar of Hooker's argument was the elevation of reason to an authority on a par with Scripture and tradition. Unlike the Anglicans, the Westminster Divines did not exalt reason; but, by defending logical deduction from Scripture, they maintained the Bible as the essential authority over reason.[1]

The following examples show how the authors of the Confession defended good and necessary consequence. The most important example of these defenses occurs in the minutes of the Westminster Assembly. Because of the influence of good and necessary consequence on members of the Assembly, and the influence this discussion had on the formation of the Confession, the portions of the minutes discussing this method will be cited in detail. The context of these examples is the discussion concerning whether or not divine warrant can be found for a divine rule of church government. The minutes of session number 640 answer the question: "Is necessary consequence a sufficient argument of Christ's will?"

> *Resolved* upon the Q., First proof; Christ proves the resurrection in Matt. xxii. 31, 32: "As touching the resurrection of the dead, have you not read

> that which was spoken unto you by God, saying, I am the God of Abraham, and the God of Isaac, and the God of Jacob? God is not the God of the dead, but of the living;" which is proof of the resurrection of the dead by a consequence only.
>
> This proof; Christ, John x., refutes the Jews reproaching Him with blaspheming for saying that He and the Father were one, by a consequence drawn from Scriptures," calling princes gods.
>
> *Resolved* upon the Q., Acts xiii. 34, "And as concerning that He raised Him up from the dead, now no more to return to corruption, He said on this wise, I will give you the sure mercies of David," which proves the resurrection of Christ by a consequence only.
>
> *Resolved* on the Q., Hebrews i.6, "And again, when He bringeth in the first Begotten into the world, He saith, And let all the angels of God worship Him," where it is proved that Christ is the Son of God by a consequence.[2]

The deliberations on this topic continued in session 649. The minutes give a series of resolutions. The first resolution is that there are Old Testament examples of *jus divinum* by implication. The examples used were the building of altars to God and the offering of sacrifices by men from Adam to Abraham, which was done in faith, but for which there is no command recorded in the Bible. The second resolution deals with the duty of the surviving brother to marry the wife of his deceased childless brother. There is no evidence that this was God's law before Moses except the example of Judah's sons in Genesis 38. The third resolution appeals to the "Jews having of synagogues and worshipping of God in them, and in particular of their reading of Moses and the prophets there every Sabbath-day." Next came the observation of the first day of the week as the Christian Sabbath. The following concluded the Assembly's resolutions:

> *Resolved* upon the Q., "and of baptizing persons but once. . . ."
>
> *Resolved* upon the Q., "In all which examples, as we have cause to believe that the fathers at the first had a command from God of those things whereof we now find only their example for the ground of their posterities' like practice for many generations, so likewise, though we believe that Christ, in the time that He conversed with His disciples before and after His resurrection, did instruct them in all things concerning the kingdom of God, yet nothing is left recorded to show His will and appointment of the things instanced in, but the example and the practice of the Apostles and churches in their time."[3]

In session 654, the Westminster Assembly finally reached the conclusion based on the proofs above. The Assembly concluded that the Bible teaches a divinely appointed form of church government, or a *jus divinum*. The minutes read,

> *Resolved* upon the Q., "Those examples, either of the apostles, evangelists, or of the Church planted and ordered by them, which are recorded in the New Testament, and are nowhere therein disallowed, and the particular reason whereof still abides, do show a *jus divinum*, and the will and appointment of Jesus Christ so as still to remain."[4]

The conclusion that the implications of the Bible are binding along with the explicit statements played an important role in determining the positions of the Westminster Assembly on issues such as baptism, worship, and the church polity. The citations above from the Assembly's Minutes used the three types of proofs of good and necessary consequence commonly used by the authors of the Confession, namely Christ's use of good and necessary consequence, its use in catholic doctrines, and examples from the Bible where the practices prove the existence of commands not found in the text. These proofs will now be examined in the writings of the authors of the Confession.

First, we consider Christ's use of good and necessary consequence. In his refutation of the Antinomians who rejected the consequences of Scripture, Samuel Rutherford appealed to Matthew 22:29-33, where Jesus used logical consequence to refute the Sadducees. Samuel Rutherford wrote:

> *God is the God of dead Abraham,* ergo *the dead shall rise,* by the very name of scripture, which yet was but a consequence drawn from Exo. chap. 3.6. *yee erre, not knowing the Scriptures,* and further he rebuketh the *Saduces* as ignorant, who did not make use of the like logicall consequence to see the truth of the doctrine of the resurrection, *yee erre, not knowing the scriptures.* Matthew 22.31. *Have yee not read that which was spoken to you? &c. ergo* it was their unbeleife and dulnesse that they did not read and understand the logick of the *Holy Ghost,* and they ought to have read the article of the resurrection, *Exodus 3.6.* in the consequence of it, as the Scripture it selfe.[5]

Rutherford continued in the same context, observing that Paul also used good logic in drawing arguments from the Old Testament (e.g., "Isaiah says," "Hosea says" and thus with other prophets).

The second defense of good and necessary consequence came from the ecumenical doctrines or practices derived by the method of good and necessary consequence. In addition to being an example of the second defense, the quotation below also shows the *key* assumption behind good and necessary consequences, namely that God knew the implications of his words when he spoke them. As a result, believers must accept both the literal message and the implications of the Bible. George Gillespie observed,

> If we say that necessary consequences from Scripture prove not a *jus divinum*, we say that which is inconsistent with the infinite wisdom of God; for although necessary consequences may be drawn from a man's word which do not agree with his mind and intention, and so men are often times ensnared by their words; yet (as Cameron well noteth) God being infinitely wise, it were a blasphemous opinion to hold that anything can be drawn by a certain and necessary consequence from his holy word which is not his will.

Gillespie concluded the result of this logic was to make God look as foolish as men, who are unable to see all the implications of their words. Therefore, one must believe that the mind of God follows necessarily from the Word of God. He continued his argument with widely accepted examples based on the use of necessary consequence, such as the admission of women to the Lord's Supper.[6]

Other authors of the Confession also used good and necessary consequence to defend and derive doctrines, like infant baptism. Cornelius Burgess, for example, used good and necessary consequence to defend infant baptism. He admitted that there is no text of Scripture that explicitly teaches infant baptism, however, men should be satisfied "that by like sound and necessary consequences I have from the scriptures made good this point in hand."[7]

Robert Baillie also used good and necessary consequence to defend infant baptism. He commented on the baptist rejection of good and necessary consequence as follows:

> When in their debates against the baptism of infants they are straited with consequences from the

> circumcision of infants, and the promises of the Covenant made with *Abraham,* and his children; many of them do run out so far as to deny all scripturall consequences: refusing with the Jesuit *Veron* in their reasonings all deductions though never so necessary and clear, requiring for every thing they will admit, expresse and syllabicall Scriptures.[8]

A less controversial use of good and necessary consequence was to support church discipline. George Gillespie took note of Bible passages "as either directly, or at least by consequence, prove that notorious and scandalous sinners were not admitted into the temple or to partake in the ordinances." Gillespie used the example of Deuteronomy 23:18, where the law forbids one from bringing the hire of a whore to the house of God, drawing the consequence, that it was even more "contrary to the will of God, that the whore herself, being known to be such, should be brought to the house of the Lord?"[9]

Gillespie also used good and necessary consequence in understanding the apostolic practice and doctrine of church polity. He wrote below that the existence of a church officer proved the institution of that office by God. He wrote, "That Scripture which supposeth an institution, and holds out an office already instituted, shall to me (and, I am confident, to others also) prove an institution; for no text of Scripture can suppose or hold out that which is not true."[10]

As is now evident, the Westminster Divines frequently used good and necessary consequence to defend their doctrines. They defended this hermeneutical practice on three bases: (1) that Jesus and the inspired authors of the Bible used it, (2) that its historical use in deriving doctrines from the Bible had precedent, and (3) that practices commanded by God are legitimate when the commands are not found in the Bible. They also assumed that God wrote the Bible in such a way that he determined the consequences of the words as well as the words themselves. Hence, the implications of Scripture are of equal authority with Scripture's literal readings.

The Rejection of Allegorical Interpretation

With the Assembly's adoption of good and necessary consequence as a criterion of interpretation taught by the Bible, there was a corresponding rejection of allegorical interpretation. Allegorical interpretation was used by two movements that the Westminster Assembly opposed: the Roman Catholics and the Sectarians. The latter used it to justify some unusual interpretations. Thomas Gataker, an author of the Confession, rejected allegorical interpretation especially where the literal interpretation was clear. He wrote that believers should not use allegorical interpretation of the Scriptures when a literal reading yielded a clear interpretation, and condemned groups like the Enthusiasts who tried to "obtrude on us their vain and profane fancies in stead of God's sacred Oracles."[11]

Rutherford did more than reject the allegorical method, he also described its problems. He listed them as follows:

> This makes 1 The Scripture a mass of contradictions and lyes. 2 This turnes our faith and knowledge into a phancie, for the scripture it selfe cannot be a rule of exponing [expounding] scripture, if the glosse destroy the text. 3 The scripture shall not Judge all controversies, as *Christ* referres the gravest question that ever was, *Whether he be the sonne of God or no,* to this tribunall: *Search the Scriptures for they testifie of me,* Ioh. 5 [sic John 5:39]. 4 All the articles touching *Christ,* his birth, life, death, buriall, resurrection, ascending to heaven . . . shall teach nothing, an Allegory shall cause scripture say the contrary.[12]

Rutherford rejected the view of the Antinomians and Enthusiasts that there are two senses of Scripture, a literal that proved nothing, and another spiritual and allegorical that only "spiritual" persons could understand. As proof of the literal position, Rutherford observed that Christ and Paul proved both the resurrection of the dead and the Messiahship of Christ by the literal use of the Bible. When the Pharisees and Sadducees, who denied these truths, opposed Jesus and Paul, the two men referred the opposition to the literal sense of the Bible, not its allegorical interpretation. Jesus and Paul taught that, "the scriptures hold forth not spirituall, might understand."[13]

The next aspect of good and necessary consequence is the limitations of it. Jack Rogers observed that there were problems in the application of good and necessary consequence. Responding to Gillespie's teaching on the subject, Professor Rogers said that Gillespie drew a distinction between natural and regenerate reason. Gillespie concluded that, because God was wholly consistent with Himself, man's deductions from the Scripture would correspond to God's will which tended to underestimate man's subjectivity in drawing consequences. Rogers concluded that Gillespie was not sufficiently sensitive to the possibility of men making errors.[14] Like any method of Biblical interpretation, the drawing of implications can be abused. One method used by the authors of the Confession to prevent this abuse was comparing their conclusions with other theologians. For example, Cornelius Burges said concerning his use of Scriptural implications about baptism,

> Nor haue I beene mine owne iudge, or expounded them out of mine head, but take such expositions as the most Learned Iudicious, Reuerend, and eminene Diuines of this last age, as well as others of lesse note . . .[15]

As the above evidence has shown, the acceptance of good and necessary consequence as a method of interpreting the Bible also involved a rejection of the allegorical form of interpretation because it was inaccurate, and not used by Jesus and Paul in the Bible.

The Role of Reason

The last item discussed under the heading of good and necessary consequence is the role of reason. Rogers observed that the place of reason to the Westminster Divines was subordinate to that of Scripture.

> The Westminster Divines give a definite, if restricted, place to the right use of reason whether under the name of light of nature, Christian prudence or conscience. But they make it clear that reason, in whatever form, never has an independent authority, but only an authority subordinate to and dependent on the Word of God.[16]

The following examples show how the authors of the Confession used reason as a servant to interpret the Bible and not as an authority independent of Scripture. In the first example, George Gillespie used reason to go from the effect—spiritual fruit—to the cause—salvation—as an application of the biblical doctrine of the assurance of salvation. He said, "It is a consequence no less sure and infallible,—here is unfeigned love to the brethren, therefore here is regeneration; here are spiritual motions . . . therefore here is spiritual life."[17]

Edward Reynolds, in his discussion of the nature of faith, allowed for the use of reason as a tool in understanding biblical content, but not as an independent authority. His argument concluded that Scripture was a more sure source of knowledge than reason. He wrote that all faith is not saving faith, for there is a faith that makes the devils tremble (James 2:19). "Faith, in general, is an assent of the reasonable soul unto revealed truths." Every inducement to assent comes either from the "light" of the object or from the authority of a narrator, upon whom men rely without evidence. He used an analogy from John 4 to show the Bible was a better source of knowledge than reason. The Samaritans first assented to Christ's miracles by the woman's testimony or by faith. Later they assented because they had heard and seen Christ, and this was sight. Both kinds of assent have attached to them either certainty or probability. The certainty of faith, "even above the evidence of demonstrative conclusions," is universally agreed, because men often are weak and untrusting. However, if faith depends on God's Word, which is near to the one who is the fountain of truth, whose properties include certainty and infallibility, this faith is more sure than anything produced by natural reason alone.[18] To summarize the analogy: The Samaritans depended upon the empirical or reasonable evidence of a fallible eyewitness. When they heard Christ, the evidence for their belief shifted from empirical evidence to a belief in the infallible living Word. Likewise, the infallible Word is a more certain source of belief than fallible reason.

In his defense of the Church of Scotland, Alexander Henderson, after defending the high place of Scripture, observed that the place of reason was a lower one than that of Scripture. He saw reason as a useful tool for guidance in circumstances where the Bible gave general rules, and men were to fill in details. Examples of these details were seating arrangements, times of services, locations of churches and the like. He wrote that the Scottish reformers had no pattern and rule of Reformation other than the Bible and the practices of the early church in the Word. While the Bible is perfect, and a perfect directory of church activities,

> it presupposeth the light and law of nature, or the rules of common prudence, to be our guide in circumstances or things locall, temporall and personall, which being *Ecclesiastico Politica*, are common to the church with civill societies, and concerning which, the word giveth generall rules to be universally and constantly observed by all persons, in all times and places:

Henderson used two rules to apply his point. First, the physician cannot determine the patient's diet and bath by a letter—the pulse must be touched. Second, when a change is not for the better, it is without and against reason to make a change. It is without reason because, when the change is made to something equally good, the reasons are equal. It is against reason because, in the case of an equal change, it hinders edification, favors the love of innovation, and downgrades the authority that made the constitution.[19]

The authors of the Confession gave a definite but restricted place to the proper use of reason. They used reason to interpret the Bible and to determine specific circumstances where the Bible left guidelines. They regarded reason, however, as subordinate to and dependent upon the Holy Scriptures. The authors view of reason as a tool to interpret and apply the Bible contrasted with the Anglicans who viewed reason as one of their three sources of authority, the others being Scripture and tradition.

Jack Rogers summarized the position of the authors of the Confession on reason when he said, "They did not deny the use of human reason, nor did they wholly discount the opinions of theologians, either individually or in council. But they claimed all opinions of men were valid only insofar as they agreed with the Scripture.[20]

The Analogy of Faith

In Chapter 1:9 of the Confession, another hermeneutical principle is taught, "The infallible rule of interpretation of Scripture is the Scripture itself." This principle is called the "analogy of faith." The Westminster Divines used the analogy of faith against errors in biblical interpretation, appealing to the whole of the Bible against those who would take passages out of context, or introduce rules of interpretation external to the Scriptures.

In his discussion on Scripture, James Ussher gave reasons why Scripture must interpret Scripture. From his examination of Scripture, he concluded that men can only know with certainty the teaching of the Holy Spirit by confirming it in the Bible. He said that the Spirit of God is the only certain interpreter of God's Word, which was written by His Spirit, for no man is able to know the things of God, but the Spirit of God (1 Corinthians 2:11). The Bible's prophesies are not of human interpretation, for their source was not the will of man, but holy men spoke as they were led by the Holy Spirit (2 Peter 1:20-21). The interpretation of Scripture must therefore be by the same Spirit that revealed the Bible, and men's interpretations are only acceptable as far as they can be confirmed by the Holy Scriptures.[21]

In the following quotation, Archbishop Ussher gave more detail concerning how the analogy of faith was to be used to interpret the Bible, namely more obscure places were to be interpreted by less obscure. He wrote,

> According to the Analogie of Faith, *Romans* 12.6. and the scope and circumstance of the present place, and conference of other plain, and evident places, by which all such as are obscure and hard to bee understood, ought to bee interpreted; for there is no matter necessary to eternall life, which is not plainely, and sufficiently set forth in many places of Scripture, . . .

He also showed that Jesus used the analogy of faith when he was tempted by the devil. Ussher wrote that the texts abused by the devil and his ministers may properly be interpreted using the example of Christ in the Temptation. When the devil tempted Christ, he abused Psalm 91:11. Christ replied that the Psalm passage must be understood in the light of the clearest and most expressive commandment, Deuteronomy 6:16, "Ye shall not tempt the LORD your God."[22]

The analogy of faith presupposes several assumptions about the Bible, among them its truthfulness, clarity, and consistency. Thomas Gataker observed that the analogy could not be properly used without these assumptions being consistently applied. Gataker wrote that the Bible is the source of all Christian doctrine. The collation of Scripture with Scripture gives many insights into the obscure places. No part of Scripture can contradict or take away the truthfulness of any other part.[23]

George Gillespie agreed with Gataker on the use of the analogy of faith.[24] For example, he argued against a position on the basis that it broke the noncontradiction assumption of the analogy. He wrote, "That exposition which now I argue against, tendeth to make one scripture contradict another, and to make that lawful by one scripture which another scripture makes unlawful, even some of themselves being judges."[25]

The Confession calls the analogy of faith the only "infallible" interpreter of Scripture. The authors of the Confession were reacting against the infallibility of the papacy. By calling the Scripture infallible *truth* in Section 1:5 and calling Scripture the infallible *rule* of interpretation in Section 1:9, the Divines were setting an infallible book against an infallible papacy. One modern scholar stated the Westminster Assembly's position in this way,

> It is almost cliche to say that Protestantism revolted against an "infallible Pope" only to set up an "infallible Book.". . . the Westminster Confession leaves no lingering doubts: There are two "infallibles". The first, already noted, is the infallible foreknowledge of God. The second is closer to hand: 'The infallible rule of interpretation of Scripture is the Scripture itself' (I.9, cf. XVIII.2).[26]

The discussion above has shown that the authors of the Confession believed that the only reliable way to interpret the Bible was by using the Bible. This method, called the analogy of faith, served as the Puritan-Presbyterian answer to the Roman doctrine of papal infallibility. The infallibility of Scripture thus lays a logical basis for Section

1:10 of the Confession—Scripture as the Supreme Judge.

The Holy Spirit Speaking in Scripture

The final authority is not the Scriptures, but the "Holy Spirit speaking in the Scripture," as Confession 1:10 states. Jack Rogers observed that the Westminster Divines

> claimed that all opinions of men were valid only insofar as they agreed with the Scripture. Furthermore, the Scripture was only rightly understood by those whose minds were enlightened by the Holy Spirit. But neither the reason apart from Scripture, nor the Spirit apart from Scripture was authoritative in religious matters. Only the Spirit speaking in the Scripture was the "supreme judge" in controverted points.[27]

As Scripture interprets Scripture, so the Confession interprets the Confession. This topic will be treated briefly here. Section 6 says, "Nevertheless, we acknowledge the inward illumination of the Spirit of God to be necessary for the saving understanding of such things as are revealed in the Word . . ." Section 5 on the same topic says, "our full persuasion and assurance of the infallible truth and divine authority thereof, is from the inward work of the Holy Spirit bearing witness by and with the Word."

Professor John Murray argued that the Confession is treating the Bible as the supreme judge of controversies, and gave the phrase "the Holy Spirit speaking in the Scripture" a different meaning than the Spirit's bearing witness in the hearts of believers. Murray said, "This phrase was put in the Confession to answer Rome, who insisted that the voice of the church was necessary as well as Scripture, and the enthusiasts who argued for a special revelation in coordinate with Scripture."[28]

While Murray is correct that placing the Holy Spirit with Scripture offered a valuable corrective against the Romanists and Sectarians, it appears to this writer that the authors of the Confession wished to say more than this about roles of the Spirit and the Word as judge. One must admit, however, from the quotations above concerning councils and tradition, that the authors of the Confession frequently did not mention the Holy Spirit when they discussed the Bible and other authorities, possibly implying that the use of Spirit here referred to the authorship of the Bible.

In contrast to Professor Murray, Edward Reynolds, an author of the Confession, showed great insight into the working of Spirit and Word. He saw the Word as absolute truth from God, yet it was a truth the Spirit worked within the soul to help men hear and to make the truth of the Word effectual by working to seal the truth. While Reynolds here is referring to conversion, man's need for truth does not stop at conversion:

> So then a true faith hath its evidence and certainty, grounded upon the authority of the Word, as the instrument, and of the Spirit of God raising and quickening the soul to attend, and acknowledge the things therein revealed, to set its own seal unto the truth and goodness of them.

How did a believer know the Word to be God's Word and the Spirit to be God's Spirit? Reynolds continued,

> undoubtedly the Spirit brings a proper, distinctive, uncommunicable majesty and lustre into the soul, which cannot be, by any false spirit, counterfeited: and this Spirit doth open first the eye, and then the Word, and doth in that discover *"notas insitas veritatis,"* those marks of truth and certainty there, which are as apparent as the light, which is, without any other medium, by itself discerned.[29]

Agreeing with Reynolds' belief that Word and Spirit work together, Dr. Wayne Spear notes the ways in which

Word and Spirit work together as supreme judge. Discussing the phrase, "the Holy Spirit speaking in the Scripture," Prof. Spear says negatively that this phrase denies that any human being or institution can give a final verdict in controversies. Positively, this phrase teaches that the Spirit is the "living judge who renders decisions in disputed cases." The Spirit who reveals the Word is illuminating the minds of believers so that they can correctly interpret it. "Thus it is not the Spirit apart from Scripture, nor the Scripture without the teaching of the Spirit, but *both* together." Religious disputes are to be settled by use of a prayerful and humble appeal to the Spirit and the Word.[30]

This paper has discussed some of the hermeneutical methods used by the members of the Westminster Assembly to write the Westminster Standards. These methods show both how the members interpreted the Bible and how they used the Bible to determine their hermeneutical methodology. One is impressed by their desire to use the same methods of biblical interpretation as their Savior, by their faithfulness to Scripture in making it the supreme authority in matters of religion, and by their realization that a humble reliance on the Holy Spirit is necessary for accurate biblical interpretation. One is also impressed that all the methods of interpretation mentioned above remain foundational for evangelical biblical interpretation today.

Endnotes

[1]Jack Rogers, *Scripture in the Westminster Confession: A Problem of Historical Interpretation for American Presbyterianism* (Kampen: J.H. Kok, 1966), 339. Following the example of Professor Rogers, all my 17th century sources except James Ussher were members of the committee that wrote the Westminster Confession. These men are called the authors of the Confession.

[2]Westminster Assembly of Divines, *Minutes of the Sessions of the Westminster Assembly of Divines (November 1644 to March 1649)*, ed. Alexander F. Mitchell and John Struthers (Edinburgh and

London: William Blackwood and Sons, 1874), 231-32. The spelling and emphasis of the original quotations has been followed.

[3]Ibid., 237-38. The argument concerning worship in the synagogue is also used as an argument for the regulative principle of worship.

[4]Ibid., 241.

[5]Samuel Rutherford, *A Survey of the Spirituall Antichrist. Opening the Secrets of Familisme and Antinomianisme in the Antichristian Doctrine of John Saltmarsh, and Will. Del, the Present Preachers of the Army Now in England, and of Robert Town, Rob. Crisp, H. Denne, Eaton, and Others. In Which Is Revealed the Rise and Spring of Antinomians, Familists, Libertines, Swenck-feldians, Enthysiasts, &c.* (London: Printed by J.D. & R.I. for Andrew Crooke, 1648), pt. 1, 50.

[6]George Gillespie, *A Treatise of Miscellany Questions; Wherein Many Useful Questions and Cases of Conscience are Discussed and Resolved, for the Satisfaction of Those Who Desire Nothing More than to Search for and Find Out Precious Truths in the Controversies of these Times* (Edinburgh: Printed by George Lithgow for George Swintoun, 1649; reprint ed. in *The Presbyterian's Armoury*, vol. 1, Edinburgh: Robert Ogle, and Oliver & Boyd, 1844 *Treatise of Miscellany Questions*), 102-03.

[7]Cornelius Burges, *Baptismall Regeneration of Elect Infants, Professed by the Church of England, according to the Scriptures, and Primitiue Church, the Present Reformed Churches and Many Particular Divines Apart* (Oxford: Printed by I.L. for Henry Curteyn, 1629), 113-14.

[8]Robert Baillie, *Anabaptism, the Trve Fovntaine of Independency, Antinomy, Brownisme, Familisme, and the Most of the Other Errours, Which for the Time Doe Trouble the Church of England, Vnsealed* (London: Printed by M.F. for Samuel Gellibrand, 1646), 37.

[9]George Gillespie, *Aaron's Rod Blossoming; or The Divine Ordinance of Church Government Vindicated* (London: Printed by E.G. for Richard Whitaker, 1646; reprint ed. in *The Presbyterian's Armoury*, vol. 1, Edinburgh: Robert Ogle, and Oliver & Boyd, 1844), 44.

[10]George Gillespie, *Male Audis; or, An Answer to Mr. Coleman's Male Dicis* (London: Printed for Robert Bostocke, 1646; reprint ed. in *The Presbyterian's Armoury*, vol. 2, Edinburgh: Robert Ogle, and Oliver & Boyd, 1844), 7.

[11]Thomas Gataker, *Shadowes without Substance, or, Pretended New Lights: Together, with the Impieties and Blasphemies That Lurk under Them, Further Discovered and Drawn Forth into the Light: In Way of Rejoynder unto Mr Iohn Saltmarsh His Reply: Entituled Shadowes Flying away* (London: Robert Bostock, 1646), 69.

[12]Rutherford, *Survey of the Spirituall Antichrist*, pt. 1, 67.

[13]Ibid., pt. 1, 23.

[14]Rogers, *Scripture in the Westminster Confession*, 335-36.

[15]Burges, *Baptismall Regeneration of Elect Infants*, 114. The writings of the authors of the Confession are filled with quotations, notes or allusions to other theologians.

[16]Rogers, *Scripture in the Westminster Confession*, 365.

[17]Gillespie, *Treatise of Miscellany Questions*, 104. Gillespie used reason as a tool for determining the "good and necessary consequences" of Bible passages.

[18]Edward Reynolds, *The Whole Works of the Right Rev. Edward Reynolds, D.D.* (London: Printed for B. Holdsworth, 1826), 3:141.

[19]Alexander Henderson, *Reformation of Church-Government in Scotland, Cleered from Some Mistakes and Prejudices, by the Commissioners of the Generall Assembly of the Church of Scotland, Now at London* (n.p.: Robert Bostock, 1644), 5.

[20]Rogers, *Scripture in the Westminster Confession*, 430.

[21]James Ussher, *A Body of Divinitie, or the Svmme and Svbstance of Christian Religion* (London: Printed by M.F. for Tho: Dovvnes and Geo: Badger, 1645), 24. While Ussher was not a member of the Westminster Assembly, he exercised a great influence on it.

[22]Ibid., 25.

[23]Gataker, *Shadowes without Substance*, 29.

[24]Gillespie, *Treatise of Miscellany Questions*, 21.

[25]Gillespie, *Aaron's Rod Blossoming*, 184.

[26]Charles K. Robinson, "Philosophical Biblicism: The Teaching of the Westminster Confession Concerning God, the Natural Man, and Revelation and Authority." *Scottish Journal of Theology* 18 (March 1965): 37.

[27]Jack B. Rogers and Donald K. McKim, *The Authority and Interpretation of the Bible* (San Francisco: Harper and Row, 1979), 217-18.

[28]John Murray, "The Theology of the Westminster Confession," in *Scripture and Confession*, ed. John H. Skilton (n.p.: Presbyterian and Reformed Publishing Co., 1973), 130.

[29]Reynolds, *Whole Works*, 1:462-63.

[30]Wayne R. Spear, "The Westminster Assembly and Biblical Interpretation" in *The Book of Books*, ed. John H. White (n.p.: Presbyterian and Reformed Publishing Co., 1978), 51-52.

Hermeneutics: With History or with Hubris

David W. Hall

"Historiam esse vitae magistram, vere dixerunt ethnicic &c."

Calvin on Romans 4:23-24.

"History is philosophy teaching by example."

Lord Bolingbroke

Even though widely esteemed as one of the premier commentators on Scripture in his day, in the preface to his commentary on Job (first published in English in 1587) Theodore Beza confessed: "I am minded to expound the *histories* [emphasis added] of Job, in which . . . there are many dark and hard places, insomuch as I must here of necessity sail, as it were, among the rocks; and yet I hope I shall not make any shipwreck."[1]

Beza's awareness of the past—along with its complexity—led him to a humble assessment of his own ability as an exegete. The two prominent options for him were: (1) a historically informed hermeneutic ("the histories of Job"), or (2) a shipwreck resulting from an unawareness of the previous interpretations of Job. In this instance, Calvin's disciple saw the choice between a hermeneutic *cum* history, or a hermeneutic with pride of discovery (hubris)—but capable of shipwreck. He chose the former, and with an appreciation for the history of interpretation, found not only a sounder platform, but also evidenced much more humility than many moderns. Many today would also profit from a similar history-induced humility.

Indeed the hermeneutical enterprise would be vastly strengthened by an improved working knowledge of the history of interpretation of any event, theory, or text. If such is confirmed, then it is also predicted that—in any endeavor at interpretation, whether in science or religious or philosophical hermeneutics—not only will sounder interpretation result, but also humility will be a by-product as well. Or in terms of a recipe: History (*historia*) added to hermeneutic (*hermeneia*) will yield more humility or less *hubris*.

Any interpreter who approaches his text, theory, or subject unfamiliar with what has gone before, will predictably be less progressive (having to dedicate much time to basic rediscoveries, which others have already documented), but also will be more proud of his eventual discoveries. Such pride of discovery, while exhilarating and fulfilling, is also a fine fit with the self-centeredness that so characterizes our age. If one adopts a humbler position, holding out the possibility that prior interpreters may have been equal to or greater than ourselves, then one can more readily benefit from their previous foundation, and as a result have a more sober assessment of one's own originality. In both cases, progress and humility go hand in hand, whereas on the other model, hubris and static conditions characterize the approach that arrogantly and automatically discounts those who have preceded us. A preferred model, therefore, will value history as an interpretive variable over the hubris associated with claims to original (or novel) discovery.

Biblical interpretations need not be ignored by each successive generation, nor rediscovered by the alternating generations. We could profit much by studying the "Old Paths" (Jeremiah 6:16 and 18:15), and attempting to mold our inchoate exegesis after the progress of our spiritual ancestors. The same may be true for scientific progress. Frequently, the greatest heuristic value is found in an approach that embraces the validity of history and other knowledge outside of the scientist alone. Such is the better part of wisdom, as we seek to rule out ill-conceived modes of interpreting.

Likewise, we can benefit from those who have already pioneered some of these paths for us. Or we can disregard their work, foolishly presuming that we are sufficient to discover all biblical truth by ourselves in our own generation. A rediscovery of the interpretations from the orthodox of the past is sorely needed in our own day. Such theological giants, exegetical exemplars, and confessions could teach us much. The choice, in the end, may be between hubris or humility.

Dutch theologian Abraham Kuyper helpfully points out how errors of interpretation can be avoided by process of elimination through the use of history and confession. Kuyper put great store in the information provided through a historical study of the church's official views: "The church tells you at once what fallible interpretations you need no longer try, and what interpretation on the other hand offers you the best chance for success."[2] Kuyper admonishes: "Take account of what history and the life of the church teach" about various theological topics. Thus history has utility to highlight "which paths [are] useless to further reconnoiter." History has heuristic value, in eliminating erroneous dead-end paths in hermeneutics, as well as in any other scientific discipline.

Thus Kuyper advised that we must not deny history. He advocated that we see the history of interpretation as a partial guarantor of "freedom from error." It would be an act of supreme arrogance to elevate our own limited experience and perspective over the sum of those who have gone before us. Rather it is "by the history of the churches" that one "shall take the dogmas of the church as his guide that he shall not diverge from them until he is compelled to do so by the Word of God."[3] For Kuyper the theological enterprise is a thoroughly historical one that greatly values church history. As an application of Santayana to hermeneutics, we may therefore say that exegetes who fail to learn the errors of past hermeneutics are doomed to repeat them. The same principle is generally true in science and philosophy.

G.K. Chesterton spoke of church tradition as a "democracy of the dead," meaning that (for those who love popular referendums) if we truly understand the unity of the church—both militant and triumphant—we will not disenfranchise those in the church who have gone home to be with the Lord. They, too, have much to say in the hermeneutical referenda of today. Though dead, they still speak (Hebrews 11:4), and to them we need to learn to listen. Perhaps we would make fewer mistakes if we returned free expression to those spiritual researchers and exegetes who have preceded us. Of course, to do so compels us to adopt the posture of John the Baptizer, accepting that they must increase, while we must decrease.

This *a priori* commitment has value in a range of academic disciplines. Recently, those in civil government have been urged to learn from history. Richard E. Neustadt and Ernest R. May in *Thinking in Time: The Uses of History for Decision Makers*[4] urge decision makers to know the "issue history, . . . a start toward using history effectively," while announcing, "Better decision-making involves drawing on history to frame sharper questions and doing so systematically, routinely." These political scientists advocate the concept of historical "placement," which involves "using historical information to enrich initial stereotypes about another person's outlook . . . Conjecturing about the world view of a stranger with whom one must deal is commonplace in government."[5] They call for historical "placing" of persons against the backdrop of "large historical events, the stuff of public history, which may mold current views . . . ." If history is useful for interpretation in the civic realm, how much more for the theologian in the ecclesiastical realm? Or for the scientist in the laboratory? Neustadt and May perceptively state: "Wrapped up in those claims, differentiating them still further, are implicit values. For the models undergirded by historical impressions are built of beliefs. . . . Many are beliefs about how fellow human beings behave. . . ."[6] Even secular experts recognize the value-ladenness of interpretive structures and the utility of history in evaluating such.

Richard Pipes recently made the same point:

> In his *Astonishing Hypothesis,* Sir Francis Crick informs the world of his discovery that we have no "soul" and that our feelings and thoughts "are in fact no more than the behavior of a vast assembly of nerve cells and their associated molecules." That this idea should strike him as a revelation indicates only that for all his scientific brilliance, Sir Francis is poorly versed in intellectual history. For this notion is over three hundred years old, having been first intimated by John Locke in his *Essay on Human Understanding* (1690), which denied the existence of "innate ideas" and therefore anything resembling a soul as an entity separate from the body. The notion was taken over and pushed to its logical extremes by French eighteenth century materialists. . . . In other words, far from being an "astonishing hypothesis," the idea is old hat. It has also proved extremely pernicious. Popularized in Russia . . . it exerted profound influence on the future Bolsheviks, who concluded that since man was nothing more than material substance, he could be molded and remade in any desired shape. It provided the philosophical justification for the

> Stalinist and Maoist attempts to create "new men." Seventy years of Communist experience, ending in utter failure, proved beyond a doubt that human beings are much more than mere matter.[7]

Who—whether in the laboratory or study—has not had the experience of extensively researching some problem or text, reaching a wonderful solution or interpretation, thinking that we are the first pioneers of this . . . phenomenon, setting forth our theory or interpretation with self-accolades for uniqueness, only to find that: (1) in science, another less known (or even heterodox) scientist has already made such discovery, or (2) in theology, that wonderful interpretation—for which we flatter ourselves with pride of discovery—was published centuries ago by Augustine, Chrysostom, Aquinas, Calvin, Luther, Wesley, a Puritan,or a papal encyclical prior to modernism? The same thing frequently happens to new pastors, graduate assistants, first-year law clerks, and anyone involved in any hermeneutical process. In each case, a little more acquaintance with the history of one's discipline leads to less hermeneutical hubris and greater appreciation for history. The history of exegesis of any passage, or the previous debates on a scientific problem, therefore is essential prior to pronouncing discovery. Those who prove to make the most enduring contributions will also be those who are more concerned with historical continuity than with headlines for purported discovery.

How unsensationally classic and non-novel is the approach revived by Thomas Oden—a humbler one, without surprise, a dusty paleo-orthodoxy in contrast to the experimental and novel so vaunted in our own day. Moreover, Oden advises interpreters:

> The weighting of references may be compared to a pyramid of sources with Scripture as the foundational base, then the early Christian writers, first

> pre-Nicene then post-Nicene, as the supporting mass or trunk, then the best of medieval followed by centrist Reformation writers at the narrowing center, and more recent interpreters at the smaller, tapering apex, but only those who grasp and express the anteceding mind of the believing historic Church. I am pledged not to try heroically to turn that pyramid upside down, as have those guild theologians who most value only what is most recent or most outrageous. Earlier rather than later sources are cited where possible, not because older is sentimentally prized but because they have had longer to shape historic consensus. Consent-expressing exegetes are referenced more confidently than those whose work is characterized by individual creativity, controversial brilliance, stunning rhetoric, or speculative genius.[8]

The central question is: Are we better off using a historically-sensitive hermeneutic, or one that is naively buttressed only by the experience of this one age? By the very framing of the question, the reader can anticipate my answer, which I will seek to support below. In so doing, I will discuss how a historical sensitivity can help in any hermeneutical enterprise,[9] and provide examples of the superiority of historical exegesis over an approach which flatters itself as original.

Nearly a century ago (1908), G.K. Chesterton wrote to the question of originality:

> I did, like all other solemn little boys, try to be in advance of the age. Like them I tried to be some ten minutes in advance of the truth. And I found that I was eighteen hundred years behind it . . . . When I fancied that I stood alone I was really in the ridiculous position of being backed up by all Christendom. It may be, Heaven forgive me, that I did try to be original; but I only succeeded in in-

> venting all by myself an inferior copy of the existing traditions of civilized religion. . . . It might amuse a friend or an enemy to read how I gradually learned from the truth of some stray legend or from the falsehood of some dominant philosophy, things that I might have learnt from my catechism—if I had ever learnt it. There may or may not be some entertainment in reading how I found at last in an anarchist club or a Babylonian temple what I might have found in the nearest parish church.[10]

Those involved in the interpretation of texts or data need such humility tempered by broader historical horizons. In short, we severely restrict our ability in hermeneutical fields if we philosophically constrain the universe to the pattern of our own experience. All along, God has given us a far more comprehensive community, which is not nearly so limited by the experience or insight of a single generation or a single interpreter. Those who have gone before us—particularly those who were best at interpreting data or texts—should be considered first in the hermeneutical enterprise, not last.

If the earlier exegetes' insights were deeper than the average paperback Christian book or pop-exegesis, then by all means we ought to refuse to be so arrogant as to cling to an indefensible bias for the modern. A more humble approach will avoid such arrogance which despises the past. This century has shown us how dangerous it is to adopt modernism wholesale. Jeremiah spoke of the "ancient paths" (Jeremiah 6:16) as those tried and trusted ruts of life, which rebels sought to destroy because they were routine. We might even find, like C.S. Lewis, that there is much we can learn from earlier works. Indeed, some of the ancient Christian examples are preferable to many unproven modern ones. As Lewis advised:

> A new book [interpretation] is still on its trial and

> the amateur is not in a position to judge it. It has to be tested against the great body of Christian thought down the ages, and all its hidden implications (often unsuspected by the author himself) have to be brought to light. . . . The only safety is to have a standard of plain, central Christianity ("mere Christianity" as Baxter called it) which puts the controversies of the moment in their proper perspective. Such a standard can be acquired only from the old books.[11]

Elsewhere Lewis exhorts: "The only palliative is to keep the clean sea breeze of the centuries blowing through our minds, and this can be done only by reading old books. Not, of course, that there is any magic about the past. People were no cleverer then than they are now; they made as many mistakes as we. But not the same mistakes . . . ."[12] This hermeneutical humility puts us in our place, so to speak, not as the first to discover something "new under the sun." It locates us in a stream of continuity, as one among many other interpreters. To those who wish to stand out and attract fame to themselves, such humility will offend. To those who value faithfulness and truth, however, a knowledge of the history of some interpretive issue is more important than their own gratification at making (or claiming) novel discoveries.

Emphasizing the value of historical studies, Elsie McKee comments: "Before one can reform or even evaluate some part of life, whether individual or corporate, it is important to understand how present practices developed. What other ages have taught and done is not necessarily normative for the twentieth century, but failure to understand what we have inherited can make us puppets of the unknown past. It can also deny us the gifts of the faith and the wisdom of the communion of the saints."[13]

Similarly, Alister McGrath tells about his grandparents in Belfast, who kept all kinds of memorabilia from their youth. When asked why, they replied that one never knows when those things might be helpful, which led McGrath to comment about one particular era:

> That is what the Reformation is like in many ways. It is about realizing that we can turn to our Christian past and rediscover things that we have neglected, that we have forgotten; things that really can be useful today. Studying history is not simply nostalgia, a sentiment that says, "Oh, they always did things better in the past." Rather, it is saying . . . reach into the past to enrich the present by discovering things that we need to hear today. . . . The reformers [said]: There is no point in going forward, forward, forward. We're not saying that the Reformation is basically something we have to repeat like parrots. We *are* not saying that, as we seek to move the church into the future. It helps to look back at those great moments in Christian history and ask, "Can we learn from that time? Is there anything that the Lord wants to say to us through those people of long ago as we face their task in today's age?"[14]

McGrath acknowledges Woody Allen's quip: "History repeats itself. It has to, nobody listens the first time around." Still McGrath reflects the perspective which will assist any hermeneutical endeavor with its humble appreciation of the past:

> The Reformation is about that process of rediscovering, and bringing to life. That is still very much our agenda. But along on our agenda . . . we are looking at a church today that very often has many of the same problems we find in the late Middle Ages. There is a need for us to think through what we can do about those problems. The Reformation gives us some bearings, some landmarks, some ideas about how to address

> today's issues, using the resources, the methods, and above all, the inspiration that comes from the past.[15]

One of the most fanciful instances of a historically-deficient hermeneutic was the popular attempt to buttress self-esteem by a dubious interpretation of Jesus' words, "Love the Lord your God with all your heart, soul, and mind. This is the first and greatest commandment. And the second is like it: Love your neighbor as yourself." In the past generation—amidst a culture infatuated with psychological counseling and its novel dogmas—Robert Schuller and others sought a biblical platform for the gospel of self-esteem. Not easily finding texts that supported that doctrine, the apostles of self-esteem were pressed to create novel interpretations of texts that did not truly support their dogma.

In one glaring instance of this mistaken (and historically-deficient) approach, some even ventured to deny the history of hermeneutics on this verse, and emphasize its final phrase, "Love your neighbor *as yourself,*" as mandating a type of self-love as a prerequisite for neighbor love. Nothing could be farther from the history of orthodox interpretation on this text. A simple knowledge of the history of interpretation of this classic and important text could have delivered the apostles of self-esteem from such exegetical error. Had history been consulted, such would not have happened easily.

Another example is the creation *ex nihilo* of the "Preferential option for the poor." The question may be legitimately asked: Does the Bible teach that the poor should be treated differently and with preference, or is it a prior philosophical commitment to the proletariat that teaches such? Certainly the Scriptures mandate giving compassion and the best help we can to the deserving poor. However, Leviticus 19:15 says, "Do not pervert justice; do not show partiality to the poor or favoritism to the great, but judge your neighbor fairly." The context of this is inter-personal relationships, and for at least a second time in Scripture (see also Exodus 23:2), the poor are not to be shown any partiality in respect to justice. While moved to help the poor and disadvantaged in light of their need, a lowering of ethical or judicial norms is not only disallowed, but explicitly condemned.

Add to this the fact that there are indeed several Old Testament texts which specifically militate against this. Exodus 23:2 is at least one instance where the poor are explicitly prohibited from receiving a preferential treatment. To the contrary we are told not to have a favoritism shown to them. It is understood that the psychology of those who would be making just decisions in this scenario is one which is apt to be sympathetic and somewhat soft on the poor. The command of God here is that jurors are to resist that normal human tendency and not show favoritism or injustice to a poor man in his lawsuit simply because of his poverty.

One final clue that this preferential option for the poor is more of a cultural innovation, than a valid biblical interpretation, is discoverable if we consult church history. Whenever we are faced with a purported new discovery of biblical teaching, it is normally illuminating to test its longevity from the history of exegesis. Specifically, it is informative to ask of a new teaching, "Has this view been held before? When and under what conditions? Did this view have an approximate moment of arrival, such that prior to it, virtually no one held that position?" If so, we can learn something about the genesis of the idea. Or has it never been advocated before the present?

In regard to this preferential option for the poor, as best as I can tell, such position was not preferred, in any period of church history, and in fact, is basically undetected prior to the 1960s. That fact, unless disproved, is as damaging to this view as any other single piece of information. It is almost like the Rogerian "unconditional positive regard," a phrase which appears to have no antecedent prior to about 1950. Could it be that the "preferential option for the poor" is to biblical social teaching, what "unconditional affirmation" is to modern psychology? Both can be dangerous, and both are devoid of historical foundation. Is it possible that the supposed "preferential option for the poor" is as innovatively fabricated as "unconditional positive regard" or other psychological chimera?

This is to raise the question, "If, all of a sudden, the 'discovery' of a new hermeneutical tidbit is proffered, upon what 'new evidence' is this founded?" If the history of orthodox interpretation does not corroborate this specific teaching, is it one we wish to advocate? I can find nowhere that great biblical scholars, like Augustine, Calvin, or Luther maintained that God had preference for the poor. Neither do the great creeds, or confessional statements affirm such. To claim such, it would be helpful to have historical analog in support. We must question the veracity of some claim, if the *analogia fides* is absent.

Nor did the reformers nor the puritans single out the poor as preferential in deserving special treatment. The poor, have always been with us, too (Jesus predicted that they would always be with us). Thus, we cannot explain the sudden epiphany of this "preferential option" in terms of a . . . phenomena. Even in the throes of the Industrial Revolution, with large-scale abuse and ill-treatment of the poor, the nineteenth century evangelicals do not speak of a preferential option of the poor as founded in Scripture. A dire call for ministry, yes, and in need of the church's constant attention, is the care for the poor; but not as a categorical difference among other needs. In the history of biblical exegesis and evangelical social interest, prior to the 20th century, there is scant evidence for any preferential treatment of the poor.

In fact, not only does this idea not appear to be supported prior to the 20th century, it is not even apparent in the theological literature in the first half of this century, making it to appear even more suspect. Is this just an innovation, invented after 1917 or 1950? Is it too much to ask that legitimate biblical claims be advocated *not solely* by our present generation, with all its respectable myopiae? Or is it too much to raise the question that if there is a legitimate biblical teaching that it be historically maintained by others than ourselves? We might not be too far off to revisit the latin *desideratum,* "held everywhere, at all times, and by everyone (*quod semper, quod ubique, quod ad omnibus*)."

If, indeed, this idea of the poor as a *summa* arose shortly after 1960, it may be that it was another case of culture determining Scripture, and not vice-versa. If no history is behind this idea, it tends to look suspiciously like a post-1960s invention. If so, we might want to recognize it as such. Most likely, that is the most reputable hermeneutical course.

Another example is the recent interpretation of the reference in First Corinthians 5 to the "handing over to Satan" of the immoral church member. There have been some fantastic interpretations of this verse. Most popular is the historically-uninformed interpretation that believes the reference above is to a prayer (or wish) that the unrepentant person would face some grave physical consequence—perhaps even death—at the hands of the unleashed evil one, if they do not repent. Some have even been encouraged to pray for their non-repentant loved ones or colleagues to be buffeted by Satan, their flesh destroyed if necessary, should they not repent. Such interpretation—although sensational and supportive of originality—does not evidence any knowledge of the previous exegesis and received interpretation of this text.

A simple scan of several leading works on the history of church discipline (or most Church Order Manuals) quickly shows that this phrase has been interpreted as synonymous with disciplinary excommunication. Johannes Wollebius interpreted First Corinthians 5:5 as "the greater excommunication by which a sinner is cast out of the church, yet not without hope of pardon and return."[16] Likewise, the Westminster Assembly's *Directory for Church*

Government (1645) alluded to First Corinthians 5:5 in its prayer attending the service of excommunication: "that this retaining of the offender's sin and shutting him out of the church, may fill him with fear and shame, break his obstinate heart, and be a means to destroy the flesh, and to recover him from the power of the devil, that his spirit may yet be saved."[17] The footnotes for the Westminster Confession of Faith's chapter on "Church Censures" (XXX:4) list First Corinthians 5:5 as a scriptural proof for excommunication. George Gillespie interpreted: "Sure I am an excommunicate person may truly be said to be delivered to Satan, who is god and prince of this world."[18] Further, in his 1644 *The Due Right of Presbyteries*, Samuel Rutherford also associated "acts of government, in rebuking, assuring, and joint consenting to deliver to Satan an incestuous man"[19] with excommunication.

Let me draw one final set of illustrations of the thesis to show the utility of history in hermeneutics. In a recent issue of the *Journal of the Evangelical Theological Society* (I am sanguine that most issues would yield the same.), I found several exegetical conclusions interesting, particularly those which were buttressed by earlier interpretations. In one article, Gerry Breshears sought to define the role of the church in modern political matters by borrowing from an ancient taxonomy of the church following the offices of Christ: Prophet, Priest and King. Breshears acknowledges that he is following the thought of Calvin. To the degree that he follows such, he has a solid tradition behind him, as well as heuristic value, in that such schema has received so little attention lately. Thus, we see a helpful categorization, but one that is not truly a unique discovery.

Like Chesterton, we might confess that such taxonomy could have been learned long ago had we known our catechism. Yet many (certainly not Breshears) are too vain to imagine that any generation prior to their enlightened one, could have possibly known anything of value.

In the same issue, T. David Gordon exposes—as unsubstantiated and biased by modernity's egalitarianism—the recent translation of Ephesians 4:12 as "equipping the saints for the work of ministry." Rather, he advocates as superior—of all things scandalous to neophiles—that the KJV and Vulgate translations, as supported by commentators on the original text, ranging from Calvin to Owen to Hodge to the present (A.T. Lincoln): "The very fact that some ancient translations do not translate the text in such a way as to permit such conclusion should produce caution and should motivate those who are otherwise convinced to frame an exegetical argument. . . . I am satisfied that the candid and unprejudiced reader will agree that the more likely translation of Ephesians 4:12 is that adopted by older translations."[20]

After helping to clarify this, he accounts for the popularity of the bastardized translation: "We cannot account for its popularity on the basis of careful Biblical study. Rather, we must attribute it to the egalitarian, anti-authoritarian, populist *Zeitgeist* so well documented by Nathan Hatch. This spirit is so pervasive and so impervious to self-criticism that it even projects itself onto others."[21]

Thus Gordon opts for the more historic hermeneutic. Most likely, Gordon is correct. Nathan Hatch has provided a critique of earlier evangelical preaching *sans* classical frame stemming from the "hermeneutics of populism" which demanded a simultaneous rejection of hierarchicalism and the elevation of the individual's conscience.[22] He observes that "American churches' profound commitment to audience in the early decades of the nineteenth century shaped the way religious thinking was organized and carried out . . . . Insurgent religious leaders . . . considered people's common sense more reliable, even in theology, than the judgement of an educated few . . . . This shift involved a new faith in public opinion as an arbiter of truth."[23] Hatch illuminates the dominant ideology of American evangelicalism under the paradigm of populism, concluding that the driving force of this Christianity is not to be found so much in its organizational styles, nor even in sociological terms, nor in the quality of its leaders, nor ideas. Instead the "central force has been its democratic or populist orientation."[24]

Francis Turretin (1623-1687)—often maligned as excessively logical—is helpful, for example, on two points of interpretation in the early chapters of Genesis. On the early population of the world—to solve a perennial dilemma, if Cain and Abel were the only sons of Adam and Eve—Turretin interprets, "The expression of Eve at the birth of Seth [Genesis 4:25] does not signify that there were absolutely no other sons of Eve, but only that none existed similar in piety and virtue to Abel recently killed, whom the pious mother hoped and desired to be in some measure restored to life in Seth."[25] Later, in Turretin's discussion of angels, he shines the light of common sense on the fantasy interpretations often given to Genesis 6:2 ("the sons of God took wives from the daughters of men"): " 'The sons of God' referred to are no other than the posterity of Seth, who on account of still retaining the purer worship of God, are distinguished from the profane posterity of Cain or 'the sons of men.' "[26] The significant point is that even at Turretin's time the exegetical option of rendering these as "giants" was present. Yet, we have in Turretin a refutation of the inferior, and an instance of superior interpretation. Is there any valid reason that such historical superiority should be ignored? Humility might thrust us back.

A correlate of this humble approach to history is that historical judgments must, of necessity, be made with some modicum of tentativeness, and be open to revision by later events. Particularly definitive of all previous history will be the *eschaton.* Anthony Hoekema likewise has served notice that a biblical view of history will manifest a certain tentativeness, respecting aspects of internal ambiguity and the bias of the interpreter: "Until the final Day of Judgment, history will continue to be marked by a certain ambiguity. . . . Cross and resurrection are both together the secret of history. Lack of appreciation for either of the two factors or the isolation of one from the other . . . must be rejected. . . . We know that in the last judgment good and evil will be finally separated, and a final evaluation of all historical movements will be given. Until that time, as Jesus said, the wheat and the tares grow together. This implies that all of our historical judgments on this side of the final judgment must be relative, tentative, and provisional."[27]

If our task is to receive updated interpretations, modified to the latest social change, then analyze it, and then re-enter it as new data for a new program, then we will by the very nature of the case always be lagging behind our cultural change. The world will be setting the agenda for the Church—even in hermeneutics. We must be careful not to become dominated by the latest discoveries or the latest trends. For if we have our ear to the drum of those outside of the church too often, we may find that, in the end, we are following in their band.

We may even find ourselves more appreciative of recycling past exegeses, than hurdling forward surrounded by so great a cloud of neo-pagan witnesses. We might even find, as some disciplines are, that the past affords more heuristic value, than many contemporaneous studies. In 1978, Robert Jastrow, one of America's foremost astronomers, concluded his book entitled *God and the Astronomers* with this soon-to-be often cited parable.

> At this moment it seems as though science will never be able to raise the curtain on the mystery of creation. For the scientist who has lived by his faith in the power of reason, the story ends like a bad dream. He has scaled the mountains of ignorance; he is about to conquer the highest peak; as he pulls himself over the final rock, he is greeted by a band of . . . theologians . . . who have been sitting there for centuries.[28]

Such is Jastrow's analogy of the way that "new scientists" seem to be discovering old truths which have been there all along. He is skeptical about the prowess of modern methods. Perhaps the theologian or scientist considering a new hermeneutic might benefit from this parable.

This parable could well be retold, in terms of the modern church's own pursuit for innovative hermeneutics. It often seems that the latest craze from the hermeneutical scientists becomes the marching order for the church. And these may be as inferior as the sincere, but deluded, efforts of secular scientists to discover God by "scaling the mountains of ignorance."

As Michael Oakeshott has asserted in the political realm, it might be more profitable for us in the ecclesiological realm to, "prefer the familiar to the unknown, to prefer the tried to the untried, fact to mystery, the actual to the possible, the limited to the unbounded, the near to the distant, the sufficient to the superabundant, the convenient to the perfect, present laughter to utopian bliss."[29]

Unfortunately, however, many of us are guilty of "chronological snobbery" which is the "assumption that whatever has gone out of date is on that account discredited" and manifests "an attitude whereby we despise our Christian forefathers for not having the [unprecedented] insights or experiences we have."[30] Because of chronological snobbery, "the past is rarely seen as offering any real wisdom for our more 'enlightened' age. The belief that new-is-better predominates our twentieth century culture."

Thomas Oden warns the maturing evangelical community against an abandonment of the past:

> Modern scholarly habits, fixated upon novelty, often betray an underlying value premise I call "modern chauvinism"—the assumption that old ways are predictably oppressive and that new ways are intrinsically morally superior. This is a tragic shift that seems to be taking place throughout the evangelical community . . . the special form of creeping modern chauvinism that

> has gained more than a toehold in evangelical institutions—a step backward toward a deteriorating modernity, not forward toward a postmodern inquiry into orthodoxy.[31]

Oden, as a spokesman for the tradition of historically-sensitive exegesis, discloses his intent:

> To make no new contribution to theology, and to resist the temptation to prefer modern writers less schooled in the whole counsel of God than the best ancient classic exegetes. I seek quite simply to express the one mind of the believing Church that has been ever attentive to that apostolic teaching to which consent has been given by Christian believers everywhere, always, and by all. . . . I have been passionately dedicated to unoriginality. . . . The focus is upon setting forth sound layers of argument traditionally employed in presenting in connected order the most commonly held points of Biblical teaching as classically exegeted by the leading teachers of its first five centuries. I am doggedly pledged to irrelevance insofar as relevance implies a corrupt indebtedness to modernity. What is deemed most relevant in theology is often moldy in a few days.[32]

This is the humble option for hermeneutics: a hermeneutics *cum* history, rather than the hubris of the Enlightenment. One might be reminded of words over a century earlier by Charles Hodge who had boasted that Princeton Seminary had not heard a single original doctrine in all his years of teaching. Oden in championing the classic almost seems to endorse the well known proverb, "He who marries the science of today, is a widower tomorrow." In his allergic reaction to modernity, the result is a definite return to humility and respect for those who have gone before us.

One of Oden's personal turning points is described as,

> I would remain densely uneducated until I had read deeply in patristic writers . . . where it at length dawned on me that ancient wisdom could be the basis for a deeper critique of modern narcissistic individualism than I had yet seen. Then I fancied that I was formulating unprecedented insights and ordering them in an original way. Later, while reading John of Damascus on the *oikonomia* ("arrangement, plan") of God . . . I began belatedly to learn that all my supposed new questions were much-investigated amid the intergenerational wisdom of the *communio sanctorum* and that what I had imagined myself to be just recently inventing had been largely well understood as a received tradition in the eighth century.[33]

In closing, I argue that there are at least three additional reasons to be more humble and historical in one's hermeneutic. If for no other reasons, should we employ a more historically-sensitive hermeneutic, the following result.

1) Such tames some of the arrogance of perceived uniqueness. All too often, we think of ourselves in a self-centered fashion. We tend to believe that the world revolves around our own lives, and that the discoveries we make in our labs are the first and the finest. Some of this stems from an acceptable joy of discovery. However, even in this, a little more humility would cause us to be more cautious in our announcements, and more circumspect in allowing for other possibilities in our interpretation.

The best scientists and exegetes will avoid the "You're so special" syndrome, which does appeal to me-centeredness. But in light of biblical wisdom (1 Corinthians 10:13), claims to utter uniqueness must be refracted through other truths. History added to any hermeneutic will strip it of some of the aggrandizement attendant with the pride of discovery.

2) Such recognizes that others (prior to us) may possibly be as wise as we are. An acquaintance with history forces us to admit that other scholars have preceded us. Church historians are fond of citing, "We stand upon the shoulders of others." Might not scientists, with a greater appreciation of the history of science begin to echo some such similar saying? If we can learn to agree with Solomon (that there is nothing new under the sun), then prior to trumpeting our discoveries, we may wish to seek out other earlier pioneers to see if they have beaten us to the punch. Moreover, a preference is given to that which is the received judgment as opposed to new discovery. The burden of proof rests on the shoulders of the novel, not the already-proven.

3) Such leads to a healthy tentativeness in pronouncing novel judgment. Accordingly, we will have to learn to make friends out of provisionality in some areas. Often, we will have to wait, patiently—as well as humbly—on further confirmation. And indeed, some of our theorizing will have to be jettisoned and revised. Tentativeness in pronouncing judgment may be a sign of a mature scholar or scientist. Wolfhart Pannenberg has urged that scientific conclusions be subjected to ongoing revision, and also is helpful in reminding of the need to submit one's pre-understanding to the ontological flow of history.[34]

Lest it be construed that the above intends to sublimate discovery, a reminder from Karl Popper—to both theologians and scientists—is in order:

> Although I believe that in the history of science it is always the theory and not the experiment, always the idea and not the observation, which opens up the way to new knowledge, I also believe that it is always the experiment which saves us from following a track that leads nowhere; which helps us out of the rut, and which challenges us to find a new way.[35]

On the utility of history in general, James Packer eulogized D.M. Lloyd-Jones in words borrowed from Hilaire Belloc: "[H]istory adds to a man, giving him, as it were, a great memory of things—like a human memory, but stretched over a longer space than one human life." Such longevity of perspective helps in hermeneutics—legal, biblical, scientific, or otherwise. History is indeed our friend, as Norman Geisler has similarly remarked: "But can a seven-hundred-year-old thinker still be relevant today? Students of logic will recognize the implication of the question as the fallacy of 'chronological snobbery.' 'New is true' and 'old is mold,' we are told. Logic informs us, however, that time has no necessary connection with truth. Or at least, if there were any kind of connection, then the time-honored thought ought to have the edge."[36] All in all, history appears to be the friend of humility, not to mention, the friend of hermeneutics.

Endnotes

[1]Derek Thomas, "Calvin's Exposition of the Book of Job," *The Banner of Truth*, no. 366 (March 1994): 13.

[2]Abraham Kuyper, *Principles of Sacred Theology* (reprinted Grand Rapids: Baker Book House, 1980), 576.

[3]Ibid., 577.

[4]New York Free Press, 1986, 90-91 and 32.

[5]*Thinking in Time*, 159.

[6]Ibid., 204.

[7]*National Review*, Aug. 15, 1994, 2.

[8]Thomas Oden, "The Long Journey Home," *Journal of the Evangelical Theological Society*, vol. 34, no. 1 (March 1991), 81.

[9]Although this essay mainly deals with examples from theological hermeneutics, hermeneutics is not the exclusive possession of religion. Any exercise in interpretation—be it legal hermeneutics (e.g., in seeking to determine original intent), literary hermeneutics, philosophical hermeneutics, or scientific hermeneutics—will find the thesis of this essay beneficial.

[10]G.K. Chesterton, *Orthodoxy* (New York: Doubleday, 1990), 12.

[11]Cited in *Table Talk* (Orlando: Ligonier Ministries), Jan. 1993, 7.

[12]*Table Talk*, Jan. 1993, 7.

[13]Elsie McKee, *Diakonia in the Classical Reformed Tradition and Today*, (Grand Rapids: Eerdmans Co, 1989), xi.

[14]Alister McGrath, "The State of the Church Before the Reformation" *Modern Reformation* (March/April 1994): 4, 11.

[15]Ibid., 11.

[16]Cited in David W. Hall and Joseph H. Hall, *Paradigms in Polity* (Grand Rapids: Eerdmans, 1994), 164.

[17]*Paradigms in Polity*, 270.

[18]George Gillespie, *Aaron's Rod Blossoming* (1646, rpr. Harrisonburg, VA: Sprinkle Publications, 1985), 198.

[19]*Paradigms in Polity*, 315.

[20]T. David Gordon, " 'Equipping' Ministry in Ephesians 4?," *Journal of the Evangelical Theological Society*, Vol. 37, no. 1, 70.

[21]Gordon, op. cit., 77.

[22]*The Democratization of American Christianity* by Nathan Hatch (New Haven: Yale Univ. Press, 1989).

[23]Hatch, 162.

[24]Ibid., 213.

[25]Francis Turretin, *Institutes of Elenctic Theology*, ed. by James T. Dennison (Phillipsburg, NJ: Presbyterian and Reformed, 1992), vol. I, 461.

[26]Ibid., 548.

[27]Anthony Hoekema, *The Bible and the Future* (Grand Rapids: Eerdmans, 1979), 34-35, 37.

[28]Robert Jastrow, *God and the Astronomers* (New York: Warner Books, 1978), 104-106.

[29]Cited in R. Emmett Tyrell, Jr.'s *The Conservative Crack-Up* (New York: Simon and Schuster, 1992), 280 as one definition of a conservative, in tandem with Abraham Lincoln's famous definition of conservativism as "adherence to the old and tried, against the new and untried."

[30]Norman Geisler, *Thomas Aquinas: An Evangelical Reappraisal* (Grand Rapids: Baker, 1991), 11.

[31]Oden, "Long Journey Home," 82-83.

[32]Ibid., 79.

[33]Ibid., 83-4.

[34]See, e.g., W. Pannenberg, *Theology and the Philosophy of Science* (Philadelphia: Fortress, 1976). Pannenberg, as part of the hermeneutic movement in late twentieth century philosophy, sees any process of understanding—whether it is science or theology—as involving hermeneutic. He as much as says, "Where there is science there is hermeneutic and where there is hermeneutic there is science."

[35]Karl Popper, *The Logic of Scientific Discovery*, 268.

[36]Geisler, op. cit., 11.

Galatians 3:28: A Test Case for Sound Hermeneutics

Virgil Warren

Introduction

"There is no male and female because you are all one in Christ Jesus" (Galatians 3:28). The wording of this portion of a verse has become a popular way for Christians to express the egalitarian principle that (a) *in the home and in the church there are no necessary role distinctions referenced to sex*. A man or a woman has the same "theoretical right" to lead or follow. In its healthiest form, egalitarianism calls for a "fair field and no favors" in all parts of the social arena.[1] A more extreme alternative to male headship is the belief that (b) *in the home and in the church there is only interpersonal leadership*. Not only is there no designated final responsibility in marriage and ministry referenced to sex; there is no hierarchical arrangement at all; there is only natural vs. formal leadership.[2] Cooperation rather than structure is the ideal *modus operandi*. At least the first of these viewpoints is a proposed meaning of Paul's statement to the Galatians. This study evaluates that reading in light of the evident exegetical and theological import of the passage, and addresses various ways by which women's roles have been, or might be, brought into its sphere of meaning.

Exegesis: The Salvation Topic in Galatians 3-4

In the context of Galatians 3:28, Paul's topic seems straightforward enough: Salvation through Christ is for Gentiles as surely as it is for Jews. Salvation is granted to those who have spiritual likeness to Abraham. Christ is the "seed" of Abraham. Those who are in Christ become recipients of the promise to Abraham's seed. The Old Testament concept of "seed" did not particularly envision physical descendants or those legally included in the patriarch, but those who are the "sons" of his way of life. They connect to the patriarch by having a "faith" like his. Descendants do tend to reflect their parents' values, and family values should be in all the family members. But mere physical connection is not what makes life good; it is one's values and their corresponding behaviors and attitudes. Persons who adopt Abraham's family values are closer to Abraham than are his merely physical descendants (cf. Matthew 12:46-50). "Seed," then, is both generic and collective: it refers to a type of person and by extension to all the individual persons of that type. Anyone who is of Christ is a son of Abraham by inclusion in Christ. Christ, so to speak, is the "seed-type," and everyone identified with him is a "seed-kernel" within the type; such persons are saved and blessed.

Throughout his discussion, Paul casts this salvation message in the imagery and terminology of inheritance because the original promise was conveyed in inheritance language. He deals mostly with the Jew-Greek distinction because it was the one that called forth the letter. However, in 3:28 he generalizes his point to several similar cases, adding male-female and bond-free. So the inclusion principle in salvation is not based on nationality, societal status, or sex. The statement that there is no bond-free, male-female, Jew-Greek parallels *joint heirs* in Romans 8:17; Ephesians 3:6 (re: nationality; cf. Galatians 3:14) and in First Peter 3:7 (re: wives). It parallels *no respect of persons* in Ephesians 6:9 and Colossians 3:25 (re: master-slave) and Acts 10:34; Romans 2:10-11 (re: nationality).[3] It equals Christ is *all in all* (Colossians 3:11) and there is *no distinction* (Romans 3:22; 10:12). On different occasions Paul varies the number of entries in the sets. Romans 2:10; 3:29; 9:24; 10:12; 15:9 and Ephesians 2:11-3:12 are among several that concentrate on one irrelevant distinction—Jew and Greek. First Corinthians 12:13 names two—Jew and Greek, bond and free. Colossians 3:11 lists three—Jew and Greek, barbarian and Scythian, bond and free. In all these cases the only relevancy is faith. In the kingdom of God, no one is debarred on any basis other than lack of faith.

Reasons for the Sets in Galatians 3:28

We may ask two questions about the list in Galatians 3:28. First, what is *common* to the three sets? Obviously the pairs are alike in being objects of salvation through Christ. Because Paul indicates that the only relevancy for salvation is faith, the pairs are also alike in referring to those who can have faith. Consequently, all kinds of *persons* are potential for covenant membership and inheritance of blessings. In terms of creation language, the kind of thing God intended in his promise to faithful Abraham was appropriate to everyone who has the creatable image, the interpersonal capacity.[4]

Second, is there anything *peculiar* to these sets? Did Paul have any special reason for listing these three distinctions? (a) Paul might have mentioned them, of course, simply as examples of irrelevant distinctions. He might just as well have said rich and poor, married and unmarried, old or young, barren or with children, etc.[5] Galatians 3:28 is *unique* in including male-female as an irrelevant difference. (b) Paul might have mentioned the distinctions in 3:28 because they were suggested by ancient Near Eastern inheritance customs. The inheritance theme lies in both the preceding and succeeding material (4:7).

Slaves did not inherit except perhaps after being adopted as heirs or in situations where there were no biological descendants (Genesis 15:1-4). *Non-family members did not inherit unless there was no one left in the immediate family (Num. 27:8-11); circumcision was a "family" sign. Among Jews females* did not inherit except when there were no sons (Numbers 27:1-8; 36:1-13).[6] Inheritance customs dictated that physical descendants, freemen, and sons were heirs. Since the blessing promised to Abraham was conveyed in inheritance terms, Paul may have listed these three sets as adjustments to the inheritance model for access to salvation; receiving the blessing of Abraham is not like inheritance in every way. God's blessing and promise consist of personal relationship and its consequences, and are awarded on the basis of interpersonal factors; so the objects of the blessing and promise were not affected by the kinds of distinctions that affect the transfer of physical property or family privilege.[7,8]

Another way to ask why the three items are listed is to ask why male and female are in the list. Perhaps the distinction was suggested by the covenant sign, since women were not circumcised in Judaism. Circumcision was a kind of citizenship paper that a man carried in his flesh. This kind of citizenship mark did not apply to women. The nature of the covenant and the nature of the sign of the covenant must correspond. The new covenant is not the kind where the covenant sign could be the sort it was under Mosaism or the land-and-lineage aspect of the Abrahamic covenant itself. In other words, the Christian covenant is a spiritual covenant, not a fleshly one. Because the covenant with Abraham was also with his "seed," Paul draws upon the inheritance factor in setting out his presentation. Inheritance language, then, is especially apt for explaining the 3:28 list because it offers a contextual reason for including the male-female variable.

Proscription Against Bondage

Instead of identifying Galatians 3:28 as a statement

about salvation from sin, it has been taken as a statement about salvation from bondage—bondage to Jewish laws and traditions. The verse thus warns against regressing into customs and laws based on distinctions outdated in Christ. Because male-female is one of the distinctions Paul mentions, it should be discarded as a feature of Christian practice. That means discarding male-female as a factor relevant to role assignments.[9]

This reconstruction sounds plausible because it incorporates terms and topics that do appear in the context. But it does not pick up on them the way Paul does. His "bondage" theme is not in regard to *items in the Mosaic law,* but in regard to *law itself,* especially lawkeeping ("works") as a basis for fellowship with God. Being released from law does not mean being released from the specific expectations a law contains. Those are subsequent issues determined by the new setting, by the nature of persons and personal relationship, by male-female relative gifting, and by the division of labor necessary for fulfilling kingdom purposes. Expectations and values do not have to be imbedded in law; interpersonal relationship ("faith") also contains expectations and values, perhaps just as many, perhaps the same ones; and it holds up the same perfection standard with respect to them. The "bondage" issue is not a bondage to values and legal or interpersonal expectations, but to legal perfection in such matters. If the point of release from bondage to law meant release from specific expectancies contained in a law—female submission, for example, a person could disregard moral expectations as well. The release from bondage that Paul discusses is not a release from male headship, but from personal perfection under law. The Abrahamic promise released a person from that personal perfection requirement for salvation.

Among other things, Judaizing teachers were trying to mix initial salvation through Christ ("faith," "spirit") with continued salvation by lawkeeping ("works," 3:2). They thought Gentile converts should be circumcised and keep the law of Moses (Acts 15:5, etc.). Two things were wrong with this idea. First, circumcision identified people with *national Israel*, which, coming 430 years later, was a secondary and temporary feature added to the earlier Abrahamic promise (3:17). So being included in Abraham's seed did not have anything to do with being under the Mosaic law. In a similar argument in Romans 4, Paul adds that the promise to Abraham was given even prior to circumcision. A political dimension was not essential to the people of God. Second, circumcision theoretically committed people to success at personal perfection by identifying them with the *law* of national Israel. Paul tells them in effect, "You cannot begin with trust in Christ [initial salvation] and finish with works of law [continued salvation]" (3:3). If Christ was needed because people could not maintain personal perfection before, why think they could do so now? What use would Christ be if all he gave were initial salvation? The law creates bondage to a perfection that people cannot achieve and therefore a bondage to sin they cannot escape. In Christ, people are released from the need to achieve perfect righteousness for (being viewed as righteous unto) fellowship with God. In inheritance terms, for Jews, reverting to law after being under faith is like becoming a minor again, during which time a son is no better off than a slave because he is too young to inherit the benefits of sonship (4:1-3). It is like reverting to slavery after becoming a freeman. For Gentiles it is even worse. That is the sense in which the bondage theme relates to Paul's discussion.

A point of consistency might also be raised if bondage in Galatians 3-4 means bondage to Jewish customs like sex-role distinctions. Paul denied in no uncertain terms that Christians should follow these traditions. If even an angel from heaven preached what the Judaizers were advocating, that angel should be accursed (1:6-9)! The Galatians were bewitched and foolish (3:1-3)! They were fallen from grace and separated from Christ (5:4)! Paul's message was incompatible with the Judaizing agenda. If Jewish role distinctions were included in the bondage that Paul so strenuously opposed, how could he turn around and ordain these very practices "in all the churches" (1 Corinthians 14:33-34; cf. 1 Timothy 2:8; 1 Corinthians 4:17; 7:17; 11:16) even if he did so only as a concession to cultural expectations? The adamant language of Galatians disallows such concessions even as a way to keep from hindering the progress of the gospel.

At any rate, Paul's topic is salvation; his talk about bondage deals with bondage to the law's personal perfection requirement in order to be saved. The male-female connection is that gender has no bearing on "inheriting" God's promise to Abraham through his "Seed," the Messiah.

Secondary Heterogeneity

Galatians 3:28 could involve women's roles if secondary characteristics of items in a list necessarily possessed homogeneity. The reasoning would go as follows: the Jew-Gentile and the master-slave distinctions are unnecessary and even harmful, so the male-female distinction is unnecessary and undesirable. Because we agree that Jew vs. Gentile and bond vs. free would have no place in determining roles, we can conclude that male vs. female has no place in determining roles.

But the assumption justifying such an inference is not true. That listings are not necessarily homogeneous beyond the originating principle is clear from two examples. The qualification lists for elders and deacons (1 Timothy 3:2-12; Titus 1:6-9) combine moral matters and leadership characteristics. In Acts 15:20, 29 the same list combines moral matters (fornication) and expediencies (eating things sacrificed to idols).[10] Elsewhere, eating things sacrificed to idols is treated by Paul as a matter of expediency (1 Corinthians 8; 10:23-33). Under proper conditions a person could do what Acts 15 actually prohibits, which means it is not necessarily a moral matter even though it is listed beside a moral matter. So wisdom, a larger category than commandment, is the organizing principle in Acts 15; but in Paul's treatment of the matter he includes comments about theory. Lists, then, are not necessarily homogeneous.

Because lists are not homogeneous beyond the author's point of interest, we cannot exegetically claim that some second characteristic of one or two entries must be true also of the others. If the impropriety of slavery argues for the impropriety of sex roles, it argues for the impropriety of national distinctions among Christians because there is neither Jew nor Gentile. Unlike Jew-Gentile or master-slave, male-female is not rooted in anything conceivably fallen or merely conventional. Male-female is a created difference pronounced good from the beginning. Any relative gifting or role emphases implicit in that created difference are likewise good. God created the male-female difference; he temporarily established the Jew-Gentile distinction; but man created the master-slave distinction.[11] Even within Christ, the distinctions Paul lists do in fact exist: there *are* male and female (Genesis 1:27; 5:2; etc.; Matthew 19:4 = Mark 10:6); there *are* national distinctions; there *are* slave and free. Whether any of these *ought* to exist in non-salvific matters is appropriate to ask; but that is a further question answered by other information rather than by overinterpreting Galatians 3:28.

By the *nature of language,* a statement does not mean everything it could be used to mean (linguistics), but what the writer intends it to mean here (authorial intent). "There is no male and female in Christ" should not be taken in every sense conceivable, but in the sense that Paul means it.

Galatians 3:28 is not even a free-standing proverb, but a statement embedded in a context. Consequently, it is not an absolute statement from which only provable exceptions may be subtracted; that would place undue burden on the negative, although some readings could still be eliminated by the analogy of scripture. Besides justifying (a) homosexuality, the words could affirm (b) gnostic superspirituality, an asceticism expressed in celibacy among other things (1 Timothy 4:3). It fostered a lifestyle built on hypostatic dualism that led to denying fleshly appetites as evil, sexual drives included. What proves too much does not prove what it seems to prove. Likewise, women's roles in Christ are not necessarily affirmed in Galatians 3:28, because Paul has placed his words in a context about access to Christ.

By the nature of language *convention*, lists are not necessarily homogeneous beyond their thematic principle. Consequently, the hermeneutical process must move from exegesis to theological interpretation.

Theological Interpretation

Because the "no-distinction clause" in Galatians does not refer to roles, any connection it has with roles must come from systematic inference. The proper question, then, is how an interpreter can legitimately move Galatians 3:28 onto a subject Paul is not discussing.

At this juncture, the full interpretive task becomes more subject to error because the communication between author and reader is more reader-side intensive. The reader's reasoning can be affected by incorrect pre-understandings about the nature of the case, by the impact of personality on one's application of biblical truth, by expectations in contemporary culture, by practical pressures, and so on.

Implications for Leadership Roles

Although the context of Galatians 3:28 deals with salvation instead of roles, the text connects with other subjects besides access to salvation, including marriage and formal leadership ministry. First, by generalization to like cases, we can say that the "no-distinction clause" applies to everyone created in God's image, to everyone with the interpersonal capacity. Amoral distinctions between those endowed with personhood are naturally irrelevant. Second, equal access to salvation (vertical) implies the equal basic *worth* of persons, which in turn has social implications (horizontal) because positive attitudes must operate in both directions between non-germane variants. Third, the equal worth of persons eliminates higher *rank* as a basis for superior worth. God's like attitude toward all classes of humanity removes any justification for humans themselves to distinguish between classes in regard to worth. Fourth, prioritizing the interpersonal category shapes the *manner* in which all human interaction takes place, whether in ministry, marriage, parenting, leadership, evangelism, or elsewhere. The characteristics of positive interpersonal relationship are retained rather than set aside in these more specialized settings for personal interaction. Interpersonal principles qualify operations in the specialized settings and establish boundaries on appropriate procedure. Fifth, within the ultimately interpersonal framework, *influence* precedes authority (and force) as the means by which leaders fulfill responsibility. They accomplish as much as possible by the dynamics of the fundamental reality (influence) before appealing to distinctives in the more specialized settings themselves (authority). Influence is a dynamic present with all persons, whether formal or natural leaders. Mature leadership, whether by male or female, follows the pattern dictated by the equal worth of human persons, which eliminates the correlation between relative worth and different rank or variant ability. Sixth, there is a sense in which the primary category implies something even about the *identity* of those in formal leadership roles; they are first natural leaders, people who are mature enough to lead in the manner of influence before authority.

It should be noted that this analysis appropriately derives from *any* text that implies the priority of the interpersonal category or implies the equal worth of persons in Christ. The fact that Galatians 3:28 mentions male and female in so doing gives it no extra value in this regard, because the implications for roles do not come directly from the "male and female" rubric, but indirectly from the larger human category to which the full list points.

Paralleling Rank and Worth

Much of the impetus for applying Galatians 3:28 to equal access to roles comes from the assumption that rank correlates with worth. That concept supplies the connecting link between the equal worth of persons implied by Galatians 3:28 and the otherwise unnatural inference that male and female have interchangeable roles. Long ago, when the modern women's movement began to exert its influence within the church, Virginia Mollenkott expressed the idea this way: "If woman must of necessity be subordinate, she must of necessity be inferior."[12] Calling Galatians 3:28 "The Magna Carta of Humanity," Paul Jewett proceeds to conclude against hierarchy in marriage and ministry.[13] If the assumed correlation between rank and worth is false, it does not bridge the gap.

We perceive that women's sense of personal worth is what makes gender roles such a burning issue. That is certainly understandable, because the drive for meaningfulness is a given in human nature. If we are not prepared to accept egalitarians' theological interpretation of this verse, it behooves us to state briefly the alternate construction for self-worth so as to offset the inference that might otherwise obtain.

Nature, purpose, relationship and action form an interacting set of bases for measuring the worth of persons. All human persons have an inherent worth by virtue of their common creation in the image of God. The subsequent factors of relationship, purpose, and action work together in relative fashion like members in Paul's body figure (Romans 12:3-8; 1 Corinthians 10:16-17; 12:12-30; Ephesians 3:6; 4:4, 16). The heart is not evaluated by expectations related to the purpose of the lungs. Likewise, God does not measure one person's worth by the abilities and responsibilities he gives to someone else, but by how concertedly that person fulfills his own responsibility relative to his ability to perform the role.

Success in competition is the world's model for defining self-worth, and underlies so much of the feminist rhetoric against hierarchy. It assumes individualism and equality as the highest good rather than membership and unity. It will not work very well for very many very long. It sets individuals in contrast to each other instead of drawing them together. Christianity bases self-image on being created in the divine image, on positive vertical and horizontal relationship, and on service relative to purpose. It calls for a shift from works to grace and from competition to love as a basis for objective worth and, therefore, for an appropriate sense of self-worth.

Overextending the Egalitarian Principle

By equating rank and worth, the egalitarian viewpoint overextends an otherwise crucial insight. It carries interpersonalism beyond *how* Christians lead and talks about *who* leads. By sheer principle purportedly derived from Galatians, it dismisses the possibility that divine commandment or wisdom would institute gender roles. Absolutizing most things makes them false, and egalitarianism is no exception. Equality of persons does not remove the need for assigned *responsibility* and the supervisory *authority* concomitant to it, nor does equality eliminate considering the relative *strengths* of persons in assigning roles to the best advantage so the full range of responsibilities is covered that life in the home plus the church entails. The ideal is unity, which celebrates diversity, not equality, which fosters sameness and individualism and thereby weakens the positive basis for social interdependence.

Truth tends to lie between extremes. But as with so many controversial matters, extremes beget extremes. In this case, overemphasizing order leads to overemphasizing freedom. In the past, the problem with hierarchy has been the misuse of authority; so the solution is to correct the misuse, not to get rid of authority. A problem has come from connecting worth with position and ability, and then overemphasizing ability differences between men and women. The solution is to disconnect worth from rank and ability and to affirm the differing strengths of men and women without exaggeration, not to try to eradicate gifting differences. Even as passages on the equality of persons establish no requirement to consider everyone within the same sex equally qualified for every role, so also Galatians 3:28 establishes no ideal for considering women and men equally qualified for every role—and there is no depreciation of either sex for relatively weaker capacities statistically speaking. The sexes have equal value and equal worth, but they may not have equal gifts for a given responsibility like a final leadership role. That men and women are not interchangeable is at least strongly suggested by other biblical texts beyond Galatians, and it seems to be verified also in human experience by the observation that among other things there has never been a truly matriarchal society.[14]

Egalitarianism sometimes speaks hermeneutically of identifying highest norms,[15] an acceptable idea if not done in a way that creates a canon within a canon. Doing the latter pits certain parts of Scripture against other parts, which involves the practitioner in a lower view of Scripture than we are willing to take. Furthermore, highest norms do not *oppose* lower ones, but *contextualize* them and *qualify* them. The love standard in Christianity's primary interpersonal category does qualify the way in which formal leadership operates, but it does not necessarily determine who should serve in what formal leadership roles.

Not only by generalization do roles not come into Paul's frame of reference, but they would also not come into the picture if roles were somehow viewed as a subset of membership. *Membership in a group is based on the purpose of the group*, the need people have for the purpose of the group, and their willingness to commit themselves to the purposes, values, and behaviors of that group. *Roles within the group are based on the abilities of group members*, which introduces the relative gifting concept again, circumstance needs, and the like. Salvation corresponds with the first issue, ministry with the second. We are all the same in God's eyes, but we do not do the same things. There is a difference between whether a person belongs to the body and which organ in that body he is. If membership and roles are different matters, they can be governed by different principles without contradiction. As a result, if Paul says there is no male and female relative to gaining membership *into* the body, he does not thereby lay down the principle that there is no male and female relative to serving as one organ or another *within* the body. Therefore, Galatians 3:28 does not include egalitarianism as a subset.

At the risk of stating the obvious, we note that (1) Paul says that there is no male and female, not that there is no husband and wife, father and mother, parents and children, elders and deacons, etc. Salvation as *reconciliation* is relevant to all human persons because they have the *interpersonal* capacity and the righteousness need. Sex does not affect the relevance and therefore the availability of salvation. More *specific* issues within the sexual variant become *subsequent* issues—who will mother children and who will father them. Paul's subject is interpersonal relationship, not status and role within that context. (2) The reason Paul gives for saying that there is no male and female in Christ is that "we are all one" in Christ (Galatians 3:28). The sense, then, in which Paul means there is no male-female in Christ is a sense that fits with unity, if *unity* is what Paul means by "you are all one." Because there can be diversity in unity, there can be different roles and statuses within unity, and there can be different roles and statuses based on sex within unity. By "one," however, Paul more likely means *identity*, which results in unity. Jew-Gentile, male-female, slave-free share the same identity; they are "in Christ" and "of Christ" (Galatians 3:28-29; cf. 1 Corinthians 1:12-13; 3:23). They are parts of the same "seed" even as Jews and Gentiles are part of the same olive tree (Romans 11:16b-24), the same lump/full-harvest (Romans 11:16a), the same temple court (Ephesians 2:11-18), the same citizenry (Ephesians 2:19), household (Ephesians

2:19), building (Ephesians 2:20-22), and other images New Testament writers use to express the common identity and purpose of those who are "in Christ" and "of Christ." We can infer what the statement itself means, from the reason something is stated.

The Parallel to Joel

Another way of associating Galatians 3:28 with ministry has been to consider it a restatement of Joel 2:28-32. The two texts are paralleled by connecting "no Jew/Gentile" with "all flesh" and "whoever will call on the name of the Lord." "No bond/free" corresponds with "on my servants and on my handmaidens . . . I will pour out my Spirit." No "male/female" answers to "your sons and your daughters will prophesy." The outpouring of the Spirit on men and women in Joel is in regard to revelation and proclamation, which is then compared to Galatians 3.[16]

Although the parallel is interesting, there is no reason to think that Paul had Joel in mind. Because there are only so many typical classifications of people, an undesigned overlap between Galatians and Joel is not surprising. The overlap is not complete; there is no age distinction in Galatians as there is in Joel. But the significant point is not that the lists overlap, but that the purposes of the overlapping lists are different. While Joel talks about proclamation, Galatians talks about salvation. Comments about the second do not necessarily have implications for the first. Joel does not say whether or not there will be any difference between the way sons and daughters prophesy; the "no-distinction clause" appears, not in Joel, but in Galatians, and in regard to another subject; mixing the two passages creates an artificial hybrid.

Furthermore, the point of current debate is not women in ministry, but women in authoritative ministry over men. Joel is not talking about the traditional concern raised by First Timothy 2, which supposedly contradicts Galatians. Women have any number of outlets for prophesying that have nothing to do with the limitation in First Timothy.

Galatians, First Timothy and Joel are talking about three different issues: salvation, authoritative ministry and proclamation ministry without further definition. *Prophesying* is nowhere forbidden to women and that is what Joel predicts; *authoritative teaching* is what First Timothy disallows.[17] We do not go to Joel to find out what Paul means in Galatians, because paralleling the two texts rests on the same assumption that makes Galatians speak about ministry in the first place. The approach simply restates the original claim that the "no male-female clause" in 3:28 applies to formal ministry by women over men.

Traditional Attitudes Toward Women

Another way of trying to associate Galatians 3:28 with ministry is to see it on the background of Jewish and even Hellenistic sayings that thank God for not making someone a woman.[18] Galatians becomes a corrective on such degrading views of women. Again the difficulty comes from imagining such sayings as the context for 3:28 rather than observing the context that is actually here for all to see. Furthermore, if 3:28 is correcting such Jewish notions, it corrects degrading women's *worth*, which is simply different from *roles*. Only by correlating rank and worth does abandoning negative evaluations of women pertain to abandoning the female submission principle. Finally, how apt is Paul elsewhere to advocate Jewish traditional prejudices, if he is consciously offering 3:28 as a corrective on Jewish tradition, which is one explanation for the supposed tension between Galatians 3 and First Timothy 2? Putting 3:28 in *conscious* opposition to Jewish tradition decreases the likelihood that we can account for Paul's "inconsistency" by claiming *unconscious* insight in Galatians in contrast to enjoining Jewish practices regarding women in his other writings.

The Pristine-Fallen-Restored Scenario

A further elaboration of the egalitarian reading of our text places that reading in a larger scenario about pristine, fallen and redeemed humanity. Those stages purportedly parallel an equal-subordinate-equal pattern for women. Although we cannot respond in particular to each point in this larger format, we can indicate some general comments without elaboration. (1) The New Testament seems to base the female submission principle on pre-Fall considerations (1 Corinthians 11:8-10; 1 Timothy 2:13-14). (2) Not everything mentioned in Genesis 3:7-24 necessarily differs from what it was before the Fall. (3) Christ has not—or at least not yet—reversed the aspects of "the curse" listed in Genesis 3. Furthermore, (4) Subordination need not be viewed as a cursed condition. Finally, (5) Paul also appeals to post-Fall factors as a basis for Christian practice (1 Corinthians 14:34; Genesis 3:16; cf. 1 Corinthians 11:3; Ephesians 5:23).

Crucial to the proper handling of Galatians 3:28 is the fact that Paul is not primarily talking about something that is part of a time sequence. He is not contrasting the way things are in Christ with the way they were before, but the way things are in Christ with the way they are outside of him. The principles for being "in Christ" are not a *change* from *before,* but a *contrast* to *alternatives.* It is not so much something present vs. something past as it is one sort vs. another. It is not a *change* in God's way of doing things so much as a re-affirmation of the way God has always done things. The issue involves what is secondary vs. what is primary. The promise to Abraham is a more basic frame of reference than the Mosaic law and national Israel as shown by the fact that *promise* preceded *law* (3:15-29) and even *circumcision* (Romans 4:9-12), and the law did not annul the former, more basic system (3:15-17). Mosaism was a temporary add-on for practical purposes, not theological or soteriological ones. Time comes into the picture only because in this instance what was secondary was also temporary. If we want to identify a sequence, it is not the pristine-fallen-redeemed scenario that egalitarianism wants to talk about, but the Abrahamic-Mosaic-Christian series that Paul talks about, a faith-(works)-faith series. In fact, however, salvation by faith is not in a series, because it was true before the time of the law, even during the time of the law, and in the Christian era. Faith-grace-promise has always been the governing reality for relationship to God. In other words, salvation has always been interpersonal. Paul's frame of reference returns to Abraham in his state of uncircumcision, not to Adam and Eve in their unfallen condition.

Male and Female

Related to the previous scenario is another proposal that Paul meant something significant to our question by saying male *and* female rather than male *nor* female. The other two sets in 3:28 are joined by *nor*. Placing Galatians 3:28 in the egalitarian scenario and emphasizing the use of *and* rather than *nor* has sometimes been done in the interests of calling for a supposed return to the pre-Fall condition. But that cannot explain the *and* phraseology because Paul would then be *denying* the pre-Fall condition, not affirming it: "There is *not* male and female . . . in Christ." The idea that the battle of the sexes is over is not a bad idea in and of itself, but that is not the meaning of Paul's expression. Hierarchical arrangement is not competition or a battle for worth. American individualism makes equality rather than unity the highest good among persons. With equality in first place, the basis for worth comes from success in competition instead of contribution to the common cause, creation in the image of God, and positive interpersonal behavior.

The peculiar nuances that could pertain to the format of the male-female statement, however, do not affect whether the verse has much connection with sex roles, because more likely explanations exist for that format. The male-and-female format may be due simply to the familiar creation language in Genesis 1. In all the texts of Genesis, the various LXX editions combine male and female in this order and join them by *and* whether speaking of humans or animals (11 cases). The phrase had perhaps become a *set expression* in the minds of people raised on the Greek Old Testament. It may well be that in these original contexts the "and" wording did reflect the complementary nature of the sexes.

Paul's similar listing in Colossians 3:11 puts *and* between the pairs that have nor (*oude*) between them here. First Corinthians 12:13 uses *or* (*eite*). Galatians 3:28 is the only text, however, that mixes the and/nor terminology; so the switch could be intentional. But it is doubtful whether the change of conjunctions indicates anything obvious.

The different format may imply that male and female are complements whereas Jews and Gentiles as well as bond and free were opposites. The former are conjunctive and the latter are disjunctive. In the last two sets a person could move from one alternative to the other, but that cannot happen with male and female.

The "and" format is like paralleling Galatians 3 with Joel 2, putting it on the background of traditional attitudes toward women, or making it part of a pristine-fallen-redeemed scenario. Without a correlation between worth and rank, suggestions like these cannot sustain the egalitarian viewpoint from this text.

Summary and Prospect

Earlier in this essay "no male and female" was rejected as an absolute principle because, among other things, it would then contradict Paul's clear teaching elsewhere against homosexuality and superspirituality. We did not say that it would also contradict clear teaching elsewhere about husband-wife relationships in the home and the church. We left that claim unsaid because those who use Galatians 3:28 to state the egalitarian principle do not agree that the male headship principle is indeed a clear New Testament teaching. Consequently, the study of women's roles must move beyond the scope of this study to an evaluation of the positive case for hierarchy and the female submission principle.

The case for hierarchy must be structured to address the gender-equity viewpoint in its best formulation. (a)

Hierarchy needs to be presented hermeneutically in a way that by parity of reason it appropriately handles veil-wearing and slavery as control cases. (b) It must be understood also in a way that accounts for all the activities we find women actually doing in Scripture. (c) It must conscientiously endeavor to avoid the confusing effects caused by the interpreter's own personality, cultural expectancy, previous experience with the significant women in his life, and pre-understandings that unconsciously shape the reading of relevant texts.

From the standpoint of Galatians 3, however, we express the following convictions. (1) Using "no male and female" to state the egalitarian concept *accommodates* Paul's words to a foreign concern in the reader's interests. (2) By the nature of the case, Galatians 3:28 does not establish egalitarianism as *most ideal.* (3) Much less does it *eliminate* the possibility of gender roles.

Correctly reading Galatians 3:28 is a matter of "sticking to the subject." Sometimes Paul's words are simply misquoted as a statement of gender equity, as if he were directly discussing roles. At other times the text is accommodated to gender equity because people have first misgeneralized the words to that concept through an incorrect *theory of worth*, a misformulated *theory of leadership*, or a misidentified *summum bonum* among persons. (a) Variant rank or ability does not correspond with variant worth; unequal rank or ability does not contradict equal worth. (b) Christian leadership occurs first through interpersonal influence, but secondly through responsible authority. Leadership only by influence or primarily by authority misrepresents the ideal either by omitting one factor or by putting the two factors in the wrong order theoretically and practically. (c) The highest good among persons is their harmonious relationship in the common divine purposes. Correctly understanding all three of these concepts derives from seeing interpersonalism as the ultimate reality in the Christian worldview. It is that last concept, if any, that is implied by Galatians 3:28.

Setting aside the target text as a statement of egalitarianism does not depend on first believing that other clear teaching about male headship eliminates the egalitarian reading here. If egalitarianism is true, it is not a truth learned from Paul's statement that "There is no male and female because you are all one in Christ Jesus."

Endnotes

[1]For a helpful presentation of classical feminism, see Christina Hoff Sommers, *Who Stole Feminism? How Women Have Betrayed Women* (New York: Simon & Schuster, 1994). She writes as a secular "equity feminist" against the extremes of "gender feminists." The former call for equal opportunity for women in all areas with men in contrast to a gender-roles system, affirmative action, or a sexless society. Gender feminism, however, sees patriarchy as a universal social system based on a worldview of male oppression and calls for radical restructure of society away from sex reference altogether or—even more extreme—calls for re-creating humankind in terms of feminine reality as informed by gender feminists' self-perception. The former viewpoint has most influenced the evangelical community, and is therefore the one that our study has in mind as it explores the direct and indirect meanings of Galatians 3:28.

[2]Among many authors, see Howard C. Kee, *Christian Origins in Sociological Perspective* (Philadelphia: Westminster, 1980), 91.

[3]It might correspond also with the "callings" of First Corinthians 7:10-28a: slavery, nationality and marriage. In these three respects, Paul says that each convert is to remain in the calling he had before, which amounts to the same idea. Another question is whether "male *and* female" in Galatians 3:28 may mean marriage. If so, it would eliminate the idea that the three sets are mentioned because of their connection with inheritance customs.

[4]Because Scripture uses *imago dei* terminology in more than one sense, we distinguish between "createable image" and "ethical image." The first usage occurs in Genesis 1:26; 5:1; 9:6; First Corinthians 11:7; and James 3:9; the second appears in Romans 8:29 (or eschatological image?); Second Corinthians 3:18; and Colossians 3:10. "Likeness" is not used in the ethical sense in comparisons between men and God (Genesis 1:26; 5:1; Acts

14:11; 17:29; Romans 8:3; Philippians 2:7; 1 John 3:2). We take interpersonal capacity as the meaning of the creatable image for reasons too complex to elaborate satisfactorily here. (a) Interpersonal capacity fits well with the parallelism between "us" and "them" (*relational being*; Genesis 1:26-28a); Father-Son-Spirit we understand to be the one interpersonal God (note John 14:16). (b) The "dominion mandate" calls for personal capacities (*responsible being*). (c) Forbidden fruit implies *ethical being*. (d) "God said/Satan said" deals with *communicative being*. Responsibility, ethics, communication, and the like call for the abilities we understand to be associated with personhood: primary abilities like reason, will, conscience, affection, and derivative capacities like self-transcendence, self-image and the sense of aesthetics. Interpersonal capacity has the advantage of being holistic rather than reductionistic, as views of the (creatable) image have often become historically.

[5]Besides irrelevancies to *salvation access*, Romans 14 and other texts identify a wide range of irrelevancies to *Christian practice*.

[6]Job's daughters, however, inherited equal portions with their brothers (Job 42:15).

[7]Jack Cottrell likewise concludes that the three distinctions in 3:28 are due to the inheritance metaphor. See *Gender Roles and the Bible: Creation, the Fall, and Redemption: A Critique of Feminist Biblical Interpretation* (Joplin: College Press, 1994), 272-83. He links the distinctions more specifically with Mosaic inheritance laws because Paul's point of contrast is between Christ and the law. We have taken the connection more generally with Near Eastern custom because the Abrahamic promise was conveyed in an inheritance metaphor. The metaphor itself was somewhat deficient for communicating access to a faith covenant. In light of his purpose in Galatians, Paul would not be adjusting Mosaic inheritance laws to the characteristics of the Abrahamic covenant promises; he would be adjusting the inheritance metaphor itself in the covenant promise.

[8]Inheritance imagery may also explain why Paul says Jews vs. Gentiles in Galatians 3:28 rather than circumcised vs. uncircumcised, which is often the way he puts the same point. The difference is that Jews vs. Gentiles is a family statement and therefore coextensive with inheritance patterns. Circumcision was this family's sign, which does not stress who the heirs are.

[9]See Alvera Mickelsen, *Women in Ministry: Four Views*, eds. Bon-

nidell Clouse and Robert G. Clouse (Downers Grove: InterVarsity, 1989), 204-5.

[10]Acts 15 may envision only the *sympathetic* eating of things offered to idols whereas Paul is concerned about a stronger brother misleading a weaker brother by his misunderstood example.

[11]Paul may imply something negative about slavery in First Corinthians 7:21: "But if you are indeed able to become free, use it [freedom] rather." An alternate translation might be, "Nay, although you are able to become free, use it [slavery] all the more." Since there is a translation question about the verse, the point cannot be pressed here.

[12]See the "Foreword" of Paul K. Jewett's *Man as Male and Female: A Study in Sexual Relationships from a Theological Point of View* (Grand Rapids: Eerdmans, 1975), 8.

[13]*Women in Ministry: Four Views,* 142ff.

[14]Steven Goldberg, sociologist at City University of New York, argues this viewpoint convincingly in *Why Men Rule: A Theory of Male Dominance* (Chicago: Open Court, 1993). His proposal is that the phenomenon is rooted in the chemical variants between the sexes.

[15]*Women in Ministry: Four Views,* 177ff.

[16]Gerhard Dautzenberg, "Da ist nicht männlich und weiblich," *Kairos,* N. F., p. 197; cited by Klyne R. Snodgrass, "Galatians 3:28: Conundrum or Solution?" in *Women, Authority & the Bible,* ed. Alvera Mickelsen (Downers Grove: InterVarsity, 1986), 175.

[17]Much of the difficulty in discussions about women's roles stems from the differing views of male headship and the range of activities that headship affects. We are inclined to take First Timothy 2:12 as indicating a composite act—authoritative teaching—rather than two acts—exercising authority and teaching. We suppose as well that the directive was intended at least for "standard situation" (husband-wife) especially in public settings, and referred at least to wisdom vs. commandment. The wisdom-commandment distinction means that a person who does not do a wisdom-imperative takes a risk for practical reasons, whereas a person who does not do a commandment-imperative disobeys. Finally, *prophesying* and *teaching* may differ in that the latter involves normativeness/authority in First Timothy 2.

[18]See Klyne Snodgrass, "Galatians 3:28: Conundrum or Solution?" 168-70.

The Parables of the Kingdom: A Paradigm for Consistent Dispensational Hermeneutics

Ronald N. Glass

In an attempt to refine the position of traditional dispensationalism[1] and to address lingering questions which the Darby-Scofield system left unanswered, some evangelical scholars have recently advocated a so-called "progressive dispensationalism."[2] This new form of dispensationalism, which views each dispensation as representing progress over the previous one within the unified plan of God, is really a synthesis of traditional dispensationalism and Covenant Theology.[3]

In reality, however, progressive dispensationalism raises more questions than it answers. These questions are, above all, hermeneutical.[4] The problem that needs to be addressed can be asked this way: Is compromising the principle of literal, grammatical-historical exegesis an acceptable price to pay for such rapprochement? This paper proposes that the hermeneutical problems entailed in traditional dispensationalism's approach to the prophetic

Scriptures have not been the fault of an excessively literal understanding of the text, but of a failure to maintain the literal, grammatical-historical interpretation with consistency.[5] A thoroughly dispensational hermeneutic, consistently applied, however, yields a far more satisfactory interpretation than either the non-literal methods of Covenant Theology, the compromising methods of the traditional approach, or the eclectic methods of progressive dispensationalism.

The Kingdom of Heaven and the Kingdom of God in Dispensational Thinking

No more conspicuously has the confusion of inconsistent dispensational interpretation been apparent than it has in the case of the Parables of the Kingdom, the series of seven parables recorded in Matthew 13. Over 40 years ago, Charles Ryrie correctly observed that "the details of this chapter have been a battleground for interpreters through the years."[6] It still is. The first question to be answered in approaching these parables is: what is this "kingdom of heaven" of which the Lord Jesus speaks? The identity of the kingdom is one of the major issues at stake in contemporary discussions among dispensationalists. A major problem for traditional dispensationalists is that the *Scofield Reference Bible* so confused the subject that for many the concept of the kingdom has been seriously obscured. The only satisfactory solution to this question is to define the kingdom as Scripture does.[7] By an inductive survey of the Old Testament literature, certain distinctive features attached to the kingdom concept emerge. Any kingdom in Scripture, as would be anticipated in the normal usage of the term in popular discourse, must involve a *king*, or ruler invested with sovereignty (authority). Without a reigning king, there can be no kingdom. It must also include a *realm*, a territory over which the king governs, together with the *subjects*, or the body of persons ruled. Finally, it must also entail a *system of government*, primarily revealed in a code of laws and an administrative structure.[8] With regard to the kingdom of heaven (or of God), the King is the Lord Jesus Christ Himself (Isaiah 24:23; 33:22; Ezekiel 37:24; Daniel 7:13-14; Zechariah14:9; Matthew 19:28; 1 Corinthians 15:25; Revelation 19:16; 20:6); the realm is the entire earth (Genesis 49:10; Psalm 72:8, 17; Zechariah 14:9; Revelation 11:15), governed from the Throne of David in His capital city, Jerusalem (2 Samuel 7:12-13, 16; Psalm 46-48, 96, etc.; Isaiah 2:2; 9:7; 24:23; 25:6, 10; 62; Ezekiel 40-48; etc.); the subjects are all men (Daniel 7:27; Zechariah 8:22-23; 14:16-18); and the system of government is an absolute monarchy, embracing the executive, legislative, and judicial functions in one Ruler (Isaiah 33:22), and with the Law rigidly enforced (Psalm 2:8-12; 110:5; Isaiah 66:23-24; Revelation 19:15).[9]

Moreover, regarding the time of the kingdom, the Lord Jesus early on proclaimed its imminence by virtue of His presence (Matthew 3:2; 4:17). Following His rejection by the Jewish nation, however, He made it clear that the kingdom was yet future, and would come only when He did (Matthew 19:28; 20:21; 26:29; Mark 14:25, 62; Luke 19:11-12; 21:31; 22:16, 18, 30; cf. Revelation 11:15, 17). This was also the disciples' understanding.[10] In fact, during this kingdom, even Abraham, Isaac and Jacob will be present, banqueting with those who have received the Lord Jesus as Messiah, Jews and Gentiles alike (Matthew 8:11-12).

Although an unbiased reading of the biblical text yields the conclusion that the kingdom of heaven (or God) is a future, literal, worldwide realm over which the Lord Jesus Christ shall rule with absolute authority, that is not the way it has been understood by many Christian theologians and preachers,[11] who have identified the kingdom as "spiritual," which is to say, not a literal earthly kingdom, but the rule of Christ in the hearts of His people.[12] There is, therefore, a close relationship between the kingdom of God and the Church, the Body of Christ or the people of God.[13] Other writers see the kingdom as embracing both a present and a future reality, the "redemptive reign of God."[14] To this way of thinking, although the kingdom will appear in an apocalyptic form at the end of the age, it has already entered human history in the person and work of Jesus Christ. Those who are in Him as regenerate believers are therefore currently enjoying the blessings of the kingdom. This mode of thinking, referred to as "inaugurated eschatology," has been described by recent writers with the phrase "the Already and the Not Yet."[15]

This understanding of the kingdom has been standard fare among amillenialists and covenant theologians. Progressive dispensationalists, however, are adopting much the same view,[16] which is not surprising given that traditional dispensationalists have also followed virtually the same line of thinking, and nowhere more prominently than in the *Scofield Reference Bible,* which declares that the kingdom of heaven has three aspects: the "at hand" phase proclaimed during the ministries of John the Baptist and the Lord Jesus Christ, the "mysteries of the kingdom of heaven," mentioned in Matthew 13 and which are fulfilled in the present age, and the "prophetic aspect," or future reign of Christ.[17] This second phase is problematic, since the New Testament demonstrates that the message of both John the Baptist and the Lord Jesus was "Repent, for the kingdom of heaven is at hand" (Matthew 3:2; 4:17),[18] and numerous prophecies place the kingdom in the future (see above).

The question, though, is whether or not there is such a so-called "mystery form" of the kingdom of heaven, taught by the parables of Matthew 13. Many dispensationalists firmly believe that there is. One of the clearest descriptions of it is provided by J. Dwight Pentecost, who writes:

> Within this program of God it was not the fact that God was going to establish a kingdom that was an unrevealed secret. The mystery was the fact that when the One in whom this program

was to be realized was publically presented He would be rejected and an age would fall between His rejection and the fulfillment of God's purpose of sovereignty at His second advent. The mystery form of the kingdom, then, has reference to the age between the two advents of Christ. The mysteries of the kingdom of heaven describe the conditions that prevail on the earth in that interim while the king is absent. These mysteries thus relate this present age to the eternal purposes of God in regard to His kingdom.[19]

Ryrie agrees: "It is the mystery form of this kingdom of which the Lord speaks in this chapter, and this is the form in which the kingdom is established in this present age,"[20] although he goes on to say that this kingdom of the present age is not the Church.[21] Similarly, Walvoord says that the "mystery of the kingdom of heaven is that, although Christ is absent from the earth most of the time between His first and second coming, God will nevertheless have a rule over those who are followers of Christ."[22]

I contend that these parables cannot refer to the present age, but because of this misconception commonly held by many dispensationalists,[23] the entire system of dispensationalism has been subject to intense, and sometimes justified, criticism. In fact, there is no need to interpret the Parables of the Kingdom as pointing to anything other than the future millennial reign of Jesus Christ.[24]

The Interpretation of Parables

Some fundamental interpretive guidelines are necessary to the proper understanding of the Parables of the Kingdom. For centuries, the Christian Church has acknowledged a body of rules for the interpretation of parables, rules explained by Trench in his classic work on the genre, and they are accepted as valid standards throughout this paper.[25] They can be summarized as follows:

1. **Care must be taken to identify the central**

truth as against ancillary details. Trench points out that the question as to how much of a parable is to be regarded as significant has been answered in opposite ways.[26] On the one hand, some argue that a given parable is intended only to illustrate one point and that the details must not be assigned meaning. Chrysostom, for instance, would address the main point, and then advise his hearers to "Be not curious about the rest."[27] On the other hand, however, some have sought meaning in every detail. Augustine's interpretation of the Parable of the Good Samaritan is a widely quoted example. Among those who hold that the non-essential elements must be set aside, however, there is considerable disagreement as to what is significant and what is not. Trench believes that there is significance in every part, as long as the interpretation is not forced or the details are clearly not important.[28] The details are to be interpreted in light of the central truth. If significant data must be overlooked or cannot be explained, then the proposed interpretation is surely incorrect.

2. **The introduction and application of a parable provided by the text are critical.** To neglect these is to risk serious error. In other words, the parable must be interpreted according to its context.[29]

3. **Violence must not be done to the text in order to make it conform to a preconceived understanding.** The interpretation should be natural and make sense, which is what Trench means when he says it should be "easy."[30] The expositor must not resort to exegetical contortions or allusions to such devices as vague rabbinical sources or obscure customs.

4. **Parables are never the "original or exclusive foundation of any doctrine."**[31] They must always be interpreted according to the analogy of faith. They merely illustrate, and thus must yield to passages where the doctrine is literally explained. Certainly any suggested doctrine for which the *only* proof is a parable is immediately suspect.

The Crisis[32]

Following the imprisonment of John the Baptist, the ministry of the Lord Jesus moved rapidly toward a crisis within the religious leadership of the Jewish nation. The Twelve had been sent on their first preaching tour (Matthew 11:1), and apparently word of their power in performing miracles spread rapidly. Still, the Master in whose name they did these signs was making no move toward ascending the messianic throne. From his prison cell, a perplexed John the Baptist sent a delegation of his disciples to Christ to ask whether or not he was the promised Messiah. Having answered the query by inviting John's followers to observe His works, the Lord Jesus spoke to the crowds around Him following their departure. Using the occasion to commend John, He then informed His hearers that He, the long-awaited Messiah, would face rejection at the hands of His own nation (vs. 16-24). Even though the nation at large would reject Him, however, He still held out the invitation for individuals to come to Him for spiritual rest (vs. 28-30). In a word, the approaching rejection would be no surprise to Him.

That rejection came quickly. According to Matthew's account, two incidents involving the Sabbath—the picking of grain and the healing of a man with a withered hand (12:1-13)—precipitated confrontations with the Pharisees. The climax came when a blind, mute, demon-possessed man was brought to Him. When the Lord Jesus healed him, the crowds openly conjectured that this might indeed be the Messiah. Angered at His confident defiance of their religious traditions and the people's growing fascination with His ministry, the Pharisees brazenly declared the works of the Lord Jesus to have been accomplished by the power of "Beelzebub, the ruler of the demons" (v. 24),[33] a claim Jesus demonstrated was patently absurd (vs. 25-30), but which also earned His severest censure as the unforgivable blasphemy against the Holy Spirit (vs. 31-37).

This act of blasphemous unbelief on the part of the Jewish religious authorities was the turning point in Jesus' ministry. This was apparent in at least three important ways. First, from that time forward, He ceased to preach the message of the impending advent of the kingdom. The die was cast; because the Messiah had been rejected by those who must necessarily accept Him, the messianic kingdom would be delayed. Second, He began a transition in which He concentrated on His disciples rather than on the nation, preparing them for the ministry they would have following His ascension. And third, He began to teach in parables,[34] an act of divine judgment upon Israel for their failure to receive the kingdom message. This third change is apparent immediately in Matthew's account, where the Lord Jesus not only teaches by means of these seven important Parables of the Kingdom, but also, in response to a private question from His disciples, explains the dual purpose for which He adopted this method of instruction, namely, that those who believed might receive additional light while those who had rejected Him might be hardened in their unbelief (13:10-17). Hence, by using parables, He was doing what He exhorted His followers to do; He was avoiding casting his pearls before swine (7:6).

The Contextual Key

That the seven Parables of the Kingdom were all spoken on a single occasion[35] logically points to a unity of theme surrounding them.[36] Both within the broader context of Matthew's Gospel and within this thirteenth chapter itself, there are some important clues as to the identity of this theme.[37]

The broader context points to the theme of rejection. The Lord Jesus has just faced this crisis at the hands of the Pharisees. The fact of this rejection stands behind His use of the parables as a literary device, and the events which follow the giving of the parables also involve rejection, namely, the unbelief He encounters in His hometown of

Nazareth (13:54-58) and the murder of John the Baptist 14:3-12). Thus, the entire episode of rejection is framed by an inclusion involving John the Baptist, first his imprisonment, and then his execution.

The unifying theme of the parables is thus the Lord's rejection. Their subject, however, He identifies as "the mysteries of the kingdom of heaven" (v. 11). Having determined that the consistent use of kingdom terminology in Old Testament prophecy and in the gospels is to describe the yet future messianic kingdom, what is the significance of the term "mysteries"? The best definition of this New Testament concept is that given by the Apostle Paul in Ephesians 3:4-5, where he identifies the "mystery of Christ" as that "which in other generations was not made known to the sons of men, as it has now been revealed . . . ," or in Colossians 1:26, where he refers to "the mystery which has been hidden from the past ages and generations; but has now been manifested to His saints," or again in Romans 16:25-26, where as a part of the closing doxology, he mentions "the revelation of the mystery which has been kept secret for long ages past, but now is manifested," or finally in Second Thessalonians 2:7 where he refers to "the mystery of lawlessness" which is presently at work, and which although as yet unidentified, eventually will be revealed.[38] The referent in the Ephesians and Romans passages is the Church; in the Colossians text it is the indwelling Christ; and in Second Thessalonians, it is the appearance of the Antichrist.

In each case, the common thread is that that which is revealed had formerly been unknown. Thus, Jesus' use of the term "mystery" is completely consistent with Paul's. The mysteries of the kingdom would be truth about the kingdom of heaven which previously had been unknown, but was now being revealed.[39] That this was in fact the Lord Jesus' meaning is further clarified by Matthew's editorial comment in chapter 13, verses 34-35, where he quotes Psalm 78:2:

All these things Jesus spoke to the multitudes in parables; and He did not speak to them without a parable, so that what was spoken through the prophet might be fulfilled, saying, "I will open my mouth in parables; I will utter things hidden since the foundation of the world."[40]

Consequently, there must necessarily be a relationship between the Parables of the Kingdom and the Old Testament prophetic revelation. Jesus is simply amplifying previously revealed truth.[41]

This point is so important that He Himself adds a final contextual key to interpreting the parables. At the conclusion of His discourse, He asks His disciples, "Have you understood all these things?",[42] to which they answer, "Yes" (clearly giving themselves more credit than they deserved). His comment in response is revealing: "Therefore every scribe who has become a disciple of the kingdom of heaven is like a head of a household, who brings forth out of his treasure things new and old" (vs. 51-52).[43] This is the only place in the gospel narratives where Jesus uses the term "scribe" other than to refer to the class of Jewish biblical scholars with whom He constantly clashed. His meaning here points to those who study the Scriptures, specifically the biblical revelation concerning the kingdom of heaven. Everyone who diligently studies the doctrine of the kingdom resembles the head of a household (*oikodespotes*) who, in preparing a banquet, not only uses fresh foods (such as meats and vegetables), but also aged foods (smoked meats, cheeses, and wines): something old, but also something new—or perhaps more accurately, something new about something old. This precludes any reference to the church age, for as virtually all dispensationalists admit, the church was not anticipated by the Old Testament prophetic Scriptures.[44] What this means, therefore, is that the Parables of the Kingdom are to be interpreted under the following guidelines:

1. They are concerned with the rejection of Jesus Christ by the Jewish nation.[45]

2. They contain new information about a subject concerning which there was established revelation in the Old Testament.[46]

3. That subject is the kingdom of heaven, or the personal rule of the Messiah over the earth as revealed by the Old Testament prophets.[47]

Things New and Old: The Unifying Truth Being Taught by the Parables

In light of the guidelines above, therefore, the new truth concerning the kingdom, a truth not revealed by the Old Testament, but for the first time explained by the Lord Jesus Christ, is that **the messianic kingdom will witness the parallel development of good and evil.** Throughout the Old Testament, the kingdom over which Messiah reigns is pictured as a time of peace and prosperity under the rigidly enforced righteousness of the King (for example, Micah 4:1-5 [Isaiah 2:1-11]). But nowhere did the Old Testament clearly point to an undercurrent of rebellion which would develop during the messianic dispensation.[48] In light of the rejection He had just experienced at the hands of the Jewish religious authorities, however, Jesus takes the opportunity to enlighten His disciples that they should not be surprised, for even when He reigns as King over all the earth, the opposition will still be present, and throughout His reign, even growing. This is the mystery factor in these parables.

The Parables of the Kingdom: Explanation and Validation

1. The Parable of the Seed and the Sower (vs. 3-23)

The parable of the Seed and the Sower is the only one of the seven parables that does not begin with the formula, "The kingdom of heaven is like . . . ," and is therefore both transitional and introductory to the other parables, not itself providing any new truth regarding the kingdom of heaven. It was spoken to the "multitudes" standing on the shore of the Sea of Galilee as the Lord Jesus sat in a boat (vs. 1-3). Although the parable was delivered to the crowds, it was interpreted only to the disciples (vs. 18-23), and from His comments as recorded in Mark 4:13, Jesus intended it as foundational to the rest.[49]

In the immediate context, the message of John the Baptist—and subsequently that of the Lord Jesus Himself—was being largely rejected. Those who hear the gospel of the kingdom but refuse it, therefore, are compared to the seed that falls beside the road and is eaten by birds (hard hearts); to the seed that is cast upon rocky ground, and because there is insufficient soil, springs up quickly and withers (temporary disciples who will not accept the stigma and suffering discipleship entails); and to the seed that falls upon thorny ground and is choked by weeds (the cares of life and deceitfulness [or pleasure] of wealth). The comparatively few who hear the message and receive it (see 11:25-30; 13:11-12), are described in terms of seed that falls on good ground and bears fruit in varying quantities. Even in this inhospitable environment, God's Word will not return to Him empty (Isaiah 55:11).

What makes this parable transitional is that it concerns the period of preparation leading up to the manifestation of the kingdom. The rejection experienced by the Lord Jesus Christ during the ministry of His first advent, at which time the kingdom did not come, will be repeated in the days preceding His second advent, when it shall. The "gospel of the kingdom" will be preached throughout the entire world during the early part of the Tribulation (Matthew 24:9-14), but the result will be persecution (v. 9), major apostasy (v. 10), the rise of false prophets (v. 11), and widespread lawlessness with a corresponding loss of love for God (v. 12). The character of this time will correspond to the debauchery of the antediluvian civilization (vs. 37-39). In the later, most severe, days of the Tribulation, false christs and false prophets will even do miracles which threaten to mislead the elect (vs. 21-25; Mark 13:19-23). So nothing will have changed. Thus, although the messianic kingdom has been delayed, Jesus teaches His disciples that the widespread unbelief that greeted His ministry the first time, particularly and specifically among the Jews, will mark His second advent as well.

2. The Parable of the Wheat and the Tares (vs. 24-30, 36-43)

Some dispensationalists have assumed that during the millennial reign of the Lord Jesus Christ no evil shall be found on earth.[50] This, however, is not what Scripture teaches. While the Parable of the Seed and the Sower points to the opposition that marks the advent of the messianic kingdom, the Parable of the Wheat and the Tares describes this new "mystery" of the kingdom, namely that throughout Messiah's reign, there will be a parallel development of both good and evil (see especially v. 30). Thus Jesus' words, "The kingdom of heaven may be compared to . . ." (v. 24).

The Master Himself interprets this parable in response to a request from His disciples (vs. 36-43). He is the One who sows the good seed (note the connection to the previous parable). The field is the world, the good seed "the sons of the kingdom,"[51] and the tares "the sons of the evil one," sown by the devil "while men were sleeping" (v. 25).[52] The reapers are the angels who harvest both the wheat and the darnel at the end of the age (that is, the kingdom age, or millennium).[53] The wheat is kept, the darnel burned. Jesus clearly teaches that at the end of the kingdom age, the angels will gather out of the world those who are wicked (even though they appear to have been righteous), who will then be committed to "the furnace of fire," while the righteous shine forth as the sun in the Father's kingdom.[54]

Although righteousness will be strictly enforced throughout the millennial kingdom (Psalm 2:8-12; Revelation 2:27; 12:5; 19:15), many who otherwise might appear to be righteous will ultimately prove wicked. The absence of Satan (Revelation 20:1-3) and the rigid rule of Messiah will tend to conceal the growth of evil; but it is there all the time, taking place largely unnoticed, which is apparently the implication of the sleeping men in verse 25. Once matured, this evil will be manifested in the final great rebellion of Gog and Magog (Revelation 20:7-9; cf. Ezekiel 38-39; also, Psalm 2:1-3).[55] At that point, however, all the unrighteous will be removed (note the judgment by fire, cf. Revelation 20:9), and the messianic kingdom will be delivered to the Father for all eternity (v. 43; cf. 1 Corinthians 15:24-28; the unusual "kingdom of their Father" is probably *not* the same as the "kingdom of heaven"; but see Matthew 26:29 with Mark 14:25 and Luke 22:16, 18, where "kingdom of God" translates easily to "My Father's kingdom").[56]

3. The Parable of the Mustard Seed (vs. 31-32)

Much briefer is the third parable in the series, in which the Lord Jesus compares the kingdom of heaven to a mustard seed planted by the farmer in his field. In spite of the small size of the seed, it grows into a plant larger than the others in the garden *(meizon ton lachanon)*, large enough that the birds come and rest in its branches. The figure of the tree and the birds is drawn from Old Testament prophecy (Daniel 4:10-12, 20-22, where the tree serves as a symbol for Nebuchadnezzar and the birds for the nations; Ezekiel 17:22-24, where the cedar tree represents Israel, and the birds the Gentile nations; and Ezekiel 31:3-9, which pictures Assyria as a tree and the nations as the birds resting in its boughs). The introduction of the tiny mustard seed points to the beginnings of the kingdom from a small remnant of believing Jews and Gentiles until it embraces the entire world.[57] This representation is in harmony with biblical prophecy which indicates that the kingdom will be inaugurated with the remnant of believing Jews, gathered from throughout the world, who survive the judgment at which the Lord Jesus presents

Himself to them as their Messiah (Ezekiel 20:33-44; Zechariah 12:10-13:2; cf. Psalm 50), and a remnant of righteous Gentiles who have survived the judgment of the nations (Joel 3:1-2; Matthew 25:31-46: "Come, you who are blessed of My Father, inherit the kingdom prepared for you from the foundation of the world" [v. 34]).[58]

Moreover, as biblical symbols, birds often point to that which is evil. Already in the immediate context, birds have been used as a figure representing Satan (vs. 4, 19).[59] Christ's point here, therefore, is that His kingdom will grow from its beginnings in the righteous Jewish and Gentile remnants until it encompasses the entire world (a fact which was revealed in Nebuchadnezzar's dream, Daniel 2:35). But as it grows, it will accommodate those who are evil—who oppose its principles of righteousness, and will later rebel against Messiah (Revelation 20:7-8). In fact, this is very likely the secret of the almost immediate worldwide following Satan gains among the nations upon his release from the abyss.[60]

4. The Parable of the Leaven (v. 33)

This brief parable teaches the same truth as the previous two, namely the gradual growth of evil in the kingdom of heaven. The controversy over this parable centers on the meaning of the leaven. Many have supposed it to refer to the progress of the gospel in the present age, but to see it in this way overlooks the overwhelming use of leaven as a symbol of evil. It was forbidden in the Passover meal (Exodus 12:8, 15, 18-20, 34, 39; 34:25); it was prohibited in the meal offering (Leviticus 2:11; 6:17; cf. 10:12); and it was apparently excluded from the Bread of the Presence in the Tabernacle.[61] In his epistles, Paul employs the figure of leaven to denote the corrupting influence of moral sin (1 Corinthians 5:6-8) and the dangerous inroads of doctrinal error (Galatians 5:8-9). Even more significantly, however, the Lord Jesus used the analogy of leaven in referring to the false teaching of the Pharisees and Saducees (Matthew 16:6, 11-12; cf. Mark 8:15; Luke 12:1). In fact, there is no instance in which leaven is used in Scripture as a symbol for anything other than evil of some sort.[62]

In light of the way that Jesus used leaven to refer to false doctrine, therefore, it is best to understand this parable as teaching that, in spite of the external enforcement of civil righteousness, there will be a gradual growth of errant teaching during the kingdom.[63] This does not indicate, however, that "evil will run its course and dominate the new age," or that "when the program of evil has been fulfilled, the kingdom will come."[64] Thus, while the Parable of the Wheat and the Tares primarily points to the growing presence of wicked *persons* in the world prior to the advent of the kingdom, and the Parable of the Mustard Seed to that of the evil *nations* who live under the administration of the kingdom, The Parable of the Leaven focuses on the expanding influence of the false *doctrine* that slowly penetrates the kingdom.

5. The Parable of the Hidden Treasure (v. 44)

Following the Parable of the Leaven, there is a hiatus in Matthew's account. A brief commentary on the purpose for which the Lord Jesus was using parables (vv. 34-35) is followed by the information that at this point, He left the crowds and went into a house, and that the disciples came to Him requesting an explanation of the Parable of the Wheat and the Tares, an interpretation He proceeded to provide (vv. 36-43). It is reasonable, therefore, to group the three preceding parables together. The following three parables appear to have been delivered to the disciples alone. By virtue of their content, the first two seem to be making the same point.[65] The last one differs from the first two, returning to the theme of the last three parables delivered to the crowd.

Thus, the Parable of the Hidden Treasure shifts the focus of Christ's exposition of the kingdom of heaven. The three foregoing parables have revealed that the kingdom would witness the parallel development of good and evil, but have emphasized the growing evil—the opposition to

God and to righteousness. The Lord's purpose in this and the following parable is to demonstrate something about the good which the evil opposes.[66]

Once again, the Old Testament background is critical. The nation Israel, at its very inception, was declared by YHWH to be His *sᵉgullâ,* His "personal property, or possession,"[67] His special treasure (Exodus 19:5).[68] Before entering Canaan, the Lord assured the new generation that they maintained the same status (Deuteronomy 7:6; 14:2; 26:18). The same description of Israel appears in the Psalms (135:4) and in the prophets (Malachi 3:17). So this concept would have been familiar to first-century Jews.

The peoples of New Testament times had no banks or safe deposit boxes. Especially before the threat of theft or military invasion, they would hide their valuables by burying them. The picture here is of a particularly valuable treasure which, when discovered, is buried immediately. The man who found it then sacrifices his entire fortune to purchase the field, including the right to anything hidden in it, which was acceptable under rabbinical law.[69]

The millennial kingdom, therefore, is likened to a treasure found, hidden, and redeemed.[70] The Lord Jesus uses a synecdoche, the entire kingdom representing the nation of Israel which stands at its very center.[71] The nation was "found" established by God through the patriarch Abraham and declared to be his priestly nation among the nations (Exodus 19:6), through which would come his revelation and ultimately his Messiah. But it was subsequently hidden. By virtue of their rejection of the promised Savior and Messiah, the covenant people of God were denied the kingdom (Matthew 21:43; cf. Romans 10:3; 2 Corinthians 3:14-15), the nation itself was destroyed, and its people scattered throughout the world (remember that according to v. 38, Jesus had already used a field as a symbol for the world).

And yet that treasure is not left forever hidden. Through the death of His Son, God paid the price for the redemption of the world, in order to reclaim His treasured possession. This is exactly Paul's point when, concerning the Jews, he exclaims, "Now if their transgression be riches for the world and their failure be riches for the Gentiles, how much more will their fulfillment be!" (Romans 11:12), or when he asks rhetorically, "For if their rejection be the reconciliation of the world, what will their acceptance be but life from the dead?" (v. 15). Why the salvation of the world (i.e., Gentiles)? In order that "all Israel will be saved" (v. 26; cf. John 11:51-52)! In this way, Israel becomes the centerpiece of the messianic kingdom, fulfilling at last their role as the Lord's priestly nation (Isaiah 2:2-3 [Micah 4:1-2]; 56:7-8; 61:6; Zechariah 8:20-23). As such, they become the mediator of divine truth, the foundation of righteousness in the kingdom of heaven. " 'And they will be Mine,' says the Lord of hosts, 'on the day that I prepare My own possession [treasure], and I will spare them as a man spares his own son who serves him.' So you will again distinguish between the righteous and the wicked, between one who serves God and one who does not serve him" (Malachi 3:17-18).

6. The Parable of the Pearl of Great Value (vs. 45-46)

This parable defines the treasure more precisely. The kingdom is compared to a merchant who is seeking fine (i. e., high quality) pearls. Upon finding "one pearl of great value," he sells everything he has in order to purchase it. The question here, of course, is: what does this pearl of great value represent? Most scholars, even dispensationalists, assume that it refers to the Church.[72] The context, however, argues against such an interpretation. The Church has not been in view in any of the preceding parables. Moreover, the disciples had not yet so much as heard of the Church (the first mention is in chapter 16). And yet, according to their Lord, the disciples apparently had enough information to understand what He was saying (vv. 11, 16-17, 51). Again, what He is describing was something "many prophets and righteous men desired to see" (v. 17); but since the Church was not foreseen by the Old Testament prophetic Scriptures, it cannot be under consideration here.[73]

There are only three places in Scripture where pearls are used symbolically. First, in Matthew 7:6, Jesus warns His followers against casting their pearls before swine as a means of admonishing them to use discretion in their proclamation of sacred truth. Second, there is the parable under consideration here, and finally, the description of the New Jerusalem in Revelation 21:21, where each gate is a single pearl.[74] Undoubtedly, the New Jerusalem will have twelve literal gates of pearl, but prominent parts of this city have definite symbolic significance. In this case, it is important to note that each gate of pearl is inscribed with a name of one of the 12 tribes of Israel (the foundation stones of the wall are inscribed with the names of the twelve apostles, pointing to the Church). Consistent with this imagery, then, as well as with the foregoing parable, it is best to see the pearl as pointing to Israel.

The Old Testament repeatedly describes Israel as being purchased ("redeemed") by the Lord (Exodus 15:13; Deuteronomy 15:15; Psalm 77:15; 106:10; 107:2; Isaiah 44:22-23; 48:20; 63:9; Zechariah 10:8).[75] In particular, however, several passages make the specific object of divine redemption to be Zion, or the city of Jerusalem (it is the new Jerusalem which boasts the 12 gates of pearl!). For example, Asaph pleads:

> *Remember Thy congregation, which Thou hast purchased of old,*
> *Which Thou hast redeemed to be the tribe of Thine inheritance;*
> *And this Mount Zion, where Thou has dwelt* (Psalm 74:2).

"Zion," declares YHWH through Isaiah, "will be redeemed with justice, And her repentant ones with righteousness" (Isaiah 1:27). This emphasis upon Zion as redeemed by the Lord is also seen in Isaiah 43:1, 52:7-9, and 59:20, and in Jeremiah 31:10-12. One striking example is found in Isaiah 62:11-12:

> *Behold, the Lord has proclaimed* **to the end of the earth,**
> *Say to the daughter of Zion, "Lo, your salvation comes;*
> *Behold His reward is with Him, and His recompense before Him."*
> *And they will call them, "The holy people,*
> **The redeemed of the Lord"**;
> *And you will be called,* **"Sought out,** *a city not forsaken."*
> [Emphasis added.]

The great value of Zion is underscored by the city's name, "Sought Out," and it is this city, described as purchased by the Lord, that He recovers at His coming. Its high valuation is due to the fact that during the kingdom, it is Messiah's dwelling place when He is on earth (Psalm 46:5; Isaiah 60:14; Ezekiel 48:35), and the location of the restored temple. As such, it is the repository of divine truth (Isaiah 2:2-3 [Micah 4:1-2]; cf. Zechariah 8:20-23; 14:16-17). Micah 4:6-13 expands on this prophetic insight.

In this prophecy, which ultimately looks to the end times (the "last days," [v. 1], when the nations go to Zion, or Jerusalem, to worship [v. 2]), the Lord Himself will reign in Mount Zion (the Temple Mount), which is regarded as the very center of the kingdom. The inhabitants of the city (the "daughter of Zion" or "daughter of Jerusalem") will have been gathered from Babylon, the capital of Antichrist's empire, and from "the field," which is the nations of the world. This rescue is described as the nation's *redemption.* Hence, the Lord repurchases His people, as represented by their capital city, Jerusalem, by bringing them out of worldwide dispersion to form the nucleus of the millennial kingdom. Furthermore, verses

12 and 13 point out that since the nations do not understand the Lord's thoughts or purposes, Israel will be used to chasten them and bring them under Messiah's authority, thus demonstrating Jesus' point in the parable, namely the parallel development of good and evil in the kingdom.[76]

Furthermore, as in the Parable of the Hidden Treasure, so here in this parable: the cost of the desired acquisition is "all that he had." "He" in this verse is the merchant, who must necessarily represent the Redeemer, or Messiah, with whom the kingdom is sometimes equated by the Lord Jesus via metonymy as it is here (Luke 17:21: "For behold, the kingdom of God is in your midst."). Once again, the reference can be to no other payment than that which was made through His blood (Revelation 5:9-10; cf. Ephesians1:7; Colossians 1:14; Hebrews 9:12, 15; 1 Peter 1:18-19).

7. The Parable of the Dragnet (vs. 47-50)

The final of the seven Parables of the Kingdom returns to the general theme of parables 2-4.[77] Once again, the issue is the parallel development of good and evil in the kingdom of heaven, but this time, the focus is on the final disposition of each. The Lord Jesus compares the kingdom to a dragnet, which when cast into the sea by the fisherman, produces an indiscriminate catch—"fish of every kind." When hauled ashore, however, workers empty the nets, placing the good fish in containers, while disposing of the useless fish. Similarly, declares Jesus, at the end of the age (the age under consideration, i.e., the millennial kingdom), the angels will take out the wicked from among the righteous and commit them to the judgment of eternal fire (the same truth was taught in the Parable of the Wheat and the Tares, vs. 41-43, with which this parable bears close resemblance).[78]

The reference to the judgment of fire here, of course, is to the judgment of the Great White Throne, described in Revelation 20:11-15 as "the second death," a judgment which takes place following the millennium and the final rebellion led by Gog and Magog (Revelation 20:1-9), the objects of which are the unbelieving of all ages, including those of the kingdom age.[79] It must not be confused with the judgment of the nations (Joel 3:1-2, 11-12; Matthew 25:31-46) which takes place *before* the advent of the millennial kingdom.

The Intended Response of the Hearers

As in all His teaching, the Lord Jesus was doing more than merely imparting information by telling these seven parables. He was seeking a specific response on the part of those who heard and, at least at a basic level, understood. Foremost among these were His disciples, whom He called "scribes," or scholars, who were "disciples [or students] of the kingdom of heaven." His goal was that they might understand that the Messiah would face opposition, both in the inauguration of His kingdom, as well as throughout its course. In comprehending this, they would not be misled, discouraged, or disillusioned by the rejection of the Jewish religious authorities which they had just witnessed. Furthermore, they would be able to grasp the shifting focus of their Lord as He moved away from proclaiming the gospel of the kingdom to the Jews and intensified His efforts at training His followers.

Endnotes

[1]New terms have been suggested to designate the various historical currents of dispensational thought. "Classical dispensationalism" is being used to describe the Darby-Scofield-Chafer version; the approach of McClain, Ryrie, Walvoord, Pentecost, et. al. (1950's-1980's) has been labeled "essentialist," or better, "revised dispensationalism." These two strands, both of which pre-date the so-called "progressive dispensationalism," are what is meant here by "traditional dispensationalism."

[2]The arguments for this approach have been made in three important recent books: Craig A. Blaising and Darrell L. Bock, eds., *Dispensationalism, Israel and the Church: The Search for Definition*

(Grand Rapids: Zondervan Publishing House, 1992); Craig A. Blaising and Darrell L. Bock, *Progressive Dispensationalism* (Wheaton, IL: BridgePoint, 1993) and Robert L. Saucy, *The Case for Progressive Dispensationalism* (Grand Rapids: Zondervan Publishing House, 1993). See also Craig A. Blaising, "Development of Dispensationalism by Contemporary Dispensationalists," *Bibliotheca Sacra* 145 (July-September, 1988): 254-280. The issues raised in these books have been answered by a variety of traditional dispensationalists in *Issues in Dispensationalism*, Wesley R. Willis and John R. Master, eds. (Chicago: Moody Press, 1994). Charles C. Ryrie serves as Consulting Editor for this volume. He says that this system would be better called "revised," "reconstructed," "new," or "kingdom" dispensationalism ("Update on Dispensationalism," 20). The term "covenant premillennialism" is more accurate.

[3]Saucy, *The Case for Progressive Dispensationalism*, 8.

[4]"Consequently, the hermeneutical dialogue has opened onto new levels. It is even possible to see some rapprochement taking place between dispensationalists and nondispensationalists." Blaising, "Development of Dispensationalism," 271.

[5]That consistency is the critical issue has been recognized by traditional dispensationalists. Charles Ryrie, in his classic, *Dispensationalism Today*, insists that a part of the *sine qua non* of dispensationalism is "plain hermeneutics," or hermeneutics that does not spiritualize or allegorize. The strength of dispensational interpretation, he goes on to point out, is consistency. Charles Caldwell Ryrie, *Dispensationalism Today* (Chicago: Moody Press, 1965), 45-46. The problem today, however, is that the principle of plain and consistent hermeneutics is increasingly rejected by progressive dispensationalists in favor of so-called "complementary hermeneutics," which holds "that consistently literal exegesis is inadequate to describe the essential distinctiveness of dispensationalism." Blaising, "Development of Dispensationalism," 272. The New Testament does not merely repeat Old Testament revelation, but introduces change and advance.

[6]Charles Caldwell Ryrie, *The Basis of the Premillennial Faith* (New York: Loizeaux Brothers, 1953), 94.

[7]The attempt by the editors of the *Scofield Reference Bible* to draw a hard and fast distinction between the kingdom of God and the kingdom of heaven has been almost universally rejected by contemporary scholars as pointing to a distinction without a

difference. The definition offered of the kingdom of heaven is correct: "The Messianic rule of Jesus Christ, the Son of David," and the note correctly observes that the phrase is derived from Daniel 2:34-36 (*The Scofield Reference Bible*, ed. C. I. Scofield et. al. [New York: Oxford University Press, 1909, 1917], 996). But when, a few pages later, it makes the case that the phrase, "Kingdom of God," is to be distinguished from "the Kingdom of Heaven," as "being the earthly sphere of the universal kingdom of God," which is inward and spiritual (ibid., 1003), it is unconvincing, and, in fact, sets the stage for the confusion over these terms that has existed ever since. Hence, Oswald Allis is correct when he writes that "The view generally held is that these expressions are practically synonymous, and are used interchangeably. It would be natural that they should be." Oswald T. Allis, *Prophecy and the Church* (Philadelphia: The Presbyterian and Reformed Publishing Company, 1945), 67. Similarly, George Eldon Ladd writes: "Practically all modern critical scholarship recognizes that the difference between the two phrases is one of language only." George Eldon Ladd, *Crucial Questions About the Kingdom of God* (Grand Rapids: Wm. B. Eerdmans Publishing Co., 1952), 122. As J. Barton Payne correctly points out, the "kingdom of heaven" terminology is largely Matthean, and is consistent with the Jewish reticence to use the name of deity. "Heaven " is therefore a circumlocution, in this case a metonymy, substituting the place where God's glory is manifested for His name. J. Barton Payne, *The Theology of the Older Testament* (Grand Rapids: Zondervan Publishing House, 1962), 150-151. See also Ladd, *Crucial Questions,* 122-123. The terms are therefore in fact synonymous. Similarly, see D. A. Carson, "Matthew," in *The Expositor's Bible Commentary*, vol. 8, ed. Frank E. Gaebelein (Grand Rapids: Zondervan Publishing House, 1984), 100; R. T. France, "The Gospel According to Matthew: An Introduction and Commentary," *Tyndale New Testament Commentaries* (Leicester, England: Inter-Varsity Press, 1985), 46; John MacArthur, Jr., *Matthew 8-15,* The MacArthur New Testament Commentary (Chicago: Moody Press, 1987), 348; I. H. Marshall, "Kingdom of God, of Heaven," *Zondervan Pictorial Encyclopedia of the Bible,* ed. Merrill C. Tenney, vol. 3 (Grand Rapids: Zondervan Publishing House, 1975), 803-804; George N. H. Peters, *The Theocratic Kingdom,* vol. 1 (New York: Funk and Wagnalls, 1884; reprint ed., Grand Rapids: Kregel Publications, 1952), 283-284; Saucy, *The Case for Progressive Dispensationalism,* 19; Erich Sauer,

The Triumph of the Crucified, trans. G.H. Lang (London: Paternoster Press, 1951), 23, n. 1. John Walvoord is one dispensationalist who continues to maintain the distinction. John Walvoord, *Major Bible Prophecies* (Grand Rapids: Zondervan Publishing House, 1991), 213.

[8]In popular usage, the term "kingdom" always has these components except where the usage is clearly metaphorical, as in "the animal kingdom." There is no justification for believing that the biblical "kingdom of God" is ever used in this way. Interestingly, Blaising and Bock *(Progressive Dispensationalism),* do not address the definition of the term "kingdom" at all. Saucy only touches on the problem of definition, but he himself equivocates, declaring that while the Scripture surely presupposes a realm in which God's rule is exercised, "the abstract concept is primary in the biblical words for *kingdom,* in both the Old and New Testaments . . . ." Saucy, *The Case for Progressive Dispensationalism,* 84. See the entire discussion, 82-86.

[9]See Alva J. McClain, *The Greatness of the Kingdom* (Winona Lake, IN: BMH Books, 1974), 17-19. However, McClain, one of the editors of the *New Scofield Reference Bible,* hedges on the realm as including territory, and accepts the older Scofield Bible's distinction between the kingdom of God and the kingdom of heaven. So does Walvoord, and he succinctly illustrates the problem with traditional dispensationalism's view of the kingdom: "The main concept of the kingdom is quite simple. A *kingdom* is a rule by a king (or other ruler) who exerts his authority over people and often over a territory. In the scriptural concept of kingdom, God may be king in every sense of the term without necessarily forcing recognition of this from the human race." Walvoord, "Biblical Kingdoms Compared and Contrasted," in *Issues in Dispensationalism,* 75-76. Once again, there is equivocation on the inclusion of territory in the definition of the kingdom. Moreover, the Bible gives no hint of any such "stealth" kingdom! Nonetheless, Walvoord, in his most recent thinking, insists that the concept of the kingdom is not entirely clear in the Old Testament. However, he goes on to view the kingdom of God as largely spiritual, including all saved human beings and elect angels, and the kingdom of heaven as including mere professors.

[10]It should be noted that, according to Luke, for 40 days following the resurrection, the Lord Jesus "spoke of the things con-

cerning the kingdom of God" to His disciples (Acts 1:3). When they asked Him if the time had come for Him to restore the kingdom to Israel (v. 6), their question did not arise out of a vacuum. Clearly, they had been listening to their Lord's instruction about the future kingdom which would center upon their nation.

[11]As this paper purposes to demonstrate, there is complete harmony between the Old Testament prophets and the Lord Jesus Christ as concerns the identity and nature of the kingdom. The problem for Christian theologians, however, arises from the Apostle Paul's usage of kingdom terminology (examples include Romans 14:17; 1 Corinthians 4:20; 6:9-10; 15:50; Galatians 5:21; Ephesians 5:5; Colossians 1:13; 1 Thessalonians 2:12; 2 Thessalonians 1:5; 2 Timothy 4:1, 18). Paul's epistles reflect his preaching (Acts 14:22; 19:8; 20:25; 28:23, 31). Although this subject cannot be fully explained here, the following observations should be kept in mind: 1) Paul always sees the kingdom of God as *future*, and not present, and as such, it was the focus of his preaching, even up to the end of his ministry. He saw the goal of the *parousia* of Christ as the establishment of His kingdom, and throughout his ministry, firmly held to the hope of its imminent advent. Thus, Paul never saw himself as reigning in the present age. He did, however, see believers as those whose future inheritance is so certain as virtually to place them in God's kingdom now (Philippians 3:20). 2) There are a few references where by "kingdom," Paul does not mean the future kingdom of God (millennial kingdom), but rather points to the realm of God's present authority (as, for example, opposed to Satan's, Colossians 1:13, "the kingdom of His beloved Son"). 3) The kingdom message was particularly targeted at the Jews, or at audiences with significant Jewish auditors. This is why there is virtually no mention of the kingdom in the later New Testament writers until the Apocalypse. Especially after the destruction of Jerusalem, coupled with the growth of the Church among the Gentiles, hope for the immediate restoration of the kingdom dimmed. The proper New Testament relationship of church saints to the kingdom is summarized in Revelation 5:10, where the 24 elders (representing Old Testament saints and the redeemed of the New Testament Church) worship the Lamb in heaven: "And Thou hast made them to be a kingdom and priests to our God; and they will reign upon the earth" (cf. 1:6). Christians have been appointed rulers and priests in the kingdom, but the arrival of the kingdom itself is still future.

[12]"The Kingdom announced by John and by Jesus was primarily and essentially a moral and spiritual kingdom. It was to be prepared for by repentance." Allis, *Prophecy and the Church*, 70. This generalized way of viewing the kingdom, i. e., as the spiritual life, or the "graces of the Gospel" distinguished Calvin's approach to the parables. John Calvin, *Commentary on a Harmony of the Evangelists, Matthew, Mark, and Luke*, vol. 2, trans. William Pringle (Edinburgh: Calvin Translation Society; reprint ed., Grand Rapids: Baker Book House, 1979), 97-134. John MacArthur, Jr., also accepts the concept of the kingdom as spiritual, i.e., God's rule in the hearts of His people. MacArthur, *Matthew 8-15*, 348-349.

[13]Allis, *Prophecy and the Church*, 82. Allis goes on to say that ". . . the expressions 'kingdom of heaven' and 'church' are in most respects at least equivalent, and . . . the two institutions are co-existent and largely co-extensive." Ibid., 83. The close identity of the kingdom and the church is apparent in Calvin's exposition (but see note 12, above), and was also the approach of Archbishop Trench in his classic, *Notes on the Parables of our Lord*, Second American Edition (New York: D. Appleton & Company, 1862). The same viewpoint is shared by J. C. Ryle, *Expository Thoughts on the Gospels: Matthew* (reprint ed, Cambridge: James Clarke & Co. Ltd., 1974), 140-154. More recently, John MacArthur, Jr., has written that the kingdom of heaven, in the present age, corresponds to the church. MacArthur, *Matthew 8-15*, 371. John Broadus, in his classic commentary refers the parables to the "Messianic reign," by which he means, however, the progress of Christianity. John A. Broadus, *Commentary on the Gospel of Matthew* (Philadelphia: American Baptist Publication Society, 1886), 282-309. For G. Campbell Morgan, the parables picture the kingdom "as realised in the world," which means that "The subject of the Church is involved as the means to an end and as the measure of the realisation of the kingdom." G. Campbell Morgan, *The Gospel According to Matthew* (Old Tappan, NJ: Fleming H. Revell Co., 1929), 145. See also his earlier *The Parables of the Kingdom* (New York: Fleming H. Revell , 1907), 29-31, 131. Like many traditional dispensationalists, Morgan saw the kingdom as beginning with the rejection of Matthew 12 and concluding with the second advent of Christ. William Hendriksen defines the kingdom with a menu of means which he nonetheless declares inseparable: God's rule in the hearts of His people, their complete salvation, the church, and a redeemed

universe! William Hendriksen, *Exposition of the Gospel According to Matthew*, in New Testament Commentary (Grand Rapids: Baker Book House, 1973), 249. Even the popular dispensational writer, Warren Wiersbe, refers the parables to the present age as descriptive of "Christendom." Warren Wiersbe, *Be Loyal* (Wheaton, IL: Victor Books, 1980), 82-83. Carson correctly states that "Nowhere in Matthew does 'kingdom' . . . become 'church' . . . ." Carson, "Matthew," 316 (see also 325-326). "The parable," he writes, "deals with eschatological expectation, not ecclesiological deterioration." Ibid., 317.

[14]"The kingdom of God is therefore primarily a soteriological concept. It is God acting in power and exercising His sovereignty for the defeat of Satan and the restoration of human society to its rightful place of willing subservience to the will of God." It is therefore an "abstract reign," which does not, however, preclude the full manifestation in a literal kingdom. Ladd, *Crucial Questions.* See Anthony A. Hoekema, *The Bible and the Future* (Grand Rapids: William B. Eerdmans Publishing Company, 1979), 51.

[15]Hoekema, *The Bible and the Future,* 68-75. See also Hoekema, "Amillennialism," in *The Meaning of the Millennium,* ed. Robert G. Clouse (Downers Grove, IL: InterVarsity Press, 1977), 156-187; Robert H. Stein, *The Method and Message of Jesus' Teachings* (Philadelphia: Westminster Press, 1978), 75-79. This is probably the most fruitful point of intersection between progressive dispensationalism and contemporary amillennialism. But see Saucy, *The Case for Progressive Dispensationalism,* 99, n. 56. This terminology, introduced by Werner Georg Kümmel (1943) and into evangelical theology by George Eldon Ladd and denoting an inaugurated kingdom eschatology, has its roots in the historical-critical exegesis of C.H. Dodd (*The Gospel in the New Testament,* 1926). It is the position of G.R. Beasley-Murray in his *Jesus and the Kingdom of God* (Grand Rapids: Eerdmans Publishing Company, 1986). See the useful discussion in Elliott E. Johnson, "Prophetic Fulfillment: The Already and Not Yet," in *Issues in Dispensationalism,* 183-201. This was the position of Bernard Ramm, who declared that "*the kingdom has come,*" yet it is also "*eschatological* in character"; it "is established, is progressing, and is eschatological." Ramm, *Protestant Biblical Interpretation,* third revised edition (Grand Rapids: Baker Book House, 1970), 280-281, 286.

[16]Blaising and Bock, *Progressive Dispensationalism,* 97-98.

[17]*Scofield Reference Bible,* 996. This understanding was retained in the *New Scofield Reference Bible,* ed. E. Schuyler English et. al. (New York: Oxford University Press, 1967), 994. The new edition admitted, however, that the "kingdom of heaven is similar in many respects to the kingdom of God and is often used synonymously with it, ..."

[18]"It was the Davidic kingdom which Jesus offered and not the general rule of God over the earth or His spiritual reign in individual lives." Ryrie, *Dispensationalism Today,* 173. Among older writers, Alford is unique in focusing primarily on the messianic kingdom. In commenting on Matthew 3:2, he writes that with regard to the use of the term "kingdom of heaven," ". . . we may conclude that it was used by the Jews, and understood, to mean *the advent of the Christ,* probably from the prophecy in Daniel ii. 44; vii. 13, 14, 27." In fact, he goes on to point out that wherever the term "is used in the New Testament, it signifies, not the Church, nor the Christian religion, but strictly the *kingdom of the Messiah which is to be revealed hereafter.* I should doubt this being *exclusively* true. The state of Christian men *now* is undoubtedly a part of the bringing in of the kingdom of Christ, and, as such, is included in this term." Henry Alford, *The Greek Testament,* rev. Everett F. Harrison, vol. 1 (reprint ed., Chicago: Moody Press, 1958), 19.

[19]Dwight Pentecost, *Things to Come: A Study in Biblical Eschatology* (reprint ed., Grand Rapids: Zondervan Publishing House, 1964), 143.

[20]Ryrie, *The Basis of the Premillennial Faith,* 95. Both Pentecost and Ryrie agree with the *Scofield Reference Bible,* which says: "The seven parables of Matt. xiii., called by our Lord 'mysteries of the kingdom of heaven' (vs. 11), taken together, describe the result of the presence of the Gospel in the world during the present age, that is, the time of seed-sowing which began with our Lord's personal ministry, and ends with the 'harvest' (vss. 40-43). Briefly, that result is the mingled tares and wheat, good fish and bad, in the sphere of Christian profession. It is Christendom." *Scofield Reference Bible,* 1014. Saucy concurs in assigning the parables to the present age (*The Case for Progressive Dispensationalism,* 99, 164). It is revealing to note that Allis regards this statement as surprising coming from Scofield (see Allis, *Prophecy and the Church,* 84-86). He can see the inconsistency between

the basic tenets of dispensationalism and this interpretation of the Parables of the Kingdom, even if the dispensationalists cannot!

[21]Ryrie, *The Basis of the Premillennial Faith,* 96-97. Among more recent dispensationalists, particularly those of the Dallas school of thought, the kingdom is viewed as extending from the point of Christ's rejection in Matthew 12 until the second advent. Even though the church and the kingdom exist at the same time for most of their history, they reject the notion that the kingdom is identical to the Church. For progressive dispensationalists Blaising and Bock, the mysteries of the kingdom as set forth in the parables are a new stage of the kingdom's presence "which *precedes* the apocalyptic coming of the kingdom." Blaising and Bock, *Progressive Dispensationalism,* 251. See the entire section, 251-254.

[22]Walvoord, "Biblical Kingdoms Compared and Contrasted," 81. He goes on to say, "The kingdom as it exists today is a mystery that was not revealed in the Old Testament."

[23]Among prominent traditional dispensationalists who see the Parables of the Kingdom (and therefore the kingdom itself) as referring to "the mystery form of the kingdom" are Louis A. Barbieri, Jr., "Matthew, " *The Bible Knowledge Commentary,* New Testament Edition, ed. John F. Walvoord and Roy B. Zuck (Wheaton, IL: Victor Books, 1983), 48-53; Lewis Sperry Chafer, *Systematic Theology,* vol. 5 (Dallas: Dallas Seminary Press, 1948), 349-354; also, vol. 7, 224-225; Charles L. Feinberg, *Millennialism: the Two Major Views* (Chicago: Moody Press, 1980), 253, 269-270; Arno C. Gaebelein, *the Annotated Bible,* vol. 3 (reprint ed., Neptune, NJ: Loizeaux Brothers, 1970), 33-36; I.M. Haldeman, *The Coming of Christ, Both Pre-Millennial and Imminent* (New York: Charles C. Cook, 1906), 33-47; H.A. Ironside, *Expository Notes on the Gospel of Matthew* (New York: Loizeaux Brothers, 1948), 156-157; John F. MacArthur, Jr., *The Gospel According to Jesus* (Grand Rapids: Zondervan Publishing House, 1988), 117-141; McClain, *The Greatness of the Kingdom,* 321-325; J. Dwight Pentecost, *The Parables of Jesus* (Grand Rapids: Zondervan Publishing House, 1982), 46-49; *Things to Come,* 138-149; and, *Thy Kingdom Come* (Wheaton, IL: Victor Books, 1990), 215-228, 234-237; Charles Caldwell Ryrie, *Basic Theology* (Wheaton, IL: Victor Books, 1986), 398-399; *The Basis of the Premillennial Faith,* 94-97; *Dispensationalism Today,* 145; and *The Ryrie Study Bible,*

ed. Charles Caldwell Ryrie, New American Standard Translation (Chicago: Moody Press, 1976), 1467; Sauer, *The Triumph of the Crucified,* 24; Lehman Strauss *Prophetic Mysteries Revealed* (Neptune, NJ: Loizeaux Brothers, 1980), 39-40; Paul Lee Tan, *The Interpretation of Prophecy* (Winona Lake, IN: BMH Books, 1974), 150; Stanley D. Toussaint, *Behold the King: A Study of Matthew* (Portland, OR: Multnomah Press, 1980), 176-185; John F. Walvoord, "Biblical Kingdoms Compared and Contrasted," 80-82; *Major Bible Prophecies, 205-218; Matthew: Thy Kingdom Come* (Chicago: Moody Press, 1974), 95-108; Roy B. Zuck, *Basic Bible Interpretation* (Wheaton, IL: Victor Books, 1991), 210. Although distancing himself from dispensationalsim, D. A. Carson nonetheless takes the same view ("Matthew," 307-308). Progressive dispensationalists Blaising and Bock do not hesitate to say that "the Church corresponds to that mystery form of the kingdom which Jesus revealed in the parables of Matthew 13." Blaising and Bock, *Progressive Dispensationalism,* 262. Like some of those who followed him (Ryrie, for example), the patriarch of classical dispensationalism, John Nelson Darby, rejects the notion that the parables concern the church, but also denies their reference to the millennial kingdom. J.N. Darby, "The Gospel According to Matthew," *The Collected Writings of J. N. Darby,* Expository No. 3, vol. 24, ed. William Kelly (Kingston-on-Thames: Stow Hill Bible and Tract Depot, n. d.), 5-24. He even goes so far as to describe that which is under consideration in these parables as "this confused state of the kingdom" (15). One can see why those who followed him found it necessary to invent the "mystery form of the kingdom"!

[24]Pentecost adamantly rejects this view when he insists that the mystery form of the kingdom "can not be equated with the millennial kingdom, for that kingdom was no mystery, but was clearly predicted in the Old Testament." Pentecost, *Things to Come,* 143. But as shall be demonstrated, the mysteries do not concern the existence of the kingdom. In other words, it is true that the idea of the messianic kingdom was not new, but it is also true that the reality of His coming reign was not Christ's point in delivering these parables. See also Walvoord's categorical statements that the parables do not concern the millennial kingdom. Walvoord, *Matthew,* 97; and more recently, "Biblical Kingdoms Compared and Contrasted," 82.

[25]It is not within the purview of this paper to survey the work

of recent scholarship on the interpretation of parables. For a summary, see Craig Blomberg, *Interpreting the Parables* (Downers Grove, IL: InterVarsity Press, 1990), 13-167; and Robert H. Stein, *An Introduction to the Parables of Jesus* (Philadelphia: Westminster Press, 1981), 53-71. Works dealing with the parables from a higher critical vantage point are not considered here.

[26]Trench, *Notes on the Parables,* 32. The German scholar, Adolph Jülicher, also insisted that the parables were not allegories, but simple stories with a single point (in his influential *Die Gleichnisreden Jesu,* vol. 1, 1888). Stein agrees (*An Introduction to the Parables of Jesus,* 56-58). Bernard Ramm embraced this view as well (*Protestant Biblical Interpretation,* 283), and since his text was standard for virtually an entire generation of evangelicals, many dispensationalists have concurred with this viewpoint, as for example, Zuck, in *Basic Bible Interpretation,* 215-217. But this claim is increasingly rejected today, and that certainly cannot be the proper approach to interpreting the Parables of the Kingdom which allows no place for meaning in any of the details. Since the Lord Jesus interpreted two of them Himself, we have His model as our hermeneutical paradigm (see Trench, *Notes on the Parables,* 36; Ramm, *Protestant Biblical Interpretation,* 283-284; also, Pentecost, *Things to Come,* 145), and He did assign meanings to many of the details, lending something of an allegorical nature to the parables. Zuck claims that the detail involved in these parables makes them exceptions to the way in which most of Jesus' parables are to be understood. Zuck, *Basic Bible Interpretation,* 216.

[27]Trench, *Notes on the Parables,* 33.

[28]Ibid., 36-37.

[29]See also Ramm, *Protestant Biblical Interpretation,* 284.

[30]Trench, *Notes on the Parables,* 38. "We ought not to read our theological debates back into the parables." Ramm, *Protestant Biblical Interpretation,* 285.

[31]Trench, *Notes on the Parables, 39-41. The quotation is from Irenaeus's Against Heresies.* "Parables do teach doctrine, and the claim that they may not be used at all in doctrinal writing is improper. But in gleaning our doctrine from the parables we must be strict in our interpretation; we must check our results with the plain, evident teaching of our Lord, and with the rest of the New Testament." Ramm, *Protestant Biblical Interpretation,* 285. One should say, "with the rest of the *Old* and New Testaments"!

[32]The paradigm for the interpretation of parables adopted in this paper is essentially that proposed by Roy Zuck, *Basic Bible Interpretation,* 211-218.

[33]All Scripture quotations are from the *New American Standard Bible* (La Habra, CA: The Lockman Foundation, 1960-1977).

[34]He had certainly used figurative language before, but not the parable more narrowly understood as a story illustrating a spiritual truth. Previous figurative language (more broadly regarded as parabolic by some writers) can be seen in Matthew (i.e., 7:24-27; 9:15-17; 11:16-19), but not parables.

[35]"The seven parables related in this chapter cannot be regarded as a collection made by the Evangelist as relating to one subject, the Kingdom of heaven and its development; they are clearly indicated by verse 53 to have been all spoken on *one and the same occasion,* and form indeed a complete and glorious whole in their inner and deeper sense." Alford, *The Greek Testament,* vol. 1, 137. Carson agrees ("Matthew," 300).

[36]"So, too, doubtless the seven have a certain unity, succeeding one another in natural order, and having a completeness in themselves: . . . ." Trench, *Notes on the Parables,* 123. ". . . [I]t must be borne in mind that there is harmony in the teaching in these parables. Whatever difference there might be in the figures of speech our Lord used, there is consistency in the interpretation. The seven parables form a connected and completed whole. . . . Any interpretation of one of them which contradicts that of any other cannot be the correct interpretation." Strauss, *Prophetic Mysteries Revealed,* 64.

[37]The 13th is therefore the pivotal chapter in Matthew's gospel.

[38]The mystery of the Mother of Harlots (Revelation 17:1-7), which concerns eschatological Babylon, is still largely unrevealed.

[39]Neither the Lord Jesus nor the Apostle Paul was speaking in a novel way. The New Testament *mysterion* corresponds to the Aramaic *raz* (which it translates in the LXX) in Daniel 2:18, 19, 27, 30, 47 and 4:9. In each case the word refers to something previously unknown but subsequently revealed (in these cases specifically, through revelatory dreams or visions), and in each, the "secret" is eschatological in nature (the same dynamic is at work in Paul's connection of the "mystery" of Israel's hardening to future prophetic events, Romans 11:25-27). G. Finkenrath, "Secret, Mystery," *The New International Dictionary of New Testa-*

ment Theology, ed. Colin Brown, vol. 3 (Grand Rapids: Zondervan Publishing House, 1978), 502. Carson, however, groundlessly and arbitrarily defines these "secrets of the kingdom" as "divine plans or decrees, often passed on in veiled language, known only to the elect, and usually relating to eschatological events." Carson, "Matthew," 307. Whatever else this definition is, it is not biblically derived.

[40]Psalm 78:1-3 reads:

Listen, O my people, to my instruction;
Incline your ears to the words of my mouth.
I will open my mouth in a parable;
I will utter dark sayings of old,
Which we have heard and known,
And our fathers have told us.

Truths that were previously "enigmas" (*hîdôt)*, claims Asaph, have now been heard and known. Carson thinks that the hidden things of which Christ speaks are "the righteous acts of God in redemption." Carson, "Matthew," 322. One example would be the Messiah as the Suffering Servant.

[41]Mark Saucy argues that the kingdom, which had been publicly proclaimed, is now a "secret"—a "strange fact," and so being, hints at a change in the kingdom concept itself. Mark Saucy, "The Kingdom-of-God Sayings in Matthew," *Bibliotheca Sacra* 151 (April-June, 1994), 186. In fact, says Saucy, the parables represent a "new enigma," and point to a discontinuity with the kingdom announced by Jesus at the beginning of His ministry (193). But such a view is based on a misunderstanding of the New Testament *mysterion*. Much more accurately, his father writes: "It is difficult to conceive of any aspect of God's salvation portrayed in the New Testament that is not already seen in this Old Testament hope." Saucy, *The Case for Progressive Dispensationalism*, 242.

[42]*Synekate tauta panta?* The verb *syniemi* ("understand," "perceive") originally meant "to bring together." It is used primarily in the gospels, most frequently in the passages dealing with the disciples' understanding (or lack of comprehension) of Christ's teaching in parables or figurative language (Mark 6:52; 7:18; 8:17, 21), or their lack of insight into the OT prophetic Scriptures (Luke 18:34). It is also used of Jesus' insight, as a boy of 12, into the Scriptures, and the lack of understanding on the part of Mary and Joseph (Luke 2:47, 50). In verses 13 and 15, it is used

in conjunction with Isaiah's prophecy (cf. also Acts 28:26). The nuance here appears to be, "Have you put all of this together?", implying that understanding comes from assimilation of the Old Testament Scriptures with the parables He had just told. Henry George Liddell and Robert Scott, *A Greek-English Lexicon* (Oxford: Clarendon Press, 1883), 1494; Hans Conzelmann, *"syniemi, etc." Theological Dictionary of the New Testament,* ed. Gerhard Friederich, trans. and ed. Geoffrey W. Bromiley, vol. 7 (Grand Rapids: Wm. B. Eerdmans Publishing Company, 1971), 888-896; J. Goetzmann, *"synesis," The New International Dictionary of New Testament Theology,* ed. Colin Brown, vol. 3 (Exeter: The Paternoster Press, 1971), 130-133.

[43]A number of scholars regard this as the eighth parable of the kingdom. The reason for rejecting this interpretation is twofold: 1) this comment does not share the common theme of the other parables, and 2) it is concerned with the interpretation of the parables, and not with the kingdom itself.

[44]Perhaps Carson is as clear as any who hold to the "mystery form" view when he writes: "The new truth, now given to men by revelation in the person and mission of Jesus, is that the kingdom which is to come finally in apocalyptic power, as foreseen by Daniel, has in fact entered the world in advance in a hidden form to work secretly within and among men." Carson, "Matthew," 307. The contrast, then, is between an "inaugurated kingdom," and its "apocalyptic culmination." Ibid., 310.

[45]Thus, Barbieri declares that the " 'mystery' concerning the kingdom Jesus presented here was the truth that the good news was rejected by the majority. This had not been revealed in the Old Testament." Barbieri, "Matthew," 50. "That the parables are closely associated with rejection is attested by the significant fact that in each of the Synoptics the parables follow the clear indication of the rejection of Christ." Toussaint, *Behold the King,* 170. Among many others, see also France, *The Gospel According to Matthew,* 215; Saucy, "The Kingdom-of-God Sayings in Matthew," 182-186; Walvoord, *Major Bible Prophecies,* 206-207; and Zuck, *Basic Bible Interpretation,* 213. This rejection, however, was at least implicit in the Old Testament prophecies of Messiah's sufferings, and therefore is not the mystery of these parables.

[46]Darby is correct when he says that "What we have here is the application of lessons on the kingdom of heaven to knowledge acquired as by scribes in the Old Testament. There is nothing

about the mystery hidden and afterwards revealed by the Holy Ghost to the apostles and prophets; but we have light thrown by the kingdom and its mysteries on the promises and the government of God, which a scribe would have found in the law and the prophets. These were new things, but they were connected with the old things; they did not set them aside." Darby, "The Gospel According to Matthew," 24. Unfortunately, Darby's interpretation of the parables is inconsistent with this statement.

[47]". . . [T]he concept of the kingdom in Matthew is always millennial." Toussaint, *Behold the King,* 175. Like Darby's, however, Toussaint's interpretation of the parables is a denial of this statement.

[48]Barbieri, *Matthew,* 50. It is true that the fact that the good news would be rejected by the majority was not revealed in the Old Testament, which foresaw a kingdom of righteousness in which evil would be overcome. The difficulty with Barbieri's position, however, is that he assumes that evil will not only be overcome, but altogether eliminated in the millennial kingdom, something the Old Testament did not teach. Hence, he views the age under consideration as being "the present Age before Christ establishes the messianic kingdom."

[49]Ibid., 177.

[50]Blaising and Bock believe that the full manifestation of the kingdom will be marked by "the elimination of sin and wickedness." Blaising and Bock, *Progressive Dispensationalism,* 247.

[51]The Lord's expression, *hoi hyoi tes basileias*, seems to refer to no more than those who belong to the kingdom, i.e., those who were admitted either through judgment, or subsequently by birth. Although it refers to believers here, it is also used in Matthew 8:12, where it refers to unbelievers. Thus, in and of itself, the phrase does not define the spiritual status of the referents. Saucy, however, refers to them as "believers in the church." Saucy, *The Case for Progressive Dispensationalism,* 18.

[52]"Tares" (*zizania*) are most likely darnel (*lolium tremulentum*), a poisonous plant which looks very much like wheat until the head forms, and which has stronger roots than wheat, making it difficult to weed out once they have become entangled with the roots of the wheat. In fact, under Roman law, it was a crime to sow darnel as an act of revenge.

[53]Darby is very, and one suspects unavoidably, obscure here—an indication of the difficulties the interpreter faces when refusing to separate the biblical teaching concerning one dispensation from another. "As to the expression, *'this age,'* we are accustomed to apply it to the church; but it is not here a question of the church, but of the introduction of the kingdom of heaven, Messiah being rejected by the Jews. What was the age in which the Lord was found with His disciples? Was it the church, or the dispensation of the church? By no means. It was a certain age of this world, which was to end by the reception of the Messiah, and the re-establishment of the law as a rule by the government of this Messiah. The people of Israel having rejected Him, this age becomes purely and simply *this present evil world (age),* from which Christ delivers us, but in the course of which God has set up His kingdom, in the way we have just spoken of." Darby, "The Gospel According to Matthew," 12. Thus, it is neither the church nor the millennial kingdom, but something else, and that not very well defined!

[54]Dispensational commentators usually join nondispensational writers in viewing this parable as teaching that good and evil will distinguish the church in the present age. Ironside describes the Parables of the Kingdom as a "remarkable panorama covering the entire present age, and reaching on even into the tribulation period, ..." Ironside, *Matthew,* 174. Toussaint writes: ". . . the Lord uses this parable to instruct His disciples that this evil would coexist until the kingdom is established (Matthew 13:39-43). The whole age is in view from the ascension until the coming of the Lord to establish the kingdom." Toussaint, *Behold the King,* 181. Walvoord insists that "it describes the age between the first and second coming of Christ." Walvoord, *Major Bible Prophecies,* 212. Many commentators believe the parable teaches the coexistence of believers and non-believers in the church, and some have even gone so far as to say that it forbids church discipline in favor of final judgment! MacArthur supposes that it forbids the forcible removal of unbelievers from the world, such as in the Inquisition. MacArthur, *The Gospel According to Jesus,* 130. Carson, who rejects the identity of kingdom and church, nonetheless leans in this direction when he says that "The parable of the sower shows that though the kingdom will now make its way amid hard hearts, competing pressures, and even failure, it will produce an abundant crop. But one might ask whether

Messiah's people should immediately separate the crop from the weeds; and this next parable answers the question negatively: there will be a delay in separation until the harvest." Carson, "Matthew," 315-316. The emphasis, however, is not so much on the perseverence of the wheat as it is on the presence of the darnel. Moreover, what are the implications of Carson's view for the responsibility of maintaining the purity of the church now? Blomberg is correct when he writes that "Jesus enjoins patience and alerts them [the disciples] to expect continued hostility from those who would reject his message. At a later date, the Church could legitimately apply the same lessons within her own ranks, when false teachers or nominal adherents hindered the work of the truly redeemed. To conclude that a "mixed church" was inevitable, however, and to use this parable as a justification for doing nothing to attempt to "purify the Church (as with St. Augustine) goes well beyond anything demanded by the imagery of the narrative." Blomberg, *Interpreting the Parables,* 200. Blomberg, however, does not mention the eschatological significance of the parable.

[55]There is a recurring eschatological use of the "harvest" imagery in the Old Testament prophets (Jeremiah 51:33; Hosea 6:11; Joel 3:13). However, these all point to the judgment that inaugurates the kingdom, rather than here, where the harvest concludes it.

[56]Ladd insists that "The meaning of the parable is clear when interpreted in terms of the mystery of the Kingdom: its present but secret working in the world. The Kingdom has come into history but in such a way that society is not disrupted. The sons of the Kingdom have received God's reign and entered into its blessings. Yet they must continue to live in this age, intermingled with the wicked in a mixed society. Only at the eschatological coming of the Kingdom will the separation take place. Here is indeed the revelation of a new truth: that the Kingdom of God can actually come into the world, creating sons who enjoy its blessings without effecting the eschatological judgment. However, this separation is sure to come. The Kingdom that is present but hidden in the world will yet be manifested in glory. Then there will be an end of the mixed society. The wicked will be gathered out and the righteous will shine like the sun in the eschatological Kingdom." George Eldon Ladd, *A Theology of the New Testament* (Grand Rapids: William B.

Eerdmans Publishing Company, 1974), 97.

[57]With regard to this parable and the one that follows, Bock insists that "Whatever this kingdom is, it must refer to the present age because of the growth process. It cannot refer to the future, because when the future form of the kingdom arrives, it will be established over the entire earth immediately." Darrell L. Bock, "The Son of David and the Saints' Task: The Hermeneutics of Initial Fulfillment," *Bibliotheca Sacra* 150 (October-December, 1993), 450. Bock's mistake here, however, is that he fails to realize that the growth is not of the kingdom, but of evil within the kingdom.

[58]Thus, in contrast to the opinion of many scholars, the Lord's point is not that the kingdom (or church) grows supernaturally or that it begins inconsequentially in His ministry, developing into an eventually glorious kingdom of vast proportions. See, for example, Blomberg, *Interpreting the Parables,* 284-287; Ladd, *A Theology of the New Testament,* 97-98; and Stein, *An Introduction to the Parables of Jesus,* 94-95.

[59]Note the use of the same "birds of the air" in Acts 10:12 and 11:6 as "unholy and unclean" (10:14; 11:8), pointing back to the ceremonially unclean birds of Leviticus 11:13-19. Cf. also Revelation 18:2.

[60]Even some dispensational scholars who see this parable as pointing to the present age have trouble here, being forced to deny that the birds have any evil connotation, since in their view, the growing shrub must represent the spread of the gospel throughout the world. See Toussaint, *Behold the King,* 181. The context, however, forbids this interpretation. To his credit, Pentecost agrees that "In the first parable the birds represented that which was antagonistic to the program of God and consistency would demand that they be so interpreted here." Pentecost, *Things to Come,* 147. Ryrie provides an example of what happens when the Old Testament perspective is ignored, when he says that the birds "represent demonized human beings who are a part of Christendom." *The Basis of the Premillennial Faith,* 97.

[61]This according to Josephus, *Antiquities,* III.6.6.

[62]Against overwhelming contextual evidence, Ladd criticizes "so-called Dispensationalism," and denies that leaven must be viewed here as symbolizing evil. Ladd, *A Theology of the New Testament,* 98. And in the face of the majority premillennialist

opinion to the contrary, MacArthur agrees. MacArthur, *Matthew 8-15,* 373. Blomberg also dismisses the dispensational interpretation of the leaven as a symbol of evil. Blomberg, *Interpreting the Parables,* 286-287. In similar fashion, Carson insists that "Efforts by most dispensationalists (e.g., Walvoord) to interpret the yeast as a symbol for evil are not very convincing in this setting because they require the introduction of anachronistic ideas like 'the professing church.' " Carson, "Matthew," 319. But that is the case only if the evil is seen as growing apostasy in the Church. The argument that yeast does not symbolize evil flies in the face of every biblical use of the symbol. In fact, it is this position that is less than convincing.

[63]"Evil doctrine, according to this parable, is characteristic of the kingdom." Ryrie, *The Basis of the Premillennial Faith,* 97. Strauss correctly sees the presence of evil, as represented by leaven, during the messianic kingdom of Christ, but mentions this only in passing, preferring to interpret the parables primarily in terms of "Christendom," namely, the course of the age between Christ's two advents. Strauss, *Prophetic Mysteries Revealed,* 84. Likewise, Blaising and Bock declare that "the millennial kingdom harbors the possibility of rebellion and judgment, a possibility which becomes actual upon the release of the devil." Blaising and Bock, *Progressive Dispensationalism,* 273. Similarly, Saucy says that this "messianic reign of peace does not immediately involve the exclusion of all sin; that will take place only with the making of all things new. That sin is present during the Messiah's reign is evident in His settling disputes among the nations (cf. Isaiah 2:4) and in the possibility of punishing the disobedient (Zechariah 14:16-19). But that sin will never be able to thwart the righteous, powerful reign of the Messiah. Saucy, *The Case for Progressive Dispensationalism,* 234; also, 238. Unfortunately, these writers fail to see that the development of evil leading to rebellion is precisely the point of the parables!

[64]Toussaint, *Behold the King,* 182.

[65]As Carson observes, ". . . pairing is not uncommon in Matthew (e.g., 5:14b-16; 6:26-30; 7:6; 9:16-17; 10:24-25; 12:25; 13:31-33; 24:43-51), an excellent way of reinforcing a point." Carson, "Matthew," 327.

[66]Ladd misses the point entirely when he writes that the one thought both in this parable and the one that follows "is that the Kingdom of God is of inestimable value and is to be sought

above all other possessions." Ladd, *A Theology of the New Testament,* 100. Carson does the same thing, insisting that they both point to "the superlative worth of the kingdom of heaven" ("Matthew," 328), as do Blomberg (*Interpreting the Parables,* 279) and Stein (*An Introduction to the Parables of Jesus,* 101-104). Likewise, Blaising and Bock, who nonetheless implicitly sense the weakness of their interpretation when they write that the two parables "seem to speak of two kinds of people who come to possess the kingdom during the dispensation preceding the apocalypse." Blaising and Bock, *Progressive Dispensationalism,* 253.

[67]Walter Baumgartner, *Lexicon in Veteris Testamenti Libros,* ed. Ludwig Koehler (Leiden: E. J. Brill, 1958), 649; Francis Brown, S. R. Driver, and Charles A. Briggs, *A Hebrew and English Lexicon of the Old Testament,* trans. Edward Robinson (Oxford: The Clarendon Press, 1907), 688; *Gesenius' Hebrew and Chaldee Lexicon to the Old Testament Scriptures,* trans. Samuel Prideaux Tregelles (reprint ed., Grand Rapids: Wm. B. Eerdmans Publishing Company, 1949), 578; William L. Holladay, *A Concise Hebrew and Aramaic Lexicon of the Old Testament* (Grand Rapids: Wm. B. Eerdmans, 1971), 253; *Theological Wordbook of the Old Testament,* ed. R. Laird Harris, Gleason L. Archer, and Bruce K. Waltke, vol. 2 (Chicago: Moody Press, 1980), 617.

[68]So the KJV, NKJV, NEB and NASB (margin). Cf. the NIV's "treasured possession." The nuance "treasure" for *sᵉgullâ* is apparent in First Chronicles 29:3 and Ecclesiastes 2:8.

[69]See Stein's remarks, *An Introduction to the Parables of Jesus,* 99-100.

[70]Darby says of Christ, "He gave up everything, He emptied Himself to accomplish this work and buy the church." Darby, "The Gospel According to Matthew," 16. Alford sees the treasure as being "true faith and hope and communion with God." Alford, *The Greek Testament,* vol. 1, 148. For MacArthur, the treasure is the kingdom of heaven itself, and thus, obtaining the treasure means entering the kingdom, another way of referring to salvation. MacArthur, *The Gospel According to Jesus,* 136-139.

[71]Carson rejects this interpretation as "pressing a parable into a detailed allegory. . . ." Carson, "Matthew," 378. But he has nothing else to offer. Pentecost says that the parable depicts "the relationship of Israel to this present age." Pentecost, *Things to Come,* 148. Ryrie sees it as focusing on Israel, but as aimed

specifically at the end of the mystery form of the kingdom. Ryrie, *The Basis of the Premillennial Faith,* 97.

[72]"The pearl of great value may represent the church, the bride of Jesus Christ." Barbieri, "Matthew," 51. The church, says Darby, "is the pearl quite pure, ..." Darby, "The Gospel According to Matthew," 22. "This is the Church, ..." Ironside, *Matthew,* 173. "The parable of the pearl teaches that the Church, the body of Christ, is also a part of the kingdom of heaven in its mystery form." Ryrie, *The Basis of the Premillennial Faith,* 97. Pentecost points out that ". . . most interpreters relate the pearl to the church." Pentecost, *Things to Come,* 148. (He then goes on to allegorize, saying, for example, that "the church, like the pearl, is to be formulated by gradual accretion" [!]). "That pearl is the Church." Strauss, *Prophetic Mysteries Revealed,* 105. ". . . [T]he pearl seemed to represent the church rather than Israel." Walvoord, *Matthew,* 105. Similarly, *Major Bible Prophecies,* 216. (Strauss and Walvoord likewise speak of the church as growing out of the wounded side of Christ!). "It seems that the pearl pictures the true church of Jesus Christ." Toussaint, *Behold the King,* 184. "The pearl represents the church." Wiersbe, *Be Loyal,* 87. So also Gaebelein, *The Annotated Bible,* vol. 3, 35.

[73]MacArthur sees both the hidden treasure and the pearl as representing the "saving knowledge of God through trust in His Son and all the benefits and glory that relationship brings." MacArthur, *Matthew 8-15,* 384.

[74]In the other places where pearls are mentioned, they do not have symbolic significance (1 Timothy 2:9; Revelation 17:4; 18:12, 16).

[75]The Hebrew *ga'al,* when used in a commercial context, generally refers to buying something back (the meaning of "redeem"). In Leviticus 25:25-28, it refers "to the repurchase of a field which was sold in time of need." *Theological Wordbook of the Old Testament,* vol. 1, 300. The Greek verb used in Matthew's account (the common commercial term, *agorazo*), actually translates *ga'al* once in the LXX, in Leviticus 27:19, where once again, the subject is the repurchase of a field. This nuance of repurchasing an item previously owned is particularly appropriate to Israel, YHWH's special possession which, because of their spiritual apostasy, He had to buy back.

[76]Among additional significant texts emphasizing the central importance of Zion to the millennial kingdom are Psalm 48:1-2;

132:13-18; 146:10; 149:2; Isaiah 24:23; Joel 3:16-17, 21; Obadiah 17, 21; Zephaniah 3:14-20; Zechariach 9:9; Rev 14:1.

[77]Thus completing the chiasm so characteristic of Matthew's style.

[78]Ladd views this parable primarily in terms of the *sitz im leben* of Jesus' ministry, explaining the "strange character" of His followers, while having a more remote application to the Church. Ladd, *A Theology of the New Testament,* 101.

[79]Toussaint sees this parable as a picture of the end of the tribulation period, and the judgment as that of Israel and the nations. In his view, the judgment anticipated by the Jews prior to the coming of the new age would thus be postponed until after this unexpected intervening age, that of the Church, was completed. Toussaint, *Behold the King,* 184-185. Walvoord agrees that "this refers to the worldwide judgment at Christ's second coming when those who are not worthy to enter the kingdom will be discarded and put to death." Walvoord, *Major Bible Prophecies,* 217. The same view is endorsed by Strauss, *Prophetic Mysteries Revealed,* 112-117.

The Hermeneutics of Annihilationism: The Theological Method of Edward Fudge

Robert A. Peterson

My purpose in this essay is to evaluate the biblical hermeneutic of evangelical conditionalist, Edward William Fudge. I have chosen Fudge, author of *The Fire That Consumes: A Biblical and Historical Study of Final Punishment*, for two reasons.[1] First, his work has attracted considerable attention of late. As evidence of this fact I cite two essays in *Universalism and the Doctrine of Hell*, edited by Nigel Cameron.[2] John W. Wenham ascribes importance to Fudge's book when he includes it with three others that, in his estimation, have not been answered by traditionalist writers: "I have been waiting since 1973 for a reply to the massive work of Froom (2,476 pages), to Atkinson's closely argued 112 pages, to Guillebaud's 67 and (more important) to the one additional book which has appeared on the conditionalist side: Edward Fudge's *The Fire That Consumes*."[3]

Wenham's remarks occur in the introduction to his essay,

"The Case for Conditional Immortality." In the essay following Wenham's (in *Universalism and the Doctrine of Hell*) Kendall S. Harmon makes "The Case Against Conditionalism: A Response to Edward William Fudge."[4] Notice that when Harmon seeks to interact with a contemporary annihilationist, he chooses Fudge. Harmon gives two reasons for so doing: "First, although not as prominent as John Stott or Philip Hughes, Mr. Fudge's work is more substantial than theirs (500 pages) and is devoted exclusively to the doctrine of hell. Secondly, Mr. Fudge's book has been praised for its tone and its thoroughness."[5] Plainly, the stock of *The Fire That Consumes* is on the rise.

My second reason for choosing to evaluate the biblical interpretation of Fudge is that in the preface to *The Fire That Consumes* he says that he has given attention to hermeneutics and that he invites evaluation of his work:

> This book is written to be read—and argued with! I have no ax to grind and no cause to champion; I have tried to follow the ordinary methods of sound, biblical exegesis. Competent scholars and serious students are cordially invited to enter into dialogue. Check the statements made here. Weigh the evidence. Examine the arguments. Measure the work by every proper standard. All that matters is that we seek God's truth for His glory and the salvation of sinners![6]

I appreciate the openness Fudge here expresses. In this paper I take up one aspect of his challenge. I propose to evaluate his hermeneutic within the framework of his theological methodology.[7] Like most writers on the doctrine of hell, Fudge does not devote a section of his book to hermeneutics.[8] Nevertheless, he refers to principles of interpretation throughout *The Fire That Consumes*. By studying these stated principles and the hermeneutic implicit in his exegesis, we can discern some aspects of his hermeneutical methodology.

Instead of trying to evaluate all of his exegesis, I have chosen to base my evaluation primarily on his treatment of three New Testament passages: Matthew 25:41, 46; Revelation 14:9-11; and Revelation 20:10, 15. I have chosen these passages because they have figured most prominently in the history of the doctrine of hell. Indeed, Augustine, Aquinas, Calvin, Edwards, and Shedd, to name the stalwarts of the orthodox view of hell, all regard one or more of these passages as teaching the endless conscious torment of the wicked.[9] I have studied Fudge's treatment of these passages (within the context of his whole book) in order to evaluate his hermeneutical approach and method. As a result, I summarize Fudge's hermeneutic under the following headings.

Use of the Old Testament

Fudge devotes a 30-page chapter of *The Fire that Consumes* to a study of "The End of the Wicked in the Old Testament."[10] Contrary to the assumption of many, the Old Testament has much to say about the fate of the wicked. Fudge points to numerous biblical examples of God's judging the ungodly. I cite two: the Genesis flood and the destruction of Sodom and Gomorrah.

At the time of the flood, "God decided 'to wipe mankind . . . from the face of the earth'" (Genesis 6:5). Indeed, Fudge notes, "God told Noah his plan . . . 'to destroy . . . every creature that has the breath of life in it. Everything will perish'" (v. 17). Subsequently, God fulfilled His threat and, "When the flood came, 'Every living thing that moved on the earth perished. . . .' " (Genesis 7:21). Fudge concludes, "Here there is no doubt about the meaning of 'perish,' 'destroy,' or 'die'. . . . In this actual historical example of the end of the world, those terms were clearly literal. They meant being 'wiped out,' being 'wiped off the face of the earth.' "[11]

The fate of Sodom and Gomorrah is another example given by Fudge of God's judging the wicked in the Old Testament. In this case, "The fire fell from heaven and burned the wicked to ashes, resulting in a total desolation that would never be reversed!"[12] Indeed, as Fudge amplifies in a footnote, "The final outcome of 'fire and brimstone' in the prototypal historical judgment of Sodom was the complete extermination of every sinner. . . ."[13]

It is not necessary to multiply examples. These two enable us to understand Fudge's conception of the fate of the wicked according to the Old Testament—annihilation. Although Fudge is not the first conditionalist to reach this conclusion, as he acknowledges,[14] he has given it new visibility. Consider these words from an article he wrote in 1984:

> Is the OT silent concerning the wicked's final fate? Indeed it is not. It overwhelmingly affirms their total destruction. It never affirms or even hints at anything resembling conscious unending torment. The OT uses about 50 different Hebrew verbs to describe this fate, and about 70 figures of speech. Without exception they portray destruction, extinction or extermination. Not one of the verbs or word-pictures remotely suggests the traditional doctrine.[15]

I must give Fudge's conclusions a mixed review on the basis of a study of the major Old Testament judgment texts.[16] Such a study reveals that the punishments of God described in them are earthly and temporal, resulting in physical death. These passages do not speak of life after death or eternal destinies. This is significant in the light of Fudge's claim that the Old Testament supports his view of the extinction of the wicked.[17] Fudge correctly asserts that the judgment passages use the "vocabulary of destruction." God punishes the ungodly in the flood, Sodom and Gomorrah, the plagues and Red Sea, and the captivities by "wiping them out, cutting them off, putting them to an end, overthrowing them." As a result the wicked "perish, die, are consumed, shattered, destroyed."

Fudge errs, however, when he claims that these Old Testament texts teach the annihilation of the wicked. If that were the case, then the judgment passages would teach too much, for the "annihilation" depicted in them does not follow the resurrection and punishment of the wicked, as does the annihilation for which Fudge argues. Instead, the "annihilation" presented by the Old Testament would entail cessation of existence at death—and this is more akin to Bertrand Russell's view than to the teaching of evangelical annihilationists. Actually, however, because these passages do not speak of judgment after death, they do not teach annihilationism and pose no threat to the orthodox view of eternal punishment.[18]

I conclude that Fudge's claim that the Old Testament judgment passages teach annihilationism is false. Moreover, Fudge's error has serious repercussions in light of his theological method, for after concluding that the Old Testament teaches annihilationism, Fudge reads this conclusion into the New Testament. This is evident, for example, in his comments on "burning sulfur" in Revelation 14:10. There Fudge asserts, "In the Bible the symbol derives its meaning from the annihilation of Sodom and Gomorrah."[19]

A page later Fudge argues that the images of "burning sulfur" and of "carrion birds" eating "the corpses" both "sound out a message of utter extinction." Furthermore, "Revelation 19:20, 21 has both figures and distinguishes between them, but it gives no indication of *changing this basic meaning* of either" (italics mine). Here we see Fudge's theological method in action. The Old Testament provides the "basic meaning" of the images of God's judgment—annihilationism—and the New Testament "gives no indication of changing this basic meaning."[20]

I shall elaborate below on Fudge's habit of reading his annihilationist understanding of the Old Testament into the New Testament. For now it is sufficient to demonstrate the faulty basis for this practice. Fudge has misinterpreted the numerous Old Testament texts that use the "vocabulary of destruction" as teaching annihilationism. This is the source of his mishandling of the New Testament.

Appeal to Linguistics

Throughout *The Fire That Consumes,* Fudge appeals to linguistics in an effort to strengthen his case for conditionalism. Unfortunately, his work is marred by linguistic fallacies. I shall cite three types of such errors.

First, at times, he adopts a diachronic rather than a syncronic approach to the study of words. Fudge claims that the meaning of "punishment" in Matthew 25:46 is disputed. He then cites among other authorities Aristotle, Plutarch, and the Septuagint. Fudge would do well to heed Moises Silva's caution:

> We must accept the obvious fact that the speakers of a language simply know next to nothing about its development; and this certainly was the case with the writers and immediate readers of Scripture two millennia ago. . . . It follows that our real interest is the significance of Greek or Hebrew *in the consciousness of the biblical writers;* to put it boldly, "historical considerations are irrelevant to the investigation" of the state of the Koine at the time of Christ (italics in original).[21]

Second, Fudge commits a linguistic fallacy in his treatment of the Pauline word pair "trouble" (*thlipsis*) and "distress" (*stenochoria*) in Romans 2:9. After noting a few other occurrences of this pair in Paul's writings, Fudge remarks, "Paul is one of those who are 'hard pressed . . . but not crushed,' and he uses these same two words in participle form to say so (2 Corinthians 4:8)." So far, so good. But next Fudge draws an unwarranted conclusion: "This last translation is suggestive for our present verse [Rom 2:9]. Judgment day will find the wicked 'hard pressed'—to the point of being 'crushed.' "[22]

This is an example of what D.A. Carson calls, "Unwarranted adoption of an expanded semantic field." Carson explains: "The fallacy in this instance lies in the supposition that the meaning of a word in a specific context is much broader than the context itself allows and may bring with it the word's entire semantic range. This step is sometimes called illegitimate totality transfer."[23]

Although *stenochoroumenoi*, used metaphorically, may be rendered "crushed" in Second Corinthians 4:8 (the NIV does so), it is illegitimate to transfer this meaning to the noun *stenochoria* in Romans 2:9 and suggest that it implies the literal "crushing"—the annihilation—of the wicked on judgment day.

Third, *The Fire that Consumes* also evinces the etymological, or root, fallacy. Carson describes this error: "One of the most enduring of errors, the root fallacy presupposes that every word actually *has* a meaning bound up with its shape or its components. In this view, meaning is determined by etymology; that is, by the root or roots of a word (italics in original)."[24]

Fudge correctly teaches that Jesus' atonement "removes sin. . . ." When, however, Fudge claims as evidence for this, the fact that, "The Greek word for 'forgive' used most often by the Evangelists in reporting what Jesus said has as its root two words which mean 'to take away' (*aphiemi*),"[25] he commits "the root fallacy."[26]

I conclude that Fudge's appeal to linguistics sometimes has the opposite of his desired effect: it harms rather than helps his case for annihilationism.

Avoidance of Texts and of Opposing Arguments

Another feature of Fudge's hermeneutic is his occasional avoidance of aspects of biblical passages that are difficult to reconcile with conditionalism. Sometimes this avoidance takes the form of ignoring the strongest arguments of traditionalism.

An example of the latter is his failure to correlate Matthew 25:41 with Revelation 20:10, in spite of the fact that he dedicates 11 pages to a study of Matthew 25:41, 46.[27]

Included in Jesus' teaching concerning the sheep and the goats are his terrible words to the wicked: "Depart from me, you who are cursed, into the eternal fire prepared for the devil and his angels" (Matthew 25:41). Traditionalists since Augustine have interpreted Scripture by Scripture and gone to Revelation 20:10 for help in understanding this "eternal fire prepared for the devil." There John describes Satan's fate, "And the devil, who deceived them, was thrown into the lake of burning sulfur, where the beast and the false prophet had been thrown. They will be tormented day and night for ever and ever."

Referring to Matthew 25:41 and Revelation 20:10, Augustine concludes that, "'Eternal' in the first passage is expressed in the second by 'for ever and ever' and those words have only one meaning in scriptural usage: the exclusion of any temporal end."[28]

Many traditionalists since Augustine have regarded this as a strong argument for endless punishment. A recent example is Alan Gomes's use of this argument in his presentation of the two sets of texts (Matthew 25:41, 46; Revelation 14:9-11; 20:10) that he views as *"conclusively"* teaching eternal conscious torment (italics mine).[29]

What is Fudge's hermeneutical technique for dealing with this prominent traditionalist argument? He simply does not address it. In so doing he actually weakens his case for conditionalism, by giving the impression that he avoids the traditionalist argument because he cannot answer it.

At other times Fudge avoids biblical texts that are difficult to harmonize with conditionalism. One example is Fudge's handling of the angel's message in Revelation 14:9-11:

> If anyone worships the beast and his image and receives his mark on the forehead or on the hand, he, too, will drink of the wine of God's fury, which has been poured full strength into the cup

of his wrath. He will be tormented with burning sulfur in the presence of the holy angels and of the Lamb. And the smoke of their torment rises for ever and ever. There is no rest day or night for those who worship the beast and his image, or for anyone who receives the mark of his name.

This text is one of the pillars upon which the traditional doctrine of hell has been built. It may seem odd for me to cite Fudge's treatment of this passage as an example of his avoiding difficult texts because he devotes more than six pages to its exposition. Nevertheless, it is a striking example of avoidance. In fact, all the more so, because of the amount of space Fudge allots to it.

After briefly setting Revelation 14:9-11 in its literary context, Fudge divides it into four elements: "Wine of God's Fury," "Burning Sulfur," "Rising Smoke" and "No Rest Day or Night." He then treats the four in turn. In so doing he mentions the Old Testament more than 25 times and the New Testament more than 15 times. He regards many of these texts as teaching annihilationism and insists that we interpret Revelation 14:9-11 accordingly. Amazingly, however, other than an exposition of "There is no rest day or night" and a brief summary at the end of his discussion, Fudge does not explain Revelation 14:9-11 at all.[30] Fudge informs us of the theological method he intended to follow when he states his aim of "letting the Scripture interpret itself."[31] Certainly, interpreters are to compare Scripture with Scripture, as Luther urged. Furthermore, consulting the Old Testament background is especially important for those seeking to understand the Apocalypse, which is replete with Old Testament allusions and symbolism. Unfortunately, however, Fudge has not allowed other Scriptures to inform his exegesis of Revelation 14. Instead, he has substituted his comments on many other texts for the interpretation of Revelation 14:9-11 itself. This does not constitute exegesis of this critical text. Indeed, Fudge has not explained verses 9-11 as John has put them together. Instead, Fudge has created his own theological context for Revelation 14:9-11 out of his mosaic of biblical texts. Apparently, he assumes that the interpretation of Revelation 14:9-11 will be apparent to his readers—it teaches the same conditionalism that Fudge finds elsewhere in the Bible.

Granted, John's statements in Revelation 14:9-11 are very difficult for conditionalist interpreters to handle. But this is exactly what Fudge has to do in order to prove that annihilationism can stand up to the scrutiny of biblical exegesis. Instead, he has bombarded the reader with Scripture references. Although this may have the effect of impressing some readers, careful ones will notice that Fudge has never explained the verses at hand. The result once again is a weakening of his case for conditionalism.

I do not want to be misunderstood. I am not prying into Fudge's motives or accusing him of dishonesty. Rather, I am criticizing his theological hermeneutic. At times he simply avoids texts that are difficult for his position.

Another example is his treatment of Mark 9:43-48. Although Fudge discusses seventy New Testament passages under individual headings, he does not devote a separate heading to this significant text. Instead, he subsumes it under his treatment of Matthew 18:8, 9. There Fudge plays Matthew's and Mark's accounts against each other to avoid the verses difficult for annihilationism. For example, Fudge notes that whereas Matthew speaks of " 'eternal fire,' Mark speaks simply of being 'thrown/going into hell.' " What conclusion are we to draw from this? Fudge urges, "Matthew's language may add flavor and force, but it should not be naively interpreted in a way that contradicts Mark's."[32] I must ask why it is naive to seek to understand each passage on its own merits before doing theological systematization. And why should one regard unbelievers being thrown into hell as incompatible with endless punishment, unless one were committed *a priori* to annihilationism?

Fudge diverts his readers' attention from Jesus' strong

words about hell in Matthew 18:8, 9 and Mark 9:44, 48 by noting that Calvin in his commentary on these passages, "does not elaborate at all on final punishment."[33] I fail to understand how Calvin's omission lessens Fudge's responsibility to explain the verses at hand. Nevertheless, he simply skips Jesus' words in Mark 9:44, where he speaks of "hell, where the fire never goes out."

Fudge does treat Jesus' saying in Mark 9:48 that hell is "where their worm does not die, and the fire is not quenched." But his treatment is another example of avoidance. He instructs us that the worm here "is a devouring worm, and what it eats—in Isaiah's picture here quoted without amendment—is already dead."[34] Once more Fudge imposes his annihilationist reading of the Old Testament upon the New Testament text. Does this sufficiently explain Jesus' words about the worm's not dying? Would not the worm die when it had consumed its host? Should not a conditionalist theologian address the traditionalist arguments arising out of the biblical text? At least this traditionalist gets the impression that Fudge is reading his theology into passages that are difficult to assimilate to his position.

Moreover, my impression is only confirmed by Fudge's explanation of Jesus' description of hell as a place "where . . . the fire is not quenched" (Mark 9:48). Fudge informs us, "The devouring worm is aided by a *consuming* fire" (italics in original). As evidence he points us to biblical references already adduced along with passages in Homer and Eusebius.[35] Is this not clear avoidance of Jesus' words? Jesus says nothing in Mark 9:42-48 about a *consuming* fire; instead, he says that hell-fire "is not quenched" (v. 48). And Fudge has not interpreted these words in the context of Jesus' message.

In sum: Fudge's avoidance of the strongest traditionalist arguments and of the texts used for centuries to teach the endless punishment of the wicked damages his case for conditionalism.[36]

Logical Fallacies

In his zeal to argue for conditionalism, Fudge at times commits logical fallacies. I cite two examples. The first is the *Argumentum ad Hominem* (abusive), which Irving M. Copi defines as follows: "The phrase '*argumentum ad hominem*' translates literally into 'argument directed to the man'. . . . this fallacy . . . is committed when, instead of trying to *disprove the truth* of what is asserted, one attacks the man who made the assertion. . . . The way in which this irrelevant argument may sometimes persuade is through the psychological process of transference. Where an attitude of disapproval toward a person can be evoked, it may possibly tend to overflow the strictly emotional field and become disagreement with what the person says" (italics in original).[37]

Fudge argues in this manner in his treatment of Jesus' words in Matthew 25:46. There, speaking of the goats and sheep respectively, Jesus declares, "Then they will go away to eternal punishment, but the righteous to eternal life."

Traditionalists have often pointed to the parallelism of the fates of the righteous and unrighteous when making their case for the endless punishment for the wicked. Augustine, for example, argued this way, "Christ, in the very same passage, included both punishment and life in one and the same sentence when he said, 'So those people will go into eternal punishment, while the righteous will go into eternal life' " (Matthew 25:46). Augustine contends:

> If both are "eternal", it follows necessarily that either both are to be taken as long-lasting but finite, or both as endless and perpetual. The phrases "eternal punishment" and "eternal life" are parallel and it would be absurd to use them in one and the same sentence to mean: "Eternal life will be infinite, while eternal punishment will have an end." Hence, because the eternal life of the saints will be endless, the eternal punishment

> also, for those condemned to it, will assuredly have no end.[38]

In response, Fudge contends that eternal punishment means irreversible annihilation. "When the wicked have perished, it will be forever—their destruction and punishment is unending as well as qualitatively different from anything we now know."[39]

Second, Fudge responds to this traditionalist argument by employing an *argumentum ad hominem*. He writes, "We must be careful in pressing the parallel between 'eternal' life and 'eternal' punishment that we do not fall into any spirit of vindictiveness or ungodly joy at the fate of the wicked."[40]

The implication is that understanding Matthew 25:46 as teaching endless punishment for the wicked makes one liable to vindictiveness. Copi puts the *argumentum ad hominem* into the category of "irrelevant arguments." The premises of such arguments "are logically irrelevant to, and therefore incapable of establishing the truth of, their conclusions."[41] This is true of Fudge's argument here: whether traditionalists are vindictive or not has nothing to do with the meaning of Matthew 25:46. In fact, the defenders of the orthodox doctrine of hell have often demonstrated compassion for the lost. But whether they are compassionate or vengeful does not help us understand Jesus' words.

Fudge, by arguing in this way, seeks to persuade by "the psychological process of transference," to use Copi's description. "Where an attitude of disapproval toward a person can be evoked, it may possibly tend to overflow the strictly emotional field and become disagreement with what the person says."[42]

Unfortunately, Fudge pursues this line of argumentation in a chapter of his book titled, "Traditionalism's Problem of Pain."[43] Here he cites extreme portrayals from church history of the wicked's "everlasting torture in agony," and declares, "If the whole point is to scare the poor and the little children, why not give them a fright they will never forget?" He even paints crude Buddhist, Hindu and Muslim pictures of hell in order to heap ridicule on the traditionalist view.[44]

Fudge's argument here is as unconvincing as that employed by defenders of endless punishment who use an *argumentum ad hominem* against annihilationism by grouping conditionalists with cultists.[45]

Fudge also commits the logical fallacy of *petitio principii*. Copi describes this fallacy:

> In attempting to establish the truth of a proposition, one often casts about for acceptable premisses from which the proposition in question can be deduced as conclusion. If one assumes as a premise for his argument the very conclusion he intends to prove, the fallacy committed is that of *petitio principii*, or begging the question.[46]

Fudge commits this fallacy in his exposition of the lake of fire in Revelation 19:20. He argues that the beast and false prophet are not actual people but institutions, and hence incapable of suffering conscious, sensible pain. Their being cast into the lake of fire cannot, therefore, indicate endless punishment. Fudge then notes that Homer Hailey does not regard Revelation 19:20 as describing Christ's second coming.[47]

Fudge next appeals to Hanns Lilje, who "marvels that John gives no description here of any battle." Lilje writes of God's throwing the beast into the lake of fire: "The very moment when this purpose of God is fulfilled, the mighty power of the beast shrivels up like a collapsed balloon, as if it had never been. It has been unmasked, and its true character revealed: it was empty, futile presumption."[48]

Fudge notes that "Lilje is content to use the word 'annihilated' " to express the meaning of the lake of fire. Fudge's next sentence is revealing, "In the case of the beast and false prophet, *therefore*, the lake of fire stands for utter, absolute, irreversible annihilation" (italics mine).[49] Here Fudge commits the logical fallacy of *petitio principii*, or begging the question. Fudge does not prove that the lake of fire signifies annihilation. He merely states that Lilje thinks it means this. On that basis ("therefore") Fudge concludes that the lake of fire stands for obliteration. Fudge here assumes his conclusion. This aspect of his argument, therefore, lacks cogency.

Fudge commits the same fallacy in his comments on Hebrews 2:2, 3. There, after admitting that this passage "gives no details of that terrible and certain punishment," he nevertheless concludes that the wicked will "perish forever in the second and final death."[50]

Appeal to Systematic Theology

While commenting on the "wine of God's fury" in Revelation 14:10, Fudge speaks of the cup of God's wrath. In this context he says:

> Such was the cup Jesus accepted from God's hand in Gethsemane, and to drink it unmixed He refused even the numbing wine offered by His murderers (Matthew 26:39, 42, 44; 27:34). He suffered torment of body and soul. More than that, He drained the cup of God's wrath, passively enduring the simultaneous draining of His own life into total death.[51]

Here Fudge, following the examples of Atkinson and Froom before him, teaches that Jesus was annihilated in his death. In fact, Fudge devotes six pages to the thesis: "Jesus' Death Involved Total Destruction."[52] Here he quotes approvingly James Dunn's statements, "Man could not be helped other than through his [Jesus'] annihilation," and "This process of destruction is speeded up in the case of Jesus, the representative man, the *hilasterion*, and destroys him."[53]

Next Fudge agrees with Oscar Cullmann, who wrote that:

> [Jesus] can conquer death only by actually dying, by betaking Himself to the sphere of death, the destroyer of life, to the sphere of nothingness. . . . Whoever wants to conquer death must die; he must really cease to live—not simply live on as an immortal soul; but die in body and soul, lose life itself. . . . Furthermore, if life is to issue out of so genuine a death as this, a new divine act of creation is necessary. And this act of creation calls back to life not just a part of man, but the whole man—all that God had created and death had annihilated.[54]

Fudge insists that the Scriptures teach that Jesus was annihilated:

> The Bible exhausts the vocabulary of dying in speaking of what happened to Jesus. He "*died* for our sins" (1 Corinthians 15:3). He *laid down His "life [psyche]"* (John 10:15). He was *destroyed* (Matt 27:20, KJV) or *killed* (Acts 3:15). Jesus compared his own death to the *dissolution* of a kernel of wheat . . . (John 12:23-26). Jesus *"poured out His life [psyche] unto death"* and in so doing was "numbered with the transgressors" (Isaiah53:12; italics in original).[55]

Fudge admits, "We naturally recoil from such a thought, that the Son of God could truly have perished—even for a moment." Yet this is what Fudge believes happened. He faults Calvin for his refusal to believe that "Jesus' 'soul' truly died."[56]

In his conclusion Fudge writes: "Every scriptural implication is that if Jesus had not been raised, He—like those fallen asleep in Him—would simply have perished (1 Corinthians 15:18). His resurrection reverses every such estimation of affairs, assuring us instead of the death of Death (2 Timothy 1:10; Hebrews 2:14; Revelation 20:14)."[57]

To be precise, Fudge concurs with Edward White, who held that when Jesus died in crucifixion His humanity was annihilated, but not His divinity.[58]

Fudge, therefore, seeks to strengthen his case for annihilationism by arguing that Jesus bore the pains of hell in His death, that is, He was annihilated. What are the systematic implications of such a view? Do they strengthen or weaken Fudge's case for conditionalism?

The systematic implications of holding that Jesus was annihilated when He died are enormous. Nothing less than orthodox Christology is at stake. The definitive statement concerning the Person of Christ was made by the Council of Chalcedon in 451. Included in the Definition of the Council of Chalcedon is the following formal confession of faith:

> In agreement, therefore, with the holy fathers, we all unanimously teach that we should confess that our Lord Jesus Christ is one and the same Son, the same perfect in Godhead and the same perfect in manhood, truly God and truly man, the same of a rational soul and body, consubstantial with the Father in Godhead, and the same consubstantial with us in manhood, like us in all things except sin; begotten from the Father before the ages as regards His Godhead, and in these last days, the same, because of us and because of our salvation begotten from the Virgin Mary, the *Theotokos*, as regards His manhood; one and the same Christ, Son, Lord, only-begotten, made known in two natures without confusion, without change, without division, without separation, the difference of the natures being by no means removed because of the union, but the property of each nature being preserved and coalescing in one *prosopon* and one

> *hupostasis*—not parted or divided into two *prosopa*, but one and the same Son, only-begotten, divine Word, the Lord Jesus Christ, as the prophets of old and Jesus Christ Himself taught us about Him and the creed of our fathers has handed down.[59]

John Cooper encapsulates the teaching of Chalcedon:

> Since the Council of Chalcedon the church has officially recognized what is taught in the New Testament and held by the early church: that because of the incarnation Jesus Christ is both truly God and truly human; that he is one person with two natures, one divine and one human; and that these natures are neither mixed together nor are they separable.[60]

Next, Cooper highlights the disastrous implications of holding that Jesus was annihilated in His death:

> Now if the extinction—re-creation account of Jesus' resurrection is true, then the teaching of Chalcedon is false. The two natures of Christ are separable and were in fact separated between Good Friday and Easter Sunday. The human being Jesus completely ceased to exist. . . . So the divine-human person Jesus Christ did not exist for the interim. Only the nonincarnate Word, the wholly divine Son, the Second Person of the Trinity, existed during that time.[61]

Furthermore, if Jesus were annihilated on Calvary, and His natures separated because His humanity ceased to exist, then His resurrection constituted another incarnation. This incarnation would differ from the first in that this time the Word would take to Himself resurrected flesh. Notwithstanding, it would be a second incarnation.

I conclude: instead of Fudge's appeal to systematic theology strengthening his case for conditionalism, it weakens it considerably. Indeed, to hold that Jesus' humanity was annihilated on the cross, brings one into conflict with Chalcedonian Christology. Such a prospect ought to cause conditionalists to re-examine their views, for the Bible teaches that Christ *did* suffer the pains of hell, but not as they are conceived by annihilationists.[62]

Conclusion

Space prevents me from considering other aspects of Fudge's theological hermeneutic. Instead, I have evaluated Fudge's use of the Old Testament, appeal to linguistics, avoidance of texts and of opposing arguments, logical fallacies and appeal to systematic theology. I have pointed out deficiencies in his methodological approach in these five areas. As a result, I conclude that Fudge's case for conditionalism is not as strong as he and others have thought. In fact, evaluated in terms of hermeneutics and theological methodology, his case appears to be weak.

Endnotes

[1]Edward Fudge, *The Fire That Consumes: A Biblical and Historical Study of Final Punishment* (Houston: Providential Press, 1982). I thank Mr. Fudge for reading this paper and offering comments. I note that Fudge affirms the resurrection of the saved and the lost and rejects the teaching of Jehovah's Witnesses that hell is only the physical grave.

[2]Nigel M. de S. Cameron, ed., *Universalism and the Doctrine of Hell* (Baker, 1992).

[3]John W. Wenham, "The Case for Conditional Immortality," *Universalism and the Doctrine of Hell*, 164. My first footnote gives the bibliographical information for Fudge's book. The other three books are: Harold E. Guillebaud, *The Righteous Judge* (n.p., 1941); Basil Atkinson, *Life and Immortality* (n.p., n.d.); LeRoy Edwin Froom, *The Conditionalist Faith of Our Fathers* (Review and Herald, 1965-66). Guillebaud's and Atkinson's books were published privately and are obtainable from the Reverend B.L.

Bateson, 26 Summershard, S. Petherton, Somerset, U.K. TA13 5DP.

[4]Kendall S. Harmon, "The Case Against Conditionalism: A Response to Edward William Fudge," *Universalism and the Doctrine of Hell*, 193-224.

[5]Ibid., 195-96.

[6]Fudge, *The Fire That Consumes*, xv.

[7]Dan McCartney and Charles Clayton (*Let the Reader Understand: A Guide to Interpreting and Applying the Bible* [BridgePoint, 1994], 65-67) helpfully discuss the relation between systematic theology and hermeneutical methodology.

[8]One exception is Robert A. Morey, *Death and the Afterlife* (Minneapolis: Bethany House, 1984), 19-33.

[9]David Knowles, ed., *The City of God* (Penguin Books, 1972), XXI. 23 (1001, 1004, 1005); Vernon J. Bourke, trans., *On the Truth of the Catholic Faith. Summa Contra Gentiles*. Book Three, Providence, Part II, (Doubleday, 1956), 144. 8 (p. 216), 145.5 (p. 219); D.W. Torrance and T.F. Torrance, eds., *Calvin's New Testament Commentaries. A Harmony of the Gospels*, vol. III (Eerdmans, 1972), 117-118; John H. Gerstner, *Jonathan Edwards on Heaven and Hell* (Grand Rapids: Baker, 1980), 75; W.G.T. Shedd, *The Doctrine of Endless Punishment* (The Banner of Truth Trust, 1986; first published 1885; second edition, 1887), 89.

[10]Fudge, *The Fire That Consumes*, 87-117.

[11]Ibid., 98.

[12]Ibid., 100.

[13]Ibid., 100, n.10.

[14]Fudge approvingly cites Froom, Petavel, and Constable in the notes of his chapter on the OT in *The Fire That Consumes*. He could have added Atkinson's name as well.

[15]Edward Fudge, "The Final End of the Wicked," *JETS* 27.3 (September 1984): 326.

[16]See chapter two of my forthcoming *Hell on Trial: The Case for Eternal Punishment* (Presbyterian and Reformed, 1995) for the details of this study.

[17]Fudge is not the only one to make this claim. For another example, see Clark H. Pinnock, "The Destruction of the Finally Impenitent," *Criswell Theological Review* 4.2 (1990): 250-52.

[18]At least two Old Testament texts, Daniel 12:2 and Isaiah 66:24, do speak of the fate of the wicked after death. Fudge agrees, but then errs when he interprets these as teaching the annihilation of the wicked after resurrection (see *The Fire That Consumes,* 110-115). To the contrary, both texts suggest the endless conscious torment of the wicked. See chapter two of *Hell on Trial* for a theological exegesis of these passages.

[19]Fudge, *The Fire That Consumes,* 296.

[20]Ibid., 297.

[21]Moises Silva, *Biblical Words and their Meaning: An Introduction to Lexical Semantics* (Grand Rapids: Zondervan, 1983), 38.

[22]Fudge, *The Fire That Consumes,* 262.

[23]D.A. Carson, *Exegetical Fallacies* (Grand Rapids: Baker, 1984), 62.

[24]Ibid., 26.

[25]Fudge, *The Fire That Consumes,* 223.

[26]See Carson, *Exegetical Fallacies,* 26-32, and Silva, *Biblical Words and their Meaning,* 44-51.

[27]Fudge, *The Fire That Consumes,* 192-202.

[28]Knowles, ed., *The City of God,* XXI. 23, p. 1001.

[29]Alan W. Gomes, "Evangelicals and the Annihilation of Hell, Part One," *Christian Research Journal* 13.4 (1991), 17-18. See also Larry Dixon, *The Other Side of the Good News* (Wheaton, IL: BridgePoint, 1992), 89.

[30]Fudge, *The Fire That Consumes,* 295-301.

[31]Ibid., 299.

[32]Ibid., 184.

[33]Ibid.

[34]Ibid., 185.

[35]Ibid.

[36]How does Fudge attempt to reconcile annihilationism with Revelation 20:10, where John asserts that the devil "will be tormented for ever and ever" in the lake of fire? He admits, "There is no easy solution." He concludes, however, "Whatever the case with Satan, the final punishment of the wicked is a different subject," Ibid., 304, 307. Fudge here tries to avoid the plain sense of Revelation 20:10 and the fact that four verses later

wicked humans too are cast into the same lake of fire.

[37]Irving M. Copi, *Introduction to Logic*. 2nd ed. (New York: Macmillan, 1961), 54-55.

[38]Knowles, ed., *The City of God*, XXI. 23, pp. 1001-1002.

[39]Fudge, *The Fire That Consumes*, 195.

[40]Ibid.

[41]Copi, *Introduction to Logic*, 53.

[42]Ibid., 55.

[43]Fudge, *The Fire That Consumes*, 411-422.

[44]Ibid., 419-420.

[45]See John H. Gerstner, *Repent or Perish* (Soli Deo Gloria, 1990), 30; and Morey, *Death and the Afterlife*, 202-03.

[46]Copi, *Introduction to Logic*, 65.

[47]Fudge, *The Fire That Consumes*, 303.

[48]Ibid., 303-304.

[49]Ibid., 304.

[50]Ibid., 272-273.

[51]Ibid., 296.

[52]Ibid., 228-234.

[53]Ibid., 229.

[54]Ibid., 230.

[55]Ibid.

[56]Ibid., 231.

[57]Ibid., 233-234.

[58]Ibid., 230-231.

[59]J.N.D. Kelly, *Early Christian Doctrines*, 2nd ed. (Harper and Row, 1960), 339-340.

[60]John Cooper, *Body, Soul, & Life Everlasting: Biblical Anthropology and the Monism-Dualism Debate* (Grand Rapids: Eerdmans, 1989), 144.

[61]Ibid., 144-145.

[62]I thank my student Jimmy Agan for helping me to understand better the connection between the doctrine of hell and Christ's atonement.

Hans-Georg Gadamer and Evangelical Hermeneutics

Bruce B. Miller II

In 1960 one of the century's most prominent continental philosophers, Hans-Georg Gadamer, revitalized hermeneutics with the publication of *Truth and Method.*[1] His work transformed hermeneutics from merely a sub-discipline which methodologically interpreted texts to a way of understanding human experience. Prior to 1960, hermeneutics was largely unknown in the humanities, but in the years since the publication of *Truth and Method,* "hermeneutics" has come to be regarded as an international and interdisciplinary movement.

In the evangelical world, unfortunately, Gadamer has been dismissed prematurely. Most evangelical scholars came to know Gadamer first through E.D. Hirsch's damning critique in Appendix II to *Validity in Interpretation,*[2] where he accused Gadamer of promoting a subjectivistic, relativistic hermeneutic. Although Hirsch has recently modified his evaluation,[3] his initial dismissal of Gadamer was absorbed by most evangelical theologians and has prevented a first hand careful reading of Gadamer by the majority of the evangelical scholarly community. For instance, in his *Toward an Exegetical Theology,* Walter Kaiser expressly admits that his assessment of Gadamer is dependent on Hirsch's evaluation in *Validity in Interpretation*.[4] As a consequence, while Gadamer is commonly acknowledged as a seminal thinker by most evangelical works on hermeneutics, he is not engaged at a primary source level.

Some evangelical scholars' appraisals of Gadamer have been revised through the eyes of Anthony Thiselton in his 1982 treatment of Gadamer in *Two Horizons: New Testament Hermeneutics and Philosophical Description*.[5] In his careful reading of Gadamer, Thiselton presents a much more balanced interpretation than did Hirsch in 1965. Not only does Thiselton offer a first sympathetic and then critical reading of Gadamer, but he also works to show some helpful implications of Gadamer's work, such as for the interplay of exegesis and systematic theology. In spite of such positive work, Thiselton still moves away from Gadamer because of Gadamer's acknowledged reluctance to address method.

Most recently, in *New Horizons* (1992), Thiselton comes back to Gadamer.[6] He correctly sees Gadamer's central role in the recent history of hermeneutics and argues that Gadamer's work represents as significant a shift as did Scheliermacher's nearly two centuries before. Thiselton divides his own chronological and thematic development of hermeneutics with Gadamer. But he does not endorse the whole of his approach, because Gadamer restricts foundational, and admittedly critical issues, concerning the philosophical underpinnings of the hermeneutic enterprise. Because Thiselton chooses not to build directly from Gadamer in this most recent book, I believe the majority of evangelical scholars continue to avoid reading Gadamer.

I argue that our ignorance of Gadamer is to our detriment. Not that we ought to embrace him, but he has important insights to offer and should not be casually dismissed. In this brief essay I will point out a few valuable Gadamerian insights into the hermeneutical enterprise. At least five concepts deserve our continued exploration: tradition, awareness, openness, application and *phronesis*.

I am not arguing that we should adopt Gadamer's philosophical framework or his hermeneutical theory. We should not. I am suggesting that as a seminal thinker Gadamer has important ideas from which we can improve our own hermeneutic. Although I cannot fully develop each insight or its implications for evangelical hermeneutics, I hope to be clear enough and provocative enough to invite others to engage Gadamer and to work out from him creative approaches in dimensions that are now weak or lacking in typical evangelical hermeneutic theories and practices.

In order better to appreciate Gadamer's insights, it will be helpful briefly to survey the philosophical background of twentieth century evangelical hermeneutics.

Evangelical Hermeneutic Heritage

As heirs of the European Enlightenment, evangelicals have largely embraced a hermeneutic which breathes the air of a Cartesian, Newtonian, Baconian inductive paradigm, an ideal of absolute, certain knowledge based on scientific premises and methodology. As heirs of the Scottish enlightenment common sense tradition through Thomas Reid and others, we share a general optimism about the clarity of the text and our ability to approach it in a pure, laboratory-clean manner. In tracing our hermeneutical heritage, Roger Lundin writes, "many of us cling stubbornly to our belief that we can approach a text with Cartesian cleanliness and Baconian precision . . . [and] this Cartesian confidence has sanctioned our imposition of an unacknowledged Enlightenment tradition upon the Scripture."[7] Of course, I am over-generalizing and neglecting to explain the nuanced, sophisticated developments in recent evangelical hermeneutics. Interaction with critical scholarship, the advent of literary criticism and engaging scholars from other cultures have all helped us to nuance a rather simplistic and naive hermeneutic. Still, however, our hermeneutic remains dominated by a heavily objectivist, inductive, scientific paradigm.

Against this particular intellectual backdrop, Gadamer has some important correctives to offer us as evangelicals. I offer the following five key ideas:

1. the inevitability and value of tradition
2. enhanced awareness of pre-understanding as a better goal than its elimination
3. openness as a needed conscious goal in light of inerrancy
4. application as integral to understanding and
5. *phronesis* as a helpful model for hermeneutical judgment

The Inevitability and Value of Tradition

In the wake of the Reformation and the Enlightenment, evangelicals typically distrust tradition while embracing rationality. In the Reformation, the plain Scripture was asserted against the Roman Catholic Magisterium. In the Enlightenment, reason was raised up against the supposed superstitions of medieval traditions. The birth of science signaled the end of shadowy myths and the beginning of enlightened understanding in the pure light of reason, unshackled from the dark traditions of the past. "Progress," "new" and "discovery" capture the imagination and motivate the investment of money. In contrast, "tradition," "old" and "customary" smell stale to a modern consciousness.

As evangelicals, we want to approach texts methodically, taking nothing for granted, granting no authority to tradition or any other inclination which might affect our judgment before we encounter the object of our investigation, the text before us. We want our reading to be purely inductive and rational, rather than deductive or traditional.

Against the Enlightenment disavowal of tradition and authority for the sake of reason, Gadamer wants to restore the value of tradition in the reading of texts. To do so he coins a new phrase, *Wirkungsgeschichte,* the principle of history of effect. We are always affected by our history whether we are conscious of that effect or not. Even if our faith in method leads us to deny our historicity, it still prevails. Unrecognized, the traditions of which we are a part share our approach and understanding of texts. In explaining this reality Gadamer writes,

> If we are trying to understand a historical phenomenon [including a text] from the historical distance that is characteristic of our hermeneutical situation, we are always already affected by history. It determines in advance both what seems to us worth inquiring about and what will appear as an object of investigation, and we more or less forget half of what is really there—in fact, we miss the whole truth of the phenomenon—when we take its immediate appearance as the whole truth.[8]

In our innocent hermeneutics, we take the immediate appearance of a text as true because it seems so self-evident to us. Its very self-evidency may be a result of our reading the text from our tradition so that we read ourselves in the text. The unattainable Enlightenment ideal of inductively pure knowledge creates an illusion. We are deluded into imagining that our reading of a text is for the most part pure, innocent, unaffected by our traditions and history, and unaffected by our interests and concerns.

We interpret from eccleisial and institutional contexts. Teaching in independent educational institutions, worshipping at independent local churches and working as independent scholars can lead us down a path into excessive individualization. We can miss the incredible reality, significance and value of tradition. For most of us, because we are living in a young, new country, America, surrounded by buildings and businesses younger than we are, we can forget the richness and inevitability of historical continuity and effect. The rapid pace of change rushing us down the river of technological progress so dominates our consciousness that we tend to diminish the power of the past, the lake from which the water comes and the river flows.

In our systematic theologies, although we acknowledge the history of theology, most of our prolegomenas dealing with the nature and method of theology are weak in addressing the role of tradition. Grant Osborne concurs with this observation in *The Hermeneutical Spiral*, when he writes, "historical theology plays a critical part in the hermeneutical enterprise, though it is conspicuously absent in most commentaries or works of theology."[9] Even less evident is a developed understanding of the place of tradition in our hermeneutics.[10]

We read the biblical text as evangelicals, as Trinitarian inerrantists; and that is good. Tradition is good. Tradition can protect us from idiosyncratic and arbitrary readings. Commenting on Gadamer's view of tradition, P. Christopher Smith remarks, "Here too, Gadamer would say, history has taught us that in the end a reasonableness grounded in the tradition and not autonomous reason is the best protection from whim and excess."[11] Of course, tradition must not be accepted without critique. In reference to the past, we always face the twin perils of nostalgia and iconoclasm; either we want to worship our history or smash it. But even worse is to ignore it. And that, I fear, is a danger inherent in much of evangelical hermeneutics.

Gadamer's profound reflection on the role of tradition in hermeneutics can be an impetus and a starting place from which evangelicals can exercise creative thought in this area. We need to open our eyes to tradition. We never interpret the Bible in a vacuum unconnected to life and history; there are no white-glove, pure, laboratory contexts; the ivory tower is not clean. In practice we read the Scriptures in harmony with our doctrinal statements (evangelical creeds) and ecclesiastical traditions, but our hermeneutical theories proclaim a nearly pure inductivism.[12] Our doctrinal commitments and ecclesial traditions are not merely the final check point in validating an interpretation, but influence our interpretation right from the very beginning. As scholars we need to think more deeply and seriously about tradition in our hermeneutics, and Gadamer can help us here.

Upon recognizing the inevitability and value of tradition, I suggest with Gadamer that we pursue an enhanced awareness of pre-understanding as a better goal than its elimination.

Enhanced Awareness of Pre-understanding as a Better Goal than its Elimination

In general, our hermeneutic theories, as explained in our evangelical textbooks, teach an inductive approach in which we are to eliminate or bracket out our pre-understandings. We tell students to read the text objectively. They should practice exegesis and avoid at all costs eisegesis which would be to read their own thoughts into the text.

Ironically, however, in our admirable pursuit of theoretically pure reading, we can miss the very goal we want to achieve. We want students to hear what the text is saying rather than merely hearing their own voices played back to them in their reading of the text. Yet in trying to read the text purely they may be blind to their pre-understandings which color the text they innocently believe they are reading neutrally. When pre-understandings are unconscious, and thus unexamined, they exercise greater control over the interpreting process and can obfuscate the meaning.

Following Gadamer, I argue that instead of working to eliminate our pre-understandings, we should enhance our awareness of them. Gadamer says that a person trying to understand a text should be prepared for it to tell him something and thus from the start must be sensitive to its alterity. "But," he writes,

> This kind of sensitivity involves neither "neutrality" with respect to content nor the extinction of one's self, but the foregrounding and

> appropriation of one's own fore-meanings and prejudices. The important thing is to be aware of one's own bias, so that the text can present itself in all its otherness and thus assert its own truth against one's own foremeanings.[13]

While attempts of neutral reading can blind one to a text's unique message, awareness of one's pre-understanding can aid a clear hearing of a text's voice against one's own biases. Today, many in our evangelical scholarly community have come to see the inevitability of pre-understandings. But, some still see them as inherently bothersome hurdles to overcome in a proper reading of the Bible. Others are beginning to see their value for a healthy engagement with the biblical text. For instance, Klein, Blomberg and Hubbard, write, "Indeed, pre-understanding is desirable and essential."[14] And Osborne writes, "A close reading of the text cannot be done without a perspective provided by one's pre-understanding as identified by a 'sociology of knowledge' perspective." And a few sentences later he adds, "Here I want to stress that pre-understanding is primarily a positive (and only potentially a negative) component of interpretation. Pre-understanding only becomes negative if it degenerates into an *a priori* grid that determines the meaning of a text before the act of reading even begins."[15]

On a methodological level, I suggest we move in Gadamer's direction by pursing enhanced awareness of our pre-understandings rather than encouraging the bracketing or elimination of our pre-understandings.

We never come to the Bible with a blank slate. We carry with us our gender; most frequently a man will more quickly identify with Joseph; whereas a female reader will more readily identify with Mary. We bring with us our age, marital status, church background, cultural heritage, educational experience and political ideologies. We read from theological, denominational and sacramental traditions. We read through the eyes of the late twentieth century because we cannot do otherwise; that is where we are historically. We pick up the Bible to read it for a reason. We read for encouragement, for comfort, for guidance, for material to write a paper, for data to defend a point of view, to find God, to solve a problem and to discover hope. We read as humans, as individuals with distinctive personalities, with unique personal histories and as sinners trying to serve the living God who gave us His Word.

Rather than ignoring or covering up the factors that constitute our pre-understanding, I suggest that we work to become more aware of them. One important dimension of the interpretive process is for us to become more self-aware of who we are and why we are reading the biblical text.

This conscious awareness of our pre-understandings can better assist us in hearing the Word of God, rather than our own voice when we read the Scriptures. Gadamer's careful development of pre-understandings lays a foundation for our development of this dimension in our own hermeneutic. Recognizing our involvement in traditions and enhancing our awareness of our pre-understandings must be matched with a third insight from Gadamer: "openness" as a conscious hermeneutic goal.

Openness as a Needed Conscious Goal, Especially in Light of Inerrancy

As inerrantists we approach the biblical text with the presupposition that it is absolutely true and accurate in all that it affirms. Moreover, we believe that the Bible is the very Word of God and, as such, the final authority in every area of our lives. As noble and reverent as these beliefs are, ironically, they can prevent us from really hearing the Word of God.

Because we agree in principle that the Bible is true, and because we assume we know the text and that we agree with the text, we do not approach the text with the anticipation that we may not *now* be in full agreement with it. Too often there is no challenge to our thinking because we assume we unconsciously read our own ideas into the text as if they were the text's ideas. Many of us have such familiarity with the Scripture that we can unconsciously be closed to its radicality in exposing our false thinking and sin.

Gadamer stresses that we remain open to the meaning of the other person or text.[16] He argues that this fundamental openness involves a receptivity to the truth of the text. We must be prepared for it to tell us something and we must recognize its otherness from ourselves, which presupposes that we are aware of our own pre-understanding so that we can recognize the text's own voice as different from our own. In Gadamer's terms, we should open ourselves to the superior claim of the text and open ourselves to respond to what it has to tell us.[17] For him the rigor of hermeneutics is listening.[18]

Too often we come to the text finding what we expect. Preachers draw from the text what they have already decided to say; congregations look to the Bible to affirm their current lifestyles and personal decisions; scholars research data to substantiate their previously determined positions.

Instead, we must be open to renewing our minds with the truth, to the Holy Spirit's work in us through His Word, to be convicted, to grow, to surprise. This openness expresses a practical realization of the inerrant Scripture's authority and a correlative recognition of our own sinfulness and false understandings. For the Bible to exercise its practical authority we must be open to receive its truth and correction (2 Timothy 3:16, 17). Gadamer's understanding of the vital role of openness in hermeneutics can keep us from being lulled into a sterile familiarity which dulls the Word. This openness is not just an openness at the level of cognitive understanding, but also an openness to obey in new ways, because as Gadamer argues, in a fourth key idea, application is integral to understanding.

Application Is Integral to Understanding

Until the last few years, in evangelical hermeneutics, we have worked with a fairly clear-cut distinction between interpretation and application. We have largely followed E.D. Hirsch in distinguishing meaning from significance. We instruct our students first to discover the meaning of a text and then to work out appropriate applications of that meaning for today.

In contrast Gadamer argues, "The reader does not exist who, when he has the text before him, simply reads what is there. Rather, all reading involves application, so that a person reading a text is himself part of the meaning he apprehends. He belongs to the text that he is reading."[19] For Gadamer, application is the fundamental hermeneutic problem. He goes back to an earlier hermeneutic task, the interpretation of the oracle, to show the integration of application in meaning; he writes, "Formerly it was considered obvious that the task of hermeneutics was to adapt the text's meaning to the concrete situation to which the text is speaking. The interpreter of divine will who can interpret the oracle's language is the original model for this."[20] Interpreting the oracle required explaining its significance to the case at hand. To stop short of such application would be to stop short of understanding. It is not that applying the oracle takes place as a secondary or supplementary task, but that it is inherent to understanding the oracle. In summarizing his conclusions regarding the centrality of application Gadamer writes,

> We too determined that application is neither a subsequent nor a merely occasional part of the phenomenon of understanding, but codetermines it as a whole from the beginning. . . . The interpreter dealing with a traditionary text tries to apply it to himself. But this does not mean that the text is given for him as something universal, that he first understands it per se, and then after-

> ward uses it for particular applications. Rather, the interpreter seeks no more than to understand this universal, the text,—i.e., to understand what it says, what constitutes the text's meaning and significance. In order to understand that, he must not try to disregard himself and his particular hermeneutical situation. He must relate the text to this situation if he wants to understand at all.[21]

To explain what he means, Gadamer uses examples from the legal realm and from preaching the gospel: "A law does not exist in order to be understood historically, but to be concretized in its legal validity by being interpreted. Similarly the gospel does not exist to be understood as a merely historical document, but to be taken in such a way that it exercises its saving effect."[22] Understanding an order offers Gadamer a further illustration (and here he moves close to speech-act theory), "to understand an order means to apply it to the specific situation to which it pertains." And its real meaning is given when it is carried out. Even a person who refuses to obey an order has understood it because he applies it to the situation and knowing what obedience would mean in that situation, he refuses.[23]

Biblically, we could connect Gadamer's idea to the truth that to listen is to obey and that to obey is to understand or know. The Scripture commends obedience to the Word much more frequently and forcefully than it does merely interpreting the Word. Perhaps the Scriptures are showing the integration of application in the understanding process.

Evangelicals have been better at distinguishing interpretation from application than at showing their interrelation. In *The Doctrine of the Knowledge of God,* John Frame is one of the few evangelicals who acknowledges the integral role of application in meaning.[24] Thiselton approaches this issue through the notion of textual effects. In his newest book, *New Horizons in Hermeneutics: The Theory and Practice of Transforming Biblical Reading,* Thiselton is primarily interested in what texts do. He follows Ricoeur in paying attention to what occurs "in front of" the text.[25] Speech-act theory, as developed by John Searle and others, also leads Thiselton to this concern with the transforming power of texts.

He asks why so little attention in hermeneutical theory has been given to the capacity of biblical texts to produce certain transforming effects, rather than only to transmit certain disclosures.[26] But Thiselton is quick to note that the meanings of texts cannot be equated entirely with their pragmatic effects.[27] Nonetheless, he provides several persuasive examples of textual effect. Speech-act theory helps us see the textual effect in legal texts, covenantal texts and other features such as biblical promises, invitations, verdicts, confessions, pronouncements of blessing, commands, namings and declarations of love. Other texts' effects can better be understood through the projection of a narrative-world which shapes and transforms readers as a flow of events and feelings are imaginatively experienced at a pre-reflective level; for example, Thiselton explores the narrative world projected in the book of Jonah. Perhaps most dramatically we can see the transforming power of the cross which changes entire courses of life and systems of reference.[28]

We might note as well the role of the Holy Spirit in actualizing His Word to transform the lives of believers and bring conviction to unbelievers, leading them to faith. In this connection, Thiselton refers to Vern Poythress's work on the Divine meaning of the Scripture, "The work of the Spirit of God, he [Vern] concludes, concerns not simply the text, but also the lives and actions with which the text is interwoven."[29]

A further related issue arises from the segmentation of theological education into biblical, systematic and pastoral theology, a professional division of labor countered by Edward Farley as detrimental to the overall process.[30] Thiselton expresses concern when

> a single hermeneutical process of understanding

> the interactive horizons of past and present is split apart and segmented into "stages" in which biblical specialists are tempted to regard the texts as "objects" of historical-past enquiry; systematicians are tempted to abstract doctrine from its double-sided historical contingency; and pastoral theologians are tempted to absolutize the present as the key determinant of "relevancy" for assessing what sources and traditions of the past can meaningfully address the present.[31]

Instead we could benefit from seeing the process as one integrated whole. As Thiselton states in the conclusion of *New Horizons*, "In a co-operative shared work, the Spirit, the text, and the reader engage in a *transforming process*, which enlarges horizons and creates *new horizons*."[32]

Following Gadamer, I suggest we explore the integral role of application in understanding the biblical text. Augustine said we believe to know and perhaps it is also true that we obey to know. This is not to say that meaning is unstable or that interpretations radically shift in different readings, but that my understanding of the text relates to my application of that text to my situation and that further experience will impact my understanding of the text. For instance, I understand better now what Paul says about marriage than I did when I was single, even though Paul's words have not changed and my lexical knowledge of his terms has not substantially increased. I am aware that this is a difficult area and I have not worked out the details, but am merely arguing that we should relook at the role of application in our hermeneutic process. Two images may help communicate the relation of interpretation and application. They are like two partially overlapping movements, like two waves (one of which is the back of the other), or like one phrase of music transitioning seamlessly to the next.

Phronesis *as an Appropriate Model for Hermeneutical Judgment*

The fifth and final Gadamerian insight I will offer for consideration comes from Gadamer's reading of Aristotle's *Ethics*, where he finds a model for hermeneutical judgment in the concept of *phronesis*. In our tradition we often speak of interpretation as a science and an art, but on the whole we have been much better about describing the scientific dimension than the artistic. Gadamer turns to Aristotle's *Nichomachean Ethics* to develop a correlation between moral reasoning and hermeneutic understanding which I believe has value for evangelical hermeneutics in terms of the artistic or judgment dimension of interpretation.

Aristotle describes a kind of moral judgment which he calls *phronesis*, often translated as prudence. Although *phronesis* appears in Aristotle's work as an ethical concept, on Gadamer's reading, it can also be interpreted epistemologically as a distinctive kind of reasoning. Distinct from mathematical rationality (formal logic) and from a technical pragmatic reasoning (like that used in engineering), Aristotle understands *phronesis* as a kind of judgment relying on principles, but shaped by the concrete realities of each situation. We could profit from exploring Gadamer's retrieval of Aristotelian *phronesis*, and developing the inherent congruence of ethics and epistemology implied in Gadamer's reading of Aristotle in order to gain insight into hermeneutical judgment.

By drawing connections between ethical and hermeneutical worlds, Gadamer's retrieval of Aristotelian *phronesis* presents a form of practical-ethical rationality. Unfortunately, although his reading together of ethics and hermeneutics holds great promise, Gadamer does not fully cultivate the productive relationship he uncovers between ethical reasoning and interpretive judgment. But, as evangelicals we can build on Gadamer's seminal insights working out further in our own context the links between ethical and interpretive judgment.

Although no one has yet fully developed Gadamer's appropriation of *phronesis* as a means of addressing epistemological and ethical judgment, John Caputo, a leading thinker in the field of literary criticism, describes Gadamer's treatment of Aristotelian *phronesis* as "perhaps the most important contribution Gadamer makes."[33] Several other recent books and articles also indicate that *phronesis* is beginning to capture more attention in current humanities research. For instance, scholars such as the Scottish ethicist, Alasdair McIntyre, have rediscovered *phronesis* as an important concept helpful in thinking through what it means to make moral judgments in a post-enlightenment intellectual culture. Further evidence for the entrance of *phronesis* into contemporary scholarly discourse can be found in Thomas Guarino's recent article, "Between Foundationalism and Nihilism: Is *Phronesis* the *Via Media* for Theology?"[34] He cites Jean Greisch, "If it is necessary to designate a common denominator for the more systematic works in hermeneutics appearing over the last five years, it seems to me not inexact to identify this with the return of practical reason under the species of Aristotelian *phronesis*.[35]

Aristotle's analysis of *phronesis* provides a way of seeing human interpretation both epistemologically, as practically rational judgments and ethically, as personal acts bearing communal responsibility.

The kind of reasoning involved in *phronesis*, which can be developed from the ethical-hermeneutical concept in Gadamer and Aristotle, relates to many types of human interpretation. The legal realm offers one example. A judge in a court of law often exercises *phronesis* in applying the law to a given case. Legal judgment does not operate by simple deduction like mathematical proofs. A judge cannot judge well by ignoring the specifics of a case and merely deducing the decision from immutable relevant legal codes. Rather, a judge must interpret how legal statutes should be understood in a particular situation, at a certain time in history, in a specific jurisdiction.

Consideration of individual circumstances, however, does not abrogate the authority of the penal or civil codes. What is unjust in one case may be just in another case to which the same statutes apply. A sense of equity guides judges as they weigh their decisions. Their deliberations gain weight from the realization that they are responsible to the society for their interpretive judgments. While a judge's decision is usually not categorized as either objective or relative, it may be analyzed as prudent or foolish based on interpretation of the law, consideration of the specific facts of a case and analysis of existing socio-economic realities.

In fact, higher courts commonly reconsider a lower court's ruling and evaluate their judgment as appropriate or inappropriate. The judge, or more broadly, the one exercising *phronesis*, bears responsibility before the community for the interpretive judgments he or she makes. As actions in a human community, rational, interpretive choices entail ethical dimensions. I suggest that reviving Aristotelian-Gadamerian *phronesis* may provide a way of seeing interpretation as both an ethical and epistemological phenomenon enacted communally by individuals responsible for their linguistic acts.

As opposed to more formulaic, or alternatively, axiomatic approaches to hermeneutic theory in some of our textbooks, I suggest we explore *phronesis*, as a helpful description of hermeneutical judgment.

Conclusion

Let me reiterate, I am not arguing that we should become Gadamerians. Rather, I am simply arguing that as a seminal thinker in hermeneutics Gadamer has important insights from which we can gain help in improving our own hermeneutic. I encourage evangelical scholars to read Gadamer critically and to work out implications from some vital concepts in Gadamer's work which can strengthen our hermeneutic.

Endnotes

[1]Hans-Georg Gadamer, *Truth and Method,* Trans. and rev. by Joel Weinsheimer and Donald G. Marshall (New York: Crossroad, 1989). This revised edition is based on the revised and expanded 5th German ed., *Gessammelte Werke,* vol. 1 and on the first English trans. ed. by Garrett Barden and John Cumming (New York: Seabury Press, 1975). Hereafter references to *Truth and Method* will come from the revised English edition in the form TM.

[2]E.D. Hirsch, *Validity in Interpretation* (New Haven: Yale University Press, 1967). In Appendix II, "Gadamer's Theory of Interpretation," 245-264, first published in *The Review of Metaphysics,* March 1965. In his following book, *The Aims of Interpretation,* Hirsch makes only passing references to Gadamer, describing him as an historical relativist (Chicago: University of Chicago Press, 1976).

[3]E.D. Hirsch, "Meaning and Significance Reinterpreted," *Critical Inquiry,* 1984, 202-225. He writes, "I am now very much in agreement with Gadamer's idea that application can be part of meaning." Hirsch has expressed even fuller agreement with Gadamer in some recent informal correspondence with Darrell Bock at Dallas Theological Seminary (1994).

[4]Walter Kaiser, *Toward an Exegetical Theology* (Grand Rapids: Zondervan, 1981), 29-31.

[5]Anthony Thiselton, *Two Horizons: New Testament Hermeneutics and Philosophical Description* (Grand Rapids: Eerdmans, 1992), 293-357.

[6]Anthony Thiselton, *New Horizons in Hermeneutics: The Theory and Practice of Transforming Biblical Reading* (Grand Rapids: Zondervan, 1992).

[7]Roger Lundin, Anthony Thiselton, and Clarence Walhout, *The Responsibility of Hermeneutics* (Grand Rapids: Eerdmans, 1985), 23.

[8]TM, 300.

[9]Grant Osborne, *The Hermeneutical Spiral: A Comprehensive Introduction to Biblical Interpretation* (Downers Grove: InterVarsity Press, 1991), 265.

[10]Osborne himself does go on to develop the positive value of community understanding (tradition) in providing categories

for understanding, giving credit to Gadamer for this insight (266).

[11]*Hermeneutics and Human Finitude: Toward a Theory of Ethical Understanding* (New York: Fordham University, 1991), 197.

[12]Roger Lundin writes, "While our theory demands that we think of the pursuit of truth in the way Descartes seems to do, we live as Augustine and dream we're Descartes," in *The Responsibility of Hermeneutics*, 4.

[13]TM, 269.

[14]William W. Klein, Craig L. Blomberg and Robert L. Hubbard, *Introduction to Biblical Interpretation* (Dallas: Word, 1993), 99.

[15]Osborne, 412.

[16]TM, 268.

[17]TM, 311.

[18]TM, 465.

[19]TM, 340.

[20]TM, 308.

[21]TM, 324.

[22]TM, 309.

[23]TM, 334.

[24]John Frame, *The Doctrine of the Knowledge of God* (Philippsburg: Presbyterian and Reformed, 1987), 93-98.

[25]*New Horizons*, 26.

[26]*New Horizons*, 17.

[27]*New Horizons*, 28.

[28]*New Horizons*, 33-35.

[29]See Vern Sheridan Poythress, "The Divine Meaning of Scripture," In *Westminster Theological Journal* 48 (1986), 241-279. And "God's Lordship in Interpretation," in *Westminster Theological Journal* 50 (1988), 27-64.

[30]Edward Farly, *Theologia: The Fragmentation and Unity of Theological Education* (Philadelphia: Fortress, 1983).

[31]*New Horizons*, 605.

[32]*New Horizons*, 619.

[33]John Caputo, *Radical Hermeneutics: Repetition, Deconstruction, and the Hermeneutic Project* (Bloomington: Indiana University,

1987), 109. Consider also Joseph Dunne on Gadamer, "His other great achievement has been the way in which, more compellingly and far reaching than anyone else, he has recovered and confirmed the power of Aristotle's practical philosophy, so that mainly through his influence 'phronesis' may be said to have become naturalized in the discourse of contemporary philosophy," *Back to the Rough Ground: 'Phronesis' and 'Techne' in Modern Philosophy and Aristotle,* (Notre Dame: University of Notre Dame, 1993), 105.

[34]*Theological Studies* 54 (1993), 37-54.

[35]Thomas Guarino, "Between Foundationalism and Nihilism: Is *Phronesis* the *Via Media* for Theology?" *Theological Studies* 54 (1993), 37-54 citing Jean Greisch in "Bulletin de Philosophie: Herméneutique et Philosophie Pratique," *Revue des Sciences Philosophiques et Thélogiques* 75 (1991), 113.

The Deconstructing of the American Mind: An Analysis of the Hermeneutical Implications of Postmodernism

Luiz Gustavo da Silva Goncalves

In a recent *Chicago Tribune* article, poet and author David Lehman recapitulates quite vividly a confrontation he had with a student and a professor at Wittenberg University. Lehman had been asked to speak on the scandal surrounding the Yale guru of deconstruction, Paul de Man. The end result, however, was a debate with a female student and Professor Bob Davis, who argued that the founders of this country were white male racists. They based their position on the idea of a deconstructive interpretation of President Abraham Lincoln's address on November 19, 1863. Lehman writes:

> What with last season's Pulitzer Prize going to Garry Wills' book about the Gettysburg Address, and now a four-hour cinematic epic depicting the

> battle that inspired Lincoln's greatest speech, you'd think that this, the noblest of American orations, is enjoying the high prestige it deserves—even in academe. Guess again.[1]

This incident is an example of the destruction caused by deconstructionism. In fact, Lehman's diagnosis shows that what he faced at Wittenberg is but the tip of the iceberg:

> For the really sad thing is that the righteous students indoctrinated in deconstructive jive couldn't tell the Gettysburg Address from a Pennsylvania zip code. Ignorance is general. It is disheartening to stare at blank faces when you stand in a classroom and mention Icarus, or Thucydides, or Job, or Dante, or Robespierre, or the Gettysburg Address. We can either read the Gettysburg Address or we can deconstruct it—there isn't enough time to do both.[2]

Lehman's article is an excellent illustration of the fact that the destructive effects of both postmodernism and its more radical expression (i.e. deconstructionism) can be seen not only in the aesthetical aspects of modern life such as architecture, arts, fashion, etc, but especially in the way literature is taught in university campuses in the U.S. and abroad.

Unfortunately, history has proven that often when the evangelical Community awakens to the mortal danger of a new movement, it is too late. Even though Deconstructionism was launched in 1980, the majority of evangelicals are still unaware that in the university setting the greatest challenge to the Christian faith is no longer presented in the science department but in the literature department. Evolutionism is not the mightiest enemy anymore. It was surpassed by a more sophisticated one: i.e., the postmodern literary criticism called Deconstructionism.

Postmodernism has been recognized as a number of concurrent and parallel movements in various disciplines. Because it has many forms and shapes, it also has many meanings. It advocates the importance of finding a new way of thinking—a "new paradigm." This paradigm, however, is not a mere shift in the orientation of thought, but rather a radical transformation of the framework with which we cognitively operate.[3]

Even though several important theological issues are at stake, the most important one is hermeneutics.[4] Therefore, this paper will address the issue of the hermeneutical concept in the new paradigm. It will be divided into four sections. The first three deal with the hermeneutical implications of the paradigm shift to post-orthodoxy. It will analyze the essays presented by Küng, Tracy and Lamb at the Symposium for the Future held in Tübingen and edited under the title *Paradigm Change in Theology*[5] and the school of literary criticism known as deconstruction. Special attention will be given to Gadamer's influence on Tracy[6] and Jacques Derridá's hermeneutical reaction to structuralism inasmuch as the ethos of deconstructionism is rooted in postmodernism.[7] The fourth section relates the hermeneutical implications of deconstructionism to the evangelical arena. The undertaking of formulating a postmodern evangelical hermeneutic will be the most important aspect of this part of the work.[8]

In order to achieve such an ambitious task, I will strive to answer the following controlling question: How can one interpret the Bible without giving up the "non-negotiable" in a postmodern context?

The Importance of Hermeneutics in the Paradigm Shift

The analogy of the well-known story of the blind men and the elephant made by McGrath in his article, "The Christian Church's Response to Pluralism,"[9] nicely illustrates the agenda of pluralism. The assumption is clear that those who have accepted the idea of the new paradigm are able to see the big picture just like the king, while the rest are as blind as the beggar.[10] In the midst of such a pluralism, the issue at stake is hermeneutics.

According to Hans Küng, Scripture has a liberating role in the new paradigm.[11] Such a liberation results from a hermeneutic that goes hand in hand with historical criticism. Thus, in the new paradigm, one is allowed to talk in terms of "the way of reading the Bible of the Indian, Chinese, Japanese, African, and Latin American," as if the meaning of the text were culturally conditioned to the ethnicity of the reader.[12]

Reflection on "what interpretation itself is and how this affects every interpretation of religion and especially every theology within the new historically conscious paradigm"[13] is a vital endeavor which enabled David Tracy to design "a general hermeneutical model of theological reflection."[14]

Reasons for a New Hermeneutic

There are two main reasons for the creation of this "general hermeneutical model." The first one is an attempt to cope, according to Tracy, with the contemporary theological *status quo*:

> To read contemporary work in theology (or even to read one issue of one of the major journals or attend one session of one of the major conferences of scholars on the field) is to recognize a radical pluralism, indeed an intense conflict of interpretations, from which there can often seem no honorable exit.[15]

For Küng, the most important features of the "extra-normal theology" that is part of the new paradigm are "new models of theological interpretation."

> . . . it has become clear that new models of theological interpretation emerge, not simply be-

> cause individual theologians like to handle hot potatoes or to construct new models in their studies, but because the traditional model of interpretation breaks down, because "old thinkers," the "puzzle-solvers" of normal theology in face of the new historical horizon and its new challenge, *can find no satisfactory answer to great new questions and thus "model-testers," "new thinkers," set in motion an extra-normal, "extra-ordinary" theology alongside normal theology.*[16]

Because hermeneutics is being bombarded by modern, global, and multi-cultural issues, it plays a crucial theological role.

Hermeneutical Implications of Deconstructionism

Four dimensions of the hermeneutical model presented by postmodernists and deconstructive postmodernists need to be carefully analyzed.

A. Textual Meaning and Author's Meaning

The issue at stake here is who or what determines the meaning of the text. The new paradigm symbolizes the proposal of a combination of three views: psychologism, radical historicism and semantic autonomy.[17] The bottom line is that in pluralism there is no room for authorial intent.[18] The author has been banished.[19]

> The meaning of the text does not lie "behind" it (in the mind of the author, the original social setting, the original audience), nor even "in" the text itself. Rather, the meaning of the text lies in front of the text—in the now common question, the now common subject-matter of both text and interpreter.[20]

There is a shift taking place between the three components involved in hermeneutics, i.e., the author, the text, and the reader. Tracy calls it "conversation."

> Nor will interpretation as conversation occur if the interpreter decides that the real meaning of the text cannot be found through the text itself but must be found "behind" the text—in the mind of the author, the socio-historical conditions of the text, or the response of the original audience to the text.[21]

The influence of Gadamer on Tracy[22] has led him to accept the Hegelian gyre that the past is ontologically alien to the modern reader. Therefore, every age understands the text of the past differently. The cultural force of such an approach determines that only our own cultural entities have genuine immediacy for us. Thus the reader is the determiner of the meaning. To assume that what the author meant is what the text means "is to Gadamer pure romantic *Psychologismus*."[23] The meaning of a text lies in the *Sache*, in the subject matter that is the only element shared by both. The idea of the reader engaging in conversation with the text is formulated because the text is not considered to be a recorded speech. It is an independent piece of language with an existence of its own. The meaning of the text is found "in front of the text" (i.e., its language speaks its own meaning). Different people will understand the language of the text differently. Consequently, the doctrine of semantic autonomy, especially in the pluralistic dimensions of the new paradigm, is the doctrine of the indeterminacy of textual meaning.

Jacques Derridá investigates the texts of Plato, Rousseau, Saussure, and Lévi-Strauss until he finds an *a priori*.[24] Then he focuses on this basic contradiction, which usually consists of the usage of a metaphor, in order to distance the signifier from the signified.[25] Even when the text appears to have some referent outside itself, and the interpreter tries to work on that referent in order to understand the meaning of the text, he or she automatically introduces new text. According to Derridá, a text is always referring to text, and outside of text there is nothing.[26] Text is everything. Text does not bear witness to a referent.[27]

The indeterminacy of textual meaning has the following two pillars as its foundation: 1. Authors sometimes are not successful in conveying their meaning when they write the text. Therefore, some texts do not express what the author intended to communicate. 2. Authors are chronologically and culturally distanced from their readers. Thus, if the text has any meaning at all for the reader, it is his or her responsibility to decode it. Consequently, the reader cannot make contact with the mind of the author.

This concept that the author's meaning is locked in the past and the meaning of the text changes according to historical-cultural factors is highly problematic. Hirsch challenges it by presenting the dilemma of two contemporary interpreters who disagree about the meaning of a given text. What principle should be used in order to find out who, if either, is right?[28] Tracy would solve the matter by submitting both meanings to the scrutiny of the present culture.[29] Therefore, Tracy's new hermeneutical model requires a hierarchical structure.

A text cannot possess a meaning of its own because meaning is a product of human consciousness.[30] Meaning is a quality of thinking, and a text, which consists of black ink marks on a white page, cannot think. Therefore, unless a human consciousness is present, meaning is not possible. When Tracy suggests that the reader is the determiner of the meaning of the text, he is confusing what Hirsch calls "meaning" with "significance." Such a problem will be treated in another section.

B. The Problem of Norms

The second dimension of the hermeneutical model presented by Tracy which needs to be carefully analyzed is related to the distinction between *Sinn* and *Bedeutung*. The idea that textual meaning changes in the course of time because a text leads a life of its own, is developed by Tracy in order to accommodate different meanings which different groups have within the paradigm. They have found diverse meanings because contemporary readers share similar cultural assumptions. They naturally will agree within their cultural groups about what a text means.

> Consider, for example, the different kinds of theology that emerge when a profound sense of oppression and/or alienation, as distinct from a profound sense of fundamental trust, is explicated as *the* hermeneutical key to contemporary experience.[31]

Because of the ecumenical and political interest of the new paradigm, hermeneutical concessions have been made. Thus Lamb writes, "We can reach a genuine hermeneutical consensus only if we make our own the critical perspectives offered by the voices of the victims."[32]

The "shared hermeneutical concerns"[33] presented by Tracy function as a normative device—since the author's meaning is not normative anymore—which like an "umbrella" accommodates the social agenda of any group:

> Hermeneutics itself is grounded in conversation and thereby in a genuine community of inquiry, and thus aids the possible consensus and adjudication of the real differences among particular theologies within the shared new paradigm.[34]

The ultimate purpose for the creation of the new paradigm is to justify the frustrations of those who have found no answer in modernism. Therefore, besides engaging in dialogue with everybody, except evangelical scholars, the new paradigm also is sensitive to the experience of those who are oppressed:

> We are just beginning to formulate a duly theological hermeneutics which can retrieve the subversive memories of the tradition and criticize and interrogate the actualities of error and systemic distortion in the tradition and situation. We are just beginning to find ways to allow the different concrete, personal, social, cultural, and political contexts which impinge upon all our work to enter fully into theological reflection itself . . . to enter into a conversation serious enough to allow for mutual transformation with the other classic religions . . . and classic secular, scientific and humanistic and post-humanistic world-views.[35]

However, if for the sake of allowing pluralism one does not enunciate a normative principle for distinguishing between a valid interpretation and one which is not, there is no reason for being concerned about hermeneutics. Again, Hirsch appropriately asks the crucial question, "What constitutes a valid interpretation?"[36] According to the new paradigm, it is the one which is in harmony with the public consensus. In this case *vox populi* has become *vox Dei*!

C. The Fusion of Horizons

Tracy, who is influenced by Gadamer,[37] and Lamb solve the problem of the relationship of the actuality of history and the cultural distance by arriving at the skeptical and psychologistic conclusion that because each person is different (i.e., the author and the reader will never be perfectly identical), one must understand differently in order to understand at all.

> For many theories of interpretation, the central insight is into the actuality of historical and cultural distance (and hence our "alienation" from the classics). The central problem is the need to avoid misunderstanding, and our central hope is

> in the controls afforded by some methodology to keep us from forcing these alien texts of alien cultures or earlier periods of our own culture into the alien and alienating horizon of our present self-understanding.[38]

If the reader has understood the text only when he or she understands it differently, what follows naturally is the inference that one expresses the meaning of the text differently when one understands it at all. "What is the difference?" is one of the central issues in Derridá's literary approach. "He starts with the premise that a word gains its meaning not because of a presumed identity with an idea or a thing but because of the word's *différence* from the other words in its linguistic system."[39]

Therefore, one understands the meaning of the text only when one does not understand! The meaning of the author is lost, and the meaning of the text of the past is alien to the modern reader. Thus, the reader will interpret the meaning differently as he or she speaks with the text. This process brings the text to speech in a contemporary manner. Consequently the alien text only speaks to the modern readers through the process of explication. Hirsch again challenges the theory by asking, "What does the explicator understand before he makes his explication?"[40] What is the reader talking about when he converses with the text?

The concept that each culture is unique, and therefore people outside that culture are not able to understand it is a fallacy because interpretation is not a science which seeks to understand a different genus. Actually, hermeneutics is a methodology which endeavors to understand what another *Homo sapien* intends to convey by using sharable symbols. Each generation must seek to reapply the meaning of the author in a text to its own milieu. However, this does not imply that the author's meaning has changed. The meaning never changes. The significance of a meaning undergoes historical and cultural changes. The confusion of the concept of meaning and significance is an essential problem of the paradigm shift.

D. The Confusion of Meaning and Significance

Because meaning involves what the author meant, it is locked into time and cannot change. It is part of history, and we cannot change the past. As a result, a written text has and will always have the same meaning it had when it was written. What an author meant by his text cannot be changed. Therefore, by meaning we understand "what the author meant by his use of a particular sign sequence."[41] These signs are called language. Thus, meaning is whatever the author has willed to convey by a particular sequence of linguistic signs and which can be shared by those linguistic signs.

Significance, however, is "a relationship between the meaning and a person."[42] Heretofore, emphasis was given to the fact that when Tracy uses expressions such as "the text says to us," he is not talking about meaning but rather he is describing his response to the meaning. He has mistakenly identified significance with meaning. The inconsistency of his framework generates more multiplicity of interpretations.

The attempt of Tracy and Gadamer to fuse together past and present—*Horizontverschmelzung*—for the sake of grasping a contemporary understanding constitutes an inner contradiction in their theory. They overlook the distinction between the meaning of a text, which does not change, and the application of that meaning, which does change in a present situation. With this concept in mind, one can read Tracy's statement: "For we recognize the fate of all interpretation of all classics as a fate that can become, when embraced as a conversation, a destiny. . . . Insofar as we understand at all we understand differently (from the original author),"[43] and perceive that what he means by "understand" is implication or significance.

E. Conclusion

The ideological changes of this century have given rise to new issues. These emerging issues are assessed by Küng and Tracy and explained as the eve of the ultimate shift—a shift that constitutes a new paradigm. This paradigm does not represent a mere shift in the orientation of thought, but an alteration of the framework within which thought takes place.

As outlined in the brief analysis above, the issues of hermeneutics must be assessed on a much broader scale than ever before. This becomes evident in light of the conclusions drawn from what has been investigated so far: 1) For the new paradigm it is impossible to take an objective approach to the facts of experience. 2) Postmodern hermeneutical theories radically deny the objectivity involved in foundationalism which claims that there are some absolute tenets upon which knowledge must be developed. 3) Language is understood not as referring to objective objects because words only point to other words. 4) Meaning is found in the free play of associations of words.[44]

How can one discover the author's intended meaning in Scripture in a postmodern milieu? One cannot. Postmodernism *a priori* denies this possibility. The only strategic reason for evangelicals to engage in dialogue is the hope of eventually helping some of those who are trapped in postmodernism to realize the chaotic nature of their endeavor. Furthermore, the apologetic feature of such a task certainly forces one to sharpen one's methodology. Perhaps this can be accomplished by formulating an alternative hermeneutical method which could function as a postmodern evangelical one. This issue will be developed in the following section.

Now we are exploring dangerous territories. McGrath describes such danger well by asking, "Can one remain faithful to Christianity and engage positively with the challenge of pluralism?" Furthermore, he queries, "Is the price of such engagement an abandonment of much of what is distinctively and authentically Christian?"[45] Therefore, before rushing to the task of answering such crucial questions, we need to ponder for a moment the following warning given by D.A. Carson:

> All this is a further painful reminder of the epistemological impasse into which a substantial proportion of modern critical biblical scholarship has got itself. There is everywhere a deep desire to preserve some sort of genuinely pious attachment to Christianity, while working on historical-critical levels with such powerful post-Enlightenment impulses that no epistemologically responsible grounding for the piety is possible. The result is two-tier thinking—epistemological bankruptcy.[46]

Proposal of a Postmodern Evangelical Hermeneutic: An Attempt to Dialogue

The purpose of the symposium held in Tübingen was to offer an alternative to the view of premodernism and modernism powerful enough to displace the pillars of western society. Such a change is described as follows:

> In a word, *the paradigm or model of understanding is changed,* together with the whole complex of different methods, fields of problems and attempted solutions, as these had previously been recognized by the theological community. . . . A new view of man, world and God begins to prevail in the theological community where the whole and its details appear in a different light. In times of epochal upheavals theology thus acquires a *new shape,* even in its literary expression.[47]

Consequently, because the participants presented their method as an alternative, they have made the first move towards a dialogue—even if sometimes it sounds more like a monologue. Now it is up to the evangelical theologian to decide whether or not to wrestle with the claims of the postmodern context in order to be relevant to that situation. Such a sophisticated task ought to be constrained by some principles.

A. A Postmodern Evangelical Hermeneutic Must Discern Presupposition from Prejudice[48]

The sociology of knowledge has shown that societal values influence one's perception of reality. One's interpretation is influenced by the tradition or community to which one belongs. Because all interpreters do not belong to the same community, different opinions are predictable. Neutral exegesis does not exist. Instead of this *status quo* leading us to despair, however, it enhances the vital importance of dialogue amongst different communities. Despair leads to pluralism not to dialogue. Therefore, "we must seek controls that enable us to work with presuppositions (the positive) rather than to be dominated by prejudices (the negative)."[49]

B. A Postmodern Evangelical Hermeneutic Must Work with a Reduced Number of Foundational Items

The basic axiom of foundationalism has been questioned in light of the scientific and linguistic revolutions of this century. "Within the period of thirty years, two revolutions in physics overturned Newton's universe in a way that a nineteenth-century physicist would have said was impossible."[50] The impact caused by those revolutions shook the idea of foundational truths.

Newton dealt with measurable elements considered to be real. Einstein developed concepts related to the motion of particles, relativity, and the relationship between mass and energy. The paradigm shift brought by Einsteinan physics affects other areas of knowledge such as ethics, art, architecture, etc. In pluralism, science is not considered a discipline tied to irreducible brute facts; even science is paradigm dependent.[51]

Contrary to the pluralistic agenda, paradigm shifts are

more evolutionary than revolutionary.[52] Therefore, deconstructionism commits the self-excepting fallacy.[53] Einsteinan physics and Newtonian physics are not mutually exclusive.[54] The former qualifies the latter.[55]

Hence, one must develop a methodology that has a reduced number of foundational features. Only the linguistic assumptions that cannot be rejected without being assumed in the process must be applied.[56] Instead of demonstrating the validity of an interpretation by employing a deductive demonstration from first principles, one must prove inductively the "fitting of the facts."[57]

The presupposition is that one set of assumptions fits the wide variety of experiences better than do the hermeneutical assumptions of the new paradigm. If in reflecting on the story of the blind men we assume that the king was also blind, there would be no story! Thus, the set of assumptions must be selected carefully.

C. A Postmodern Evangelical Hermeneutic Must Examine Carefully the Significance of Linguistic Signs

In postmodern hermeneutics, the objects of words are identified as being other words. For instance, Dr. James Brooks once experienced a coughing attack in class and asked me to go to his office and bring him a cough-drop. I brought him a cup of coffee because the word cough-drop was not part of my English vocabulary. As soon as my eight-year-old daughter arrived home from school, I asked her the meaning of the English word "cough-drop." She promptly said in Portuguese, "drops!" Immediately an abstraction of cough-drops came into my mind. Concept is the reference of a language. If a cough-drop is shown to a group of international students, each one will look at it and think of the word for it in his or her own mother tongue.

Likewise, one can simultaneously preserve the concept of verbal inspiration and interpret the concepts and ideas conveyed in Scripture. Once the passage has been interpreted in its original setting, the interpreter must explain the underlying concepts embodied in it. For instance, when Jesus says in John 2:19 that he will replace the temple, the meaning of the passage is that the focal point of the manifestation of God to mankind takes place in the human body of Christ. What is being translated is not a given language, but rather the concepts which these linguistic signs represent.

If the blind men of our story were blind by birth, they would never be capable of creating a mental abstraction of the experience of touching an elephant. They would, however, be able to differentiate the animal's side from a wall, or its trunk from a pillar because the animal has body hair and a wall does not.

D. A Postmodern Evangelical Hermeneutic Must Address the Relevance of Significance

After reading Küng and Tracy's *Paradigm Change in Theology,* one inevitably concludes that in postmodernism the issue is not "What is true?" but rather "What seems to matter?" Cross cultural sensitivity becomes a very important criterion for showing the implications of the biblical truth in a relevant manner.

In a postmodern environment, experience demands interpretation. However, what interpretative framework is to be used? The dilemma created by such a question enhances the relevance of the principles presented in this section as well as the important role of biblical theology, historical theology, systematic theology, and missiology.[58] As McGrath rightly says, "there is a real need to develop genuinely Christian approaches to religions," which will serve as a "Christian framework by which religious experience in general may be interpreted."[59]

Because in postmodernism "what matters" is a very important issue, the evangelical hermeneutic must be careful not to permit human needs to set the agenda.

E. A Postmodern Evangelical Hermeneutic Will Emphasize the Meaning of Propositions in Addition to Words

In order for one to operate in a postmodern context, the

meaning of biblical concepts in propositions must be established first; then, the relationship of individual parts to that whole can be demonstrated. This is a strategic approach because in the hermeneutics of the new paradigm, the proposition, instead of the word, is the basic unit of meaning.

F. A Postmodern Evangelical Hermeneutic Must Relate Meaning to Human Needs

In postmodernism "What matters?" is more important than "What is true?" This characteristic is similar to the so-called "method of correlation," in which the interpreter begins with the ethos of the current context, draws questions out of the culture, and eventually refers to the text in order to find the answers. Thus, culture asks the questions and Scripture provides the answer; or philosophy asks the questions and theology gives the answers. There is some rightness about that procedure, but there is also some danger: it is important to pay attention to the practical significance of truth, but when one allows the culture to ask the questions, the one who sets the agenda becomes cultured. The debate between Richard Levin, professor of English at the State University at Stony Brook, New York, and Virginia Woolf regarding her feminist interpretation of Shakespeare's plays, aroused an angry response by both his feminist colleagues at the university and members of the Modern Language Association. Levin summarized his arguments by saying that "the feminists, in putting the role of sex above all else, are sifting though Shakespeare's plays in search of echoes of their own political beliefs."[60]

There must be some kind of feed-back, in biblical interpretation, where the agenda of Scripture speaks to the agenda of culture. Osborne argues that "the major difficulty in contextualizing Scripture is deciding exactly what are the cultural or time-bound elements in a passage and what are the supracultural or eternal principles."[61] To assume that culture can ask the questions and "what does matter" can go first, may allow us to presuppose that we know what the most important questions are. It may be that Scripture should tell us what are the most important questions.

The connection between the meaning of the text and fundamental human needs is made with the purpose of provoking a "dialogue" through which the meaning of the author in the text will be understood by the reader.

G. A Postmodern Evangelical Hermeneutic Must Employ Phenomenological Approach

The problems of human finitude, human fallibility, human will, and the distinctions between finitude and guilt create phenomenological dimensions that must be seriously addressed.[62]

Even though human beings are finite, fallible, and not able to have absolute knowledge of everything, an accurate knowledge—although partial—about most things in life is a fact. Mankind experiences this reality daily. People take airplanes, drive their cars above the speed limit, and allow their bodies to undergo major surgeries even though they do not have absolute knowledge of mechanics, physics, aerodynamics, medicine, etc. No one would attempt a business trip by walking from Chicago to New York due to one's lack of absolute knowledge of how aircraft operate or less than absolute certainty that such a flight would be successful.

The fallacy of absolute relativism is one of the major problems in deconstructionism.[63] Because human beings are finite and fallible, and because authors and readers are humans, texts cannot contain absolute meaning and readers are not capable of arriving at an absolute understanding of the meaning of texts.[64]

However, one does not have to understand perfectly the meaning of the text in order to achieve valid interpretation. True understanding of the meaning of the text does not mean exhaustive understanding. Therefore, the reader can overcome his or her finitude and fallibility by using a sound hermeneutical method.

> The author has produced the text and given it certain meanings that are intended to be understood by the reader. The text then guides the reader by producing certain access points that point the reader to the proper language game for interpreting that particular elocutionary act. The reader thereby aligns himself or herself with the textual world and propositional content, thus coming to understand the intended meaning of the text.[65]

A postmodern Evangelical hermeneutic ought not to fall into the same trap in which the king finds himself in our story of the blind men. Newbigin's comment on him says, "it is the immensely arrogant claim of one who sees the full truth which all the world's religions are only groping after. It embodies the claim to know the full reality which relativizes all the claims of the religions and philosophies."[66]

H. A Postmodern Evangelical Hermeneutic Must Reflect upon the Understanding of Causation Within the Time-Space Continuum

The strategy of this principle is to take advantage of the opportunities presented by modern developments in natural science.[67] Inasmuch as scientists have accommodated their conception of natural laws to the breakdown of the conception of the universe as self-sustaining, the opportunity is available to interpret a given phenomenon on the basis of other possibilities rather than solely on natural grounds.

Therefore, in order to understand the meaning of the author, the interpreter must investigate the natural factors which caused the author to write the text. The miracle portions of Scripture, for example, should be studied as historical narratives of events which actually happened.

I. A Postmodern Evangelical Hermeneutic Must Be Perceived as a Joint Effort

It is clear that one of the emphases of the symposium

held in Tübingen was the importance of collaboration within the community of scholars for the shaping and development of the "new paradigm." The participants of the symposium were seeking a core for consensus because the greatness of the challenge requires a joint effort. Likewise the task of developing a postmodern evangelical hermeneutic must be a combined effort. Individualism, which is a characteristic of this century, has penetrated the evangelical scholarly community. It appears that evangelical scholars as well as evangelical institutions are not willing to join in efforts to address issues of vital interest for the entire evangelical community. It seems that evangelical scholars like to be occupied with debating among themselves as if they were rivals. However, the emergence of this "new paradigm" brings with it such drastic changes that the emergency of the hour calls for a synergistic work by evangelical scholars.

J. A Postmodern Evangelical Hermeneutic Must Be Heavily Based on Philosophy

In order for an evangelical hermeneutic to succeed in a postmodern context, it needs to operate as a discipline that is but a part of a larger system of thought. As Erickson points out, "This means that postmodern hermeneuts will need to be more broadly prepared than in the past. . . . Today's and tomorrow's hermeneutics will require a better knowledge of linguistics."[68] The hermeneut of the future will need to display in his or her work philosophical sophistication. Anthony Thiselton's book cited above constitutes an example of the kind of philosophical, linguistic, and theological depth which evangelical hermeneutics will need to have in order to be heard in the future.

K. A Postmodern Evangelical Hermeneutic Must Be Fully Multicultural

This principle is vital in addressing the problem of the relationship of the actuality of history and the cultural distance between text and reader which creates the skeptical and psychologistic term called "fusion of horizons" by deconstructionists. Such "distanciation" becomes a hindrance when the interpreter avoids submitting his or her hermeneutic methodology to the scrutiny of biblical, historical, and systematic theologies. Therefore, in order to escape from being caught up in a hermeneutical circle, one can bridge the cultural background of the text with the background of the reader by applying the hermeneutical spiral model presented by Osborne.

> The text itself sets the agenda and continually reforms the questions that the observer asks of it. The means by which this is accomplished is twofold: grammatical-syntactical exegesis and historical-cultural background. These interact to reshape the interpreter's preunderstanding and help to fuse the two horizons. The actual contextualization then occurs as this process of fusion reaches out in another and broader hermeneutical spiral to encompass the interpreter's life and situation.[69]

Thanks to technology, the world has become a global village. The evangelical community has experienced rapid growth in non-English speaking countries. The resultant greater contact with cultural diversity has caused theologians to face the challenge of applying Scripture to global issues.

The important truths of Scripture, although themselves absolutes which are universal, will be conceptualized in different ways by different cultures. What is emphasized here is not relativism but the fact that different cultural perspectives of the truth need not be necessarily contradictory. They may be complementary. The Western cultural side of theology made in the United States i.e., the white, upper class, male interpretation will not be meaningful in Latin America.

Inasmuch as culture imposes some complex challenges

upon the hermeneutical task, the interpreter must be certain that his or her conclusions are not distorted. Therefore, the interpreter should answer the following questions before deciding for a specific interpretation: Are there supracultural indicators in the text under examination? To what degree are the cultural issues of the text restricted to cultural practices of the first century but not existent today? Is the distance between the supracultural and cultural indicators of the text sufficient to justify the decision that the surface cultural meaning applied only to the first century?[70]

Conclusion

Interpretations have a higher probability of being accurate when they are probed by biblical theology, when they are checked by systematic theology, and ultimately when they prove to be in harmony with historical theology. Any serious student of Scripture should be cautious about embracing new interpretations. If the Bible never explicitly refers to such interpretations, if the fathers of the Church never talked about such interpretations, if none of the confessions of the Church touches on such interpretations, if such interpretations have appeared *de novo*, be extremely careful! After two millennia of biblical interpretation, it is not likely that there are many unturned stones waiting for us.

Postmodernism cannot be a viable option for evangelicals because it is totally shut off to any foundational truth. Its pluralistic view embodied in the concept of "paradigm" relativizes truth causing an objective assessment of right and wrong to be inconceivable.

The problem with the paradigm shift idea is that perspectives can differ. Therefore, it is equally legitimate for one person to have a Buddhist perspective and another a Christian one. There is no way for either perspective to be judged right or wrong. All judging of right or wrong is done inside of one of those perspectives. In a postmodern context it is impossible for one to step outside of Buddhism or Christianity in order to decide which of these is correct. That is a common way of thinking today.[71] Instead of having Christian theology, we have Christian theologies, i.e., Asian theology, South African theology, Brazilian theology, etc.[72]

The whole question of whether or not all these different perspectives are equally valid or whether one can be judged better than the others, is the issue at stake. Hence, in order to do hermeneutics in a postmodern context, one needs to employ the eleven principles heretofore developed. This writer is fully reminded of Carson's warning that the greatest risk in engaging in dialogue is the danger of assimilation. However, as McGrath says, "dialogue thus implies respect, not agreement, between two parties—and, at best, a willingness to take a profound risk that the other person may be right and that recognition of this fact may lead to the changing of positions."[73]

Therefore, one must employ phenomenological methods without making Scripture a servant of experience; let us be sensitive to the effect of causation within the time-space continuum without rejecting the supernatural power of Scripture; let us join efforts and be culturally sensitive without relativizing the normative role of Scripture.

Endnotes

[1]David Lehman, "Deconstructing Abe: Fashionable Ignorance and the Gettysburg Address," *The Chicago Tribune*, 11 February 1994, section 1, 27.

[2]Ibid.

[3]This idea is further analyzed on pages 15 and 27, and in endnote 69.

[4]Alister E. McGrath in "The Christian Church's Response to Pluralism," *Journal of the Evangelical Theological Society* 35 (1992): 487-501 asserts that the pluralistic agenda also has theological implications on the doctrine of God and the doctrine of the incarnation.

[5]Hans Küng and David Tracy, eds., *Paradigm Change in Theology: A Symposium for the Future*, trans. Margaret Köhl (New York: Crossroad, 1991). This writer is not implying here that these theologians are deconstructionists. Their views are relevant for some sections of this paper because their framework was developed out of Thomas Kuhn's concept of "paradigm" as the ethos in which deconstructionism emerged.

[6]Hans-Georg Gadamer, *Truth and Method*, trans. and rev. Joel Weinsheimer and Donald G. Marshall, rev. 2d ed. (New York: Crossroad, 1989).

[7]If the reader wants to know more about Derridá and his role in deconstructionism, a good explanation and analysis is available in Anthony C. Thiselton, *New Horizons in Hermeneutics* (Grand Rapids: Zondervan, 1992), 103-113. On pages 114-123 Thiselton assesses the implications of deconstructionism for biblical interpretation. Thiselton is a fine evangelical scholar, but he is English; i.e., even when he disagrees with some scholars he is very polite. Usually he confronts his opponents by quoting others. Therefore, the reader hardly finds a paragraph without footnotes. One must plow through the book in order to arrive at Thiselton's position on different issues.

[8]This work endeavors to analyze the hermeneutics of both postmodernism and deconstructionism because the latter is a creation of the former. Since some scholars believe that deconstructionism is already cracking, postmodernism as a broader movement seems to be more relevant. According to Thomas C. Oden in *Two Worlds: Notes on the Death of Modernity in America and Russia* (Downers Grove: InterVarsity Press, 1992), 42, " . . . deconstructionism has about it the smell of death. It will not last more than a decade, or among unfeigned believers a generation." See also Allan Bloom, *The Closing of the American Mind* (New York: Simon and Schuster, 1987), 379-380.

[9]McGrath, "The Christian Church's Response to Pluralism," 493-494.

[10]One can easily find out who are the blind people by looking at the chart *Changing Paradigms in the History of Theology and Church* in Küng and Tracy, *Paradigm Change*, 291.

[11]Küng, "A New Basic Model For Theology: Divergences and Convergencies," in *Paradigm Change*, 448.

[12]Ibid., 450. See also Anthony C. Thiselton, *New Horizons in*

Hermeneutics, 27-29.

[13]Tracy, "Hermeneutical Reflection in the New Paradigm," in *Paradigm Change,* 35.

[14]Tracy, "Some Concluding Reflections on the Conference: Unity Amidst Diversity and Conflict?" in *Paradigm Shift,* 465.

[15]Tracy, "Hermeneutical Reflections," 36.

[16]Küng, "Paradigm Change in Theology: A Proposal for Discussion," in *Paradigm Change,* 19-20.

[17]Psychologism is the view in which due to the psychological differences between the author and the reader, the latter cannot understand the meaning of the former. According to radical historicism, the historical discrepancies between the author and the reader prevent the author from being understood today. Autonomism is the view which asserts that the text possesses meaning on its own. The implication of these views for postmodernism and deconstructionism will be presented in this section as well as sections B, C and D.

[18]See the chapter "To the Linguistic Abyss" in David Lehman, *Signs of the Times: Deconstruction and the Fall of Paul de Man* (New York: Poseidon Press, 1992), 94-113.

[19]This writer acknowledges his indebtedness to Dr. Robert Stein under whom he served as a teaching assistant for three years and who during that time introduced him to the hermeneutical approach developed by E.D. Hirsch, Jr. in *Validity in Interpretation* (New Haven: Yale University, 1967). Nevertheless, this writer is aware that some scholars find Hirsch's categories somehow not capable of operating in the complex environment of deconstructionism. For instance, Hirsch's discussion on "meaning" took place almost 20 years ago. Today's more complex issues associated with "meaning" are related to questions such as in which sense do you absolve any meaning from any text. The subjectiveness linked to the concept of meaning of the text is much more complex in postmodernism than it was in modernism. In fact Anthony C. Thiselton in *New Horizons in Hermeneutics,* 13, writes the following about Hirsch's approach. ". . . his largely pre-Witt-gensteinian conceptual and methodological tools do not match the complexity of the issues formulated in post-Gadamerian theory." Grant R. Osborne, in *The Hermeneutical Spiral: A Comprehensive Introduction to Biblical Interpretation* (Downers Grove: InterVarsity Press, 1991), 394

states that one of the problems in Hirsch's approach is that he "needs a much more complex validating procedure and more sophisticated reasoning. Hirsch can lead to possible meaning but it is difficult to ascertain whether his method produces probable meaning (as he claims)."

[20]Tracy, "Hermeneutical Reflections," 42.

[21]Ibid., 50.

[22]Ibid., 38.

[23]Hirsch, *Validity in Interpretation*, 247.

[24]Jacques Derridá, *Of Grammatology*, trans. Gayatri Chakravorty Spivak (Baltimore: Johns Hopkins University Press, 1976), 97-157.

[25]Tremper Longman III, *Literary Approaches to Biblical Interpretation*, Foundations of Contemporary Interpretation, vol. 3, ed. Moisés Silva (Grand Rapids: Zondervan, 1987), 42-43.

[26]Grant R. Osborne, *Hermeneutical Spiral*, 382-383.

[27]Jacques Derridá, *Of Grammatology*, 40-41.

[28]Hirsch, *Validity in Interpretation*, 249.

[29]This writer is curious to know how Tracy and Derridá react to reviewers who misunderstand the books they write! Why does Derridá write? Does he expect his readers to understand the meaning of his books? If when driving on an unknown highway, Derridá saw a traffic sign saying DEAD END AHEAD, STOP, CLIFF, would he obey the warning or deconstruct its meaning and drive through?

[30]Both Blank and Ricoeur as well as Tracy, like to use the expression "the text says." See Josef Blank, "According to the Scriptures: The New Testament Origins and Structure of Theological Hermeneutics," *Paradigm Change*, 262; and Paul Ricoeur, "Response to Josef Blank," *Paradigm Change*, 284.

[31]Tracy, "Hermeneutical Reflections," 56.

[32]Matthew L. Lamb, "Paradigms as Imperatives Towards Critical Collaboration," *Paradigm Change*, 454.

[33]Tracy, "Hermeneutical Reflections," 58.

[34]Ibid., 58-59. That this "consensus" can be maintained only by encouraging pluralism is evident in pages 61 and 440.

[35]Tracy, "Some Concluding Reflections," 470.

[36]Hirsch, *Validity in Interpretation*, 252.

[37]Tracy, "Hermeneutical Reflections," 42.

[38]Ibid., 37. For Lamb's understanding of "the fusion of horizons" and its role in the new paradigm, see Lamb, "The Dialectics of Theory and Praxis within Paradigm Analysis," *Paradigm Change*, 77.

[39]David Lehman, *Signs of the Times*, 68-69. Lehman also develops an interesting discussion on Paul de Man's interpretation of one of the episodes of *All in the Family* in which Edith Bunker asks her husband if he wants his bowling shoes laced over or laced under. Archie Bunker impatiently answers back with the question, "What is the difference?" This means that he does not care! However, Edith takes his question literally and starts to explain the difference between the two ways of tying laces. de Man uses this interchange as an example of the literal interpretation of a rhetorical question. The analysis of de Man's model of the deconstruction practiced on Archie Bunker becomes the reason Lehman names this chapter *Archie Debunking*. This is a very interesting chapter of the book.

[40]Hirsch, *Validity in Interpretation*, 253.

[41]Ibid., 8.

[42]Ibid.

[43]Tracy, "Hermeneutical Reflections," 42-43.

[44]Ibid., 40ff.

[45]McGrath, "The Christian Response to Pluralism," 489.

[46]D.A. Carson, "Selected Recent Studies of the Fourth Gospel," *Themelios* 14 (1989), 62.

[47]Küng, "Paradigm Change," 21.

[48]The reader need not think that this is an oxymoron because what is being implied here is the necessity of a hermeneutic which would allow the evangelical interpreter to use the same technical terminology used by postmodernists for the sake of being heard even if for a short period of time. One must become sensitive to the needs, weaknesses and limitations of his or her audience in order to gain a point of contact, a toehold by which the principles outlined hereafter may be applied to the postmodern mindset of a pluralistic society.

[49]Grant R. Osborne, *Hermeneutical Spiral*, 412-415.

[50]Vern Sheridan Poythress, *Science and Hermeneutics: Implica-*

tions of Scientific Method for Biblical Interpretation, Foundations of Contemporary Interpretation, vol. 6, ed. Moisés Silva (Grand Rapids: Zondervan, 1988), 39-49.

[51]Thomas S. Kuhn in *The Structure of Scientific Revolutions*, 2d ed. (Chicago: University of Chicago Press, 1970), 92, describes scientific revolutions as "non-accumulative developmental episodes" *sine qua non* to the occurrence of paradigm shift.

[52]As David Clark emphasizes in "Narrative Theology and Apologetics," *Journal of the Evangelical Theological Society* 36 (1993), 511, the apparent total discontinuity between paradigms is utopia because successive paradigms do not differ completely. Therefore, one can say that paradigms undergo organic evolution.

[53]David Clark, *Dialogical Apologetics: A Person-Centered Approach to Christian Defense* (Grand Rapids: Baker, 1993), 80.

[54]Even Kuhn's conceptual explanation of how paradigm shifts occur implies some continuity. For an assessment of his inconsistency see Maurice Mandelbaum "Subjectivity, Objectivity, and Conceptual Relativism," *The Monist* 62 (1979), 418.

[55]Imre Lakatos, "Falsification and the Methodology of Scientific Research Programmes," in *Criticism and the Growth of Knowledge*, Proceedings of the International Colloquium in the Philosophy of Science, vol. 4, eds. Imre Lakatos and Alan Musgrave (London: Cambridge University Press, 1970), 124.

[56]Perhaps this principle will focus more on the third category called by Osborne "negotiable." See Grant R. Osborne, *Hermeneutical Spiral*, 404-405.

[57]Millard Erickson, *Evangelical Interpretation: Perspectives on Hermeneutical Issues* (Grand Rapids: Baker, 1993), 114-116.

[58]Grant R. Osborne in *Hermeneutical Spiral*, 384 argues that the disregard for the historical background so peculiar in deconstructionism is present very often in modern preaching and Bible study groups. The tendency is to ask directly the biblical text, "How does this relate to my situation?" Then, Osborne writes, "The difference of course is that Derridá denies the historical referent while many evangelicals merely are unaware of it. However, the result (namely, subjective interaction with the text) is quite similar."

[59]McGrath, "The Christian Church's Response to Pluralism," 494. See also the suggestions he presents under the heading "Developing a Christian Theology of Religions" on pages 495-497.

[60]Richard Bernstein, "Shakespeare vs. Woolf: Macho by a TKO," *International Herald Tribune*, 9 March 1990.

[61]Grant R. Osborne, *Hermeneutical Spiral*, 326. Then on page 327 he rightly affirms that "all biblical statements were written in cultural guise."

[62]Thiselton, *New Horizons in Hermeneutics*, 344-350.

[63]Ibid., 318.

[64]Grant R. Osborne, *The Hermeneutical Spiral*, 382-383.

[65]Ibid., 411.

[66]L. Newbigin, *The Gospel in a Pluralist Society* (Grand Rapids: Eerdmans, 1989), 10.

[67]David Clark, *Dialogical Apologetics*, 52-75.

[68]Millard Erickson, *Evangelical Interpretation*, 123.

[69]Grant R. Osborne, *Hermeneutical Spiral*, 324.

[70]Ibid., 328-338.

[71]For a classic criticism of this kind of subjectivity, see Donald Davidson, "On the Very Idea of a Conceptual System," *Proceedings and Addresses of the American Philosophical Association*, 47 (November 1974), 5-20. This is a very difficult essay, but his basic point is that not everything can be limited to conceptual schemes. In fact, in a desconstructive postmodern setting, even talking about conceptual schemes requires that the speaker have something that is bigger and broader than a conceptual scheme. Therefore, no one can step outside of these perspectives in order to make an objective assessment of the truthfulness of the various viewpoints involved.

[72]A.E. McGrath, "The Challenge of Pluralism for the Contemporary Christian Church," *Journal of the Evangelical Theological Society* 35 (1992), 368-373.

[73]McGrath, "The Christian Church's Response to Pluralism," 490.

List of Contributors

Michael C. Bauman is Professor of Theology and Culture and Director of Christian Studies at Hillsdale College, Hillsdale, Michigan.

Craig L. Blomberg is Professor of New Testament at Denver Conservative Baptist Seminary in Denver, Colorado.

John A. Delivuk is Automation Librarian at Geneva College, Beaver Falls, Pennsylvania.

David S. Dockery is Vice President for Academic Administration and Professor of New Testament Theology at Southern Baptist Theological Seminary, Louisville, Kentucky.

Ronald N. Glass is Pastor of Wading River Baptist Church in Wading River, New York.

David W. Hall is Pastor of Covenant Presbyterian Church in Oak Ridge, Tennessee.

Bruce B. Miller II is Pastor of Leadership Development and Pastoral Care at Fellowship Bible Church in North Plano, Texas.

John Warwick Montgomery is Professor of Law and Humanities at University of Luton, England.

Robert A. Peterson is Professor of Systematic Theology at Covenant Theological Seminary, St. Louis, Missouri.

Luiz Gustavo da Silva Goncalve is a Doctoral Student at Trinity Evangelical Divinity School in Deerfield, Illinois, and a missionary for Together, Inc.

Virgil Warren is Professor of Theology at Manhattan Christian College, Manhattan, Kansas.